THE MASTER LIBRARY

The Louvre, Paris
VIII Title

THE IMMACULATE CONCEPTION
From a painting by Murillo

THE MASTER LIBRARY

PIONEERS OF THE FAITH

VOLUME EIGHT

THE FOUNDATION PRESS, INC.
CLEVELAND, OHIO.   SPRINGFIELD, MASS.   KANSAS CITY, MO.

COPYRIGHT, 1923
COPYRIGHT, 1927
BY THE FOUNDATION PRESS, INC.
CLEVELAND, OHIO
*Imperial and International
Copyright secured
All rights reserved*

PRINTED IN U. S. A.

TO
THE ONCOMING GENERATION
AND TO ALL WHO WOULD HAVE A NEW
VISION OF THE BEAUTY AND
THE POWER OF THE
MESSAGE OF
LIFE

EDITORIAL BOARD

General Editor

WALTER SCOTT ATHEARN, A.M., LL.D.

Dean, Boston University School of Religious Education and Social Service
Chairman of the Committee on Education of the International Sunday School
Council of Religious Education
Author of "The Church School," "Religious Education and American Democracy,"
"A National System of Religious Education," etc., etc.

Art Editor

HENRY TURNER BAILEY

Director of the Cleveland School of Art, and of the John Huntington Polytechnic
Institute, Cleveland
Author of "The Blackboard in Sunday School," "The Flush of The Dawn,"
"Photography and Fine Art," "Twelve Great Paintings," "Symbolism
for Artists," etc., etc.

Associate Editors

CHARLES REYNOLDS BROWN, A.M., S.T.B., D.D., LL.D., Dean, The Divinity School, Yale University, New Haven, Connecticut.

FREDERICK CARL EISELEN, A.M., B.D., Ph.D., D.D., Dean, Garrett Biblical Institute and Professor of Old Testament History and Literature, Evanston, Illinois.

JOHN RICHARD SAMPEY, D.D., LL.D., Professor of Old Testament History and Literature, Southern Baptist Theological Seminary, Louisville, Kentucky.

WILBUR FISK TILLETT, A.M., D.D., LL.D., S.T.D., Dean, Vanderbilt University, Nashville, Tennessee.

IRA MAURICE PRICE, A.M., B.D., Ph.D., LL.D., Professor of Semitic Languages and Literature, University of Chicago, Chicago, Illinois.

ALBERT EDWARD BAILEY, A.M., Professor of Religious Art and Archæology, Boston University, Boston, Massachusetts.

JAMES ISAAC VANCE, A.M., D.D., LL.D., Pastor, First Presbyterian Church, Nashville, Tennessee.

GEORGE LIVINGSTONE ROBINSON, A.M., Ph.D., D.D., LL.D., Professor of Old Testament History and Literature, McCormick Theological Seminary, Chicago, Illinois.

ELSON IRVING REXFORD, M.A., D.D., LL.D., D.C.L., Principal, Diocesan Theological College, Montreal, Canada.

PREFACE

HERE are gathered the accounts of many deeds of the great Apostles and missionaries who organized the Christian church, and who carried the message of Jesus throughout their own land and to other countries. We have also the records of their thoughts, those interpretations of the spirit and teachings of Jesus which inspired the early Christians to meet persecution, and carried them triumphantly through life and to martyrdom.

First, we see that most human and lovable of Apostles, Peter, a great and growing character, developing through responsibility, and advancing to a leadership of world outlook by reason of the wisdom with which he handled the unexpected problem resulting from the willingness of Gentiles to welcome the Gospel.

Next, we follow Paul, an Apostle who had the background and the special ability and energy to take up the work where Peter left it, and to make Christianity truly a world religion.

We read the Apocalypse, that marvelous document of faith, which shows us a church now established all over Asia Minor and in the very heart of the Roman Empire, assailed by merciless and powerful imperial antagonists, yet undaunted, and dreaming of a Holy City that was to come down from heaven and to be built up on earth. The Biblical history ends with the challenge of such a hope. This vision Christians have never outgrown, and the hope of the Book of Revelation is still the goal of Christian endeavor the world over.

CONTENTS

PETER AND THE EARLY CHURCH

	PAGE
TRIUMPHS AND DIFFICULTIES	5
The Foreword	5
The Followers of Jesus	6
The Coming of the Holy Spirit upon the Disciples	8
The First Shadow of Persecution	13
The Fellowship of the Believers	16
Imprisonment and Release of the Apostles	18
The First Christian Martyr	20
Experiences of the Apostles in Samaria	24
EXPANSION AND PERSECUTION	27
Philip and the Courtier of Ethiopia	27
The Effective Ministry of Peter	29
The Meeting of Peter and Cornelius	32
The Gospel in Antioch	39
The Storm of Persecution Breaks	41

PAUL AND THE WORLD–WIDE CHURCH

PAUL'S EARLY LIFE	55
Preparation for His Life Work	55
Paul's Active Ministry Begun	60
FIRST MISSIONARY JOURNEY OF PAUL	69
The Outward Voyage	69
The Return Voyage	78
SECOND MISSIONARY JOURNEY OF PAUL	87
The First Stage of the Journey	87
The Second Stage of the Journey	89
The Third Stage of the Journey	103

CONTENTS

	PAGE
THIRD MISSIONARY JOURNEY OF PAUL	109
The First Stage of the Journey	109
The Second Stage of the Journey	115
The Third Stage of the Journey	121
PAUL'S EXPERIENCES AT JERUSALEM	127
The Conspiracy Against Paul	127
PAUL'S JOURNEY TO ROME	145
Shipwreck and Suffering	145
The End of the Voyage	150
IMPRISONMENT AND LAST DAYS	157
Paul in Prison	157
Later Activities and Last Days of Paul	164
THE SEVEN CHURCHES OF ASIA	175
CHRISTIAN THOUGHT	
THE MANIFESTATION OF GOD'S LOVE	193
A Summary of the New Testament	193
God's Relationship to Man	193
The Gospel of Righteousness and Love	195
Jesus in Human Life	205
CHRISTIAN UNITY AND COURAGE	219
Privileges and Responsibilities	219
The Good Fight	227
THE CHALLENGE OF THE CHRISTIAN LIFE	231
Temptations and Sufferings	231
Christian Character	236
CHRISTIAN CONDUCT AND BELIEF	259
Foolish Thought and Sinful Act	259
Holy and Happy Living	266
The Life Immortal	276

PERSONAL AND SOCIAL RIGHTEOUSNESS

Principles of Righteous Living 289
- Religion in Practice 289
- Self-control in Speech 293
- Companionship and Social Intercourse . . . 297
- The Privileges of the Jew 299
- Wisdom 300

Social Ideals 305
- Family Relationships 305
- Servants and Masters 309
- Rich and Poor 311
- The Citizen and the State 314

PERSONAL LETTERS

Messages of Greeting and Friendship . . . 321
Letters of Christian Counsel 328
Three Letters About Christian Church Life . 331

CHRISTIAN WORSHIP

Christian Hymns 351
Christian Prayers 363
Sacraments and Spiritual Gifts 371

THE APOCALYPSE

The Revelation to John 381

EXPLANATORY NOTES 415

BIBLE REFERENCE INDEX 441

FROM "THE PRESENT CRISIS"

Once to every man and nation comes the moment to decide,
In the strife of Truth with Falsehood, for the good or evil side;
Some great cause, God's new Messiah, offering each the bloom or blight,
Parts the goats upon the left hand, and the sheep upon the right,
And the choice goes by forever 'twixt that darkness and that light.

Careless seems the great Avenger; history's pages but record
One death grapple in the darkness 'twixt old systems and the Word;
Truth forever on the scaffold, Wrong forever on the throne —
Yet that scaffold sways the future, and, behind the dim unknown,
Standeth God within the shadow, keeping watch above his own.

Count me o'er earth's chosen heroes; they were souls that stood alone,
While the men they agonized for hurled the contumelious stone;
Stood serene, and down the future saw the golden beam incline
To the side of perfect justice, mastered by their faith divine,
By one man's plain truth to manhood and to God's supreme design.

By the light of burning heretics Christ's bleeding feet I track,
Toiling up new Calvaries ever with the cross that turns not back;
And these mounts of anguish number how each generation learned
One new word of that grand Credo which in prophet-hearts hath burned
Since the first man stood God-conquered with his face to heaven upturned.

For humanity sweeps onward: where today the martyr stands,
On the morrow crouches Judas with the silver in his hands;
Far in front the cross stands ready and the crackling fagots burn,
While the hooting mob of yesterday in silent awe return
To glean up the scattered ashes into History's golden urn.

—James Russell Lowell

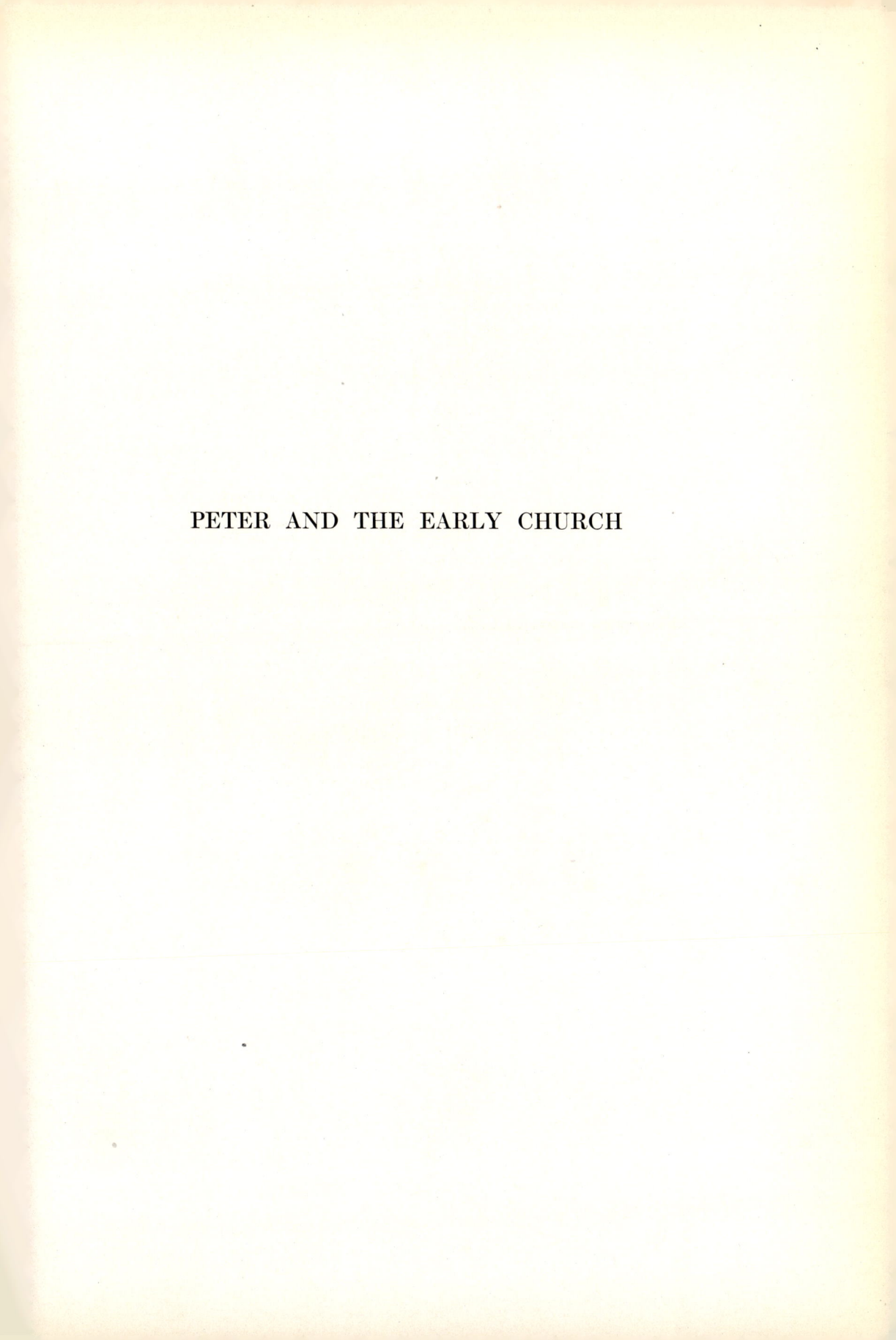

PETER AND THE EARLY CHURCH

PETER AND THE EARLY CHURCH

IN many biographies, we find that the individual portrayed is much the same throughout his entire life. The man whom we meet in his youth shows similar traits of character at the end of his career, and we receive from the narrative an impression of a consistent nature working out its abilities and influence patiently, and sometimes, perhaps, monotonously. This is true of such modern men as Carlyle, Tolstoi, Gladstone, and Roosevelt; and of Abraham, Moses, David, Cyrus, Alexander, and Cæsar, among the ancients.

But the case of Peter is different. In the great shepherd of the church at Jerusalem, we hardly recognize the ignorant, impulsive fisherman of the Lake of Galilee. Through the Gospels and through the Acts of the Apostles, we trace the steady and marvelous growth of a character that had benefited profoundly by the touch and impress of the companionship of Jesus. There is a great distance between the timorous denier of Pilate's courtyard and the aggressive leader who worked out a noble career, and whose life, according to tradition, was crowned with a martyr's death in Rome.

In the story of Peter, struggling Christians have always found encouragement. Here, they behold an Apostle with faults similar to their own: they are encouraged by his failures and recoveries; they take heart from the knowledge that he was forgiven, reinstated, and used to the utmost in his Master's service.

And yet, even Peter gave place to another, as Elijah gave place to Elisha, and John the Baptist to Christ himself. Luke graphically tells of Peter's ascendancy in the apostolic church; but he turns suddenly and completely from this episode to the main current of Christian history, which moved along the shining trail of Peter's successor, the Apostle Paul.

SIMON PETER
From a painting by Fra Bartolomeo

TRIUMPHS AND DIFFICULTIES

THE FOREWORD

The larger part of our knowledge of the life and work of the disciples of Jesus after the Ascension is given to us in the writings of Luke, who continued the account, begun in his Gospel, in what we know as the Book of Acts. The keynote of this second book is found in the message of the risen Christ, at the end of Luke's Gospel. The story of the early church, Luke here suggests, is in two parts — first, "beginning from Jerusalem," and, second, "to all the nations." The Book of Acts is divided into corresponding parts — the account of the Jewish-Christian church, whose center was Jerusalem and whose first leader was Simon Peter; and, second, the account of the world-wide church, whose leader was Paul of Tarsus.

JESUS said to them [the disciples], "These are my words which I spoke to you, while I was yet with you, how that all things must needs be fulfilled, which are written in the law of Moses, and the prophets, and the psalms, concerning me."

Then opened he their mind, that they might understand the scriptures; and he said to them: "Thus it is written, that the Christ should suffer, and rise again from the dead the third day; and that repentance and remission of sins should be preached in his name to all the nations, beginning from Jerusalem. Ye are witnesses of these things.

"And behold, I send forth the promise of my Father upon you: but tarry ye in the city, until ye be clothed with power from on high."

The above message is repeated in much the same words at the beginning of the Book of Acts, as follows:

"Ye shall receive power, when the Holy Spirit hath come upon you: and ye shall be my witnesses both in Jerusalem, and in all Judea, and in Samaria, and to the uttermost part of the earth."

THE FOLLOWERS OF JESUS

They Come Together in Jerusalem

Do we realize the courage that drew the eleven disciples back to the city where their Master had just been crucified? And do we realize that immediately after his death these fearless men were joined by Christ's own kinsmen and scores, if not hundreds, of men, women, and children from Galilee?

Jesus must have made his message most clear, inspiring, and imperative, to lead so many persons of every class to imperil their lives in order to gather in faithful expectancy for the next word of command.

Then returned they to Jerusalem[1] from the mount called Olivet, which is from Jerusalem a sabbath day's journey.

When they had come in, they went up into an upper room, where abode both Peter and John and James and Andrew, Philip and Thomas, Bartholomew and Matthew, James the son of Alpheus, and Simon the Zealot, and Judas the brother of James.

These all continued with one accord in prayer and supplication with the women, and Mary the mother of Jesus, and with his brethren.

And there was a multitude of persons gathered together, about a hundred and twenty.

Matthias Is Chosen to Succeed Judas Iscariot

The suggestion was then made by Peter, who from the beginning was acknowledged as leader, that a successor to Judas Iscariot, who in remorse had killed himself, should be chosen from among the followers of Jesus.

"Of these men who have companied with us all the time that the Lord Jesus went in and went out among us, beginning from the baptism of John, to that same day that he was taken up from us, must one become a witness with us of his resurrection."

And they put forward two, Joseph called Barsabbas, who was surnamed Justus, and Matthias. And they prayed, and said, "Thou, Lord, who knowest the hearts of all men, show

THE ASCENSION
From a painting by Gustav Biermann

of these two the one whom thou hast chosen, to take the place in this ministry and apostleship from which Judas fell away, that he might go to his own place."

And they gave forth lots for them; and the lot fell upon Matthias; and he was numbered with the eleven apostles.

THE COMING OF THE HOLY SPIRIT UPON THE DISCIPLES

They Speak with "Other Tongues"

JUDAS GOING OUT
From a painting by Henry F. Tidey

When the day of Pentecost had now come, they were all together in one place. And suddenly there came a sound from heaven as of the rushing of a mighty wind, and it filled all the house where they were sitting. And there appeared to them tongues parting asunder, like fire; and it sat upon each one of them. And they were all filled with the Holy Spirit, and began to speak with other tongues, as the Spirit gave them utterance.

Now there were dwelling at Jerusalem Jews, devout men,

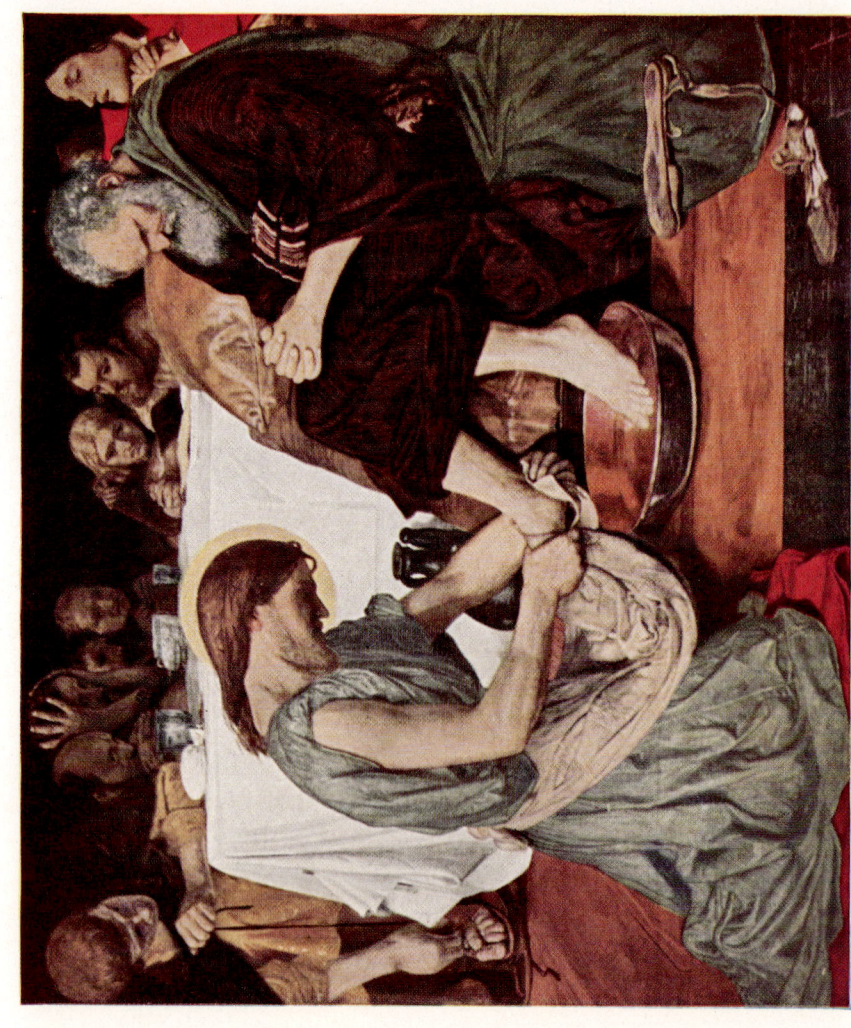

CHRIST WASHING PETER'S FEET
From a painting by Ford Madox Brown
The Tate Gallery, London, England

from every nation under heaven. And when this sound was heard, the multitude came together, and were astonished, because every man heard them speaking in his own language.

And they marveled, saying: "Behold, are not all these that speak Galileans? And how hear we every man in our own language, wherein we were born? Parthians and Medes and Elamites, and the dwellers in Mesopotamia, in Judea and Cappadocia, in Pontus and Asia,[2] in Phrygia and Pamphylia, in Egypt and the parts of Libya about Cyrene, and sojourners from Rome, both Jews and proselytes, Cretans and Arabians, we hear them speaking in our tongues the mighty works of God."

And they were all amazed, and were perplexed, saying one to another, "What meaneth this?"

Others mocking said, "They are filled with new wine."

Peter Preaches the First Christian Sermon

But Peter, standing up with the eleven, lifted up his voice, and spoke forth to them, saying:

"Ye men of Judea, and all ye that dwell at Jerusalem, be this known to you, and give ear to my words. For these are not drunken, as ye suppose; seeing it is but the third hour of the day; but this is that which hath been spoken by the prophet Joel:

"'And it shall be in the last days, saith God,
I will pour forth of my Spirit upon all flesh:
And your sons and your daughters shall prophesy,
And your young men shall see visions,
And your old men shall dream dreams:
Yea and on my servants and on my handmaidens in those days
I will pour forth of my Spirit; and they shall prophesy.
And I will show wonders in the heaven above,
And signs on the earth beneath;

Blood, and fire, and vapor of smoke:
The sun shall be turned into darkness,
And the moon into blood,
Before that great and notable day of the Lord come;
And it shall be, that whosoever shall call on the name of the Lord shall be saved.'

"Ye men of Israel, hear these words: Jesus of Nazareth, a man approved of God to you by mighty works and wonders and signs, which God did by him in the midst of you, even as ye yourselves know; him, being delivered up by the determinate counsel and foreknowledge of God, ye by the hand of lawless men did crucify and slay: whom God raised up, having loosed the pangs of death: because it was not possible that he should be held by it. For David said concerning him:

"'I beheld the Lord always before my face;
For he is on my right hand, that I should not be moved:
Therefore my heart was glad, and my tongue rejoiced;
Moreover my flesh also shall dwell in hope:
Because thou wilt not leave my soul in Hades,
Neither wilt thou give thy Holy One to see corruption.
Thou hast made known to me the ways of life;
Thou shalt make me full of gladness with thy countenance.'

"Brethren, I may speak to you freely of the patriarch David, that he both died and was buried, and his tomb is with us to this day. Therefore, being a prophet, and knowing that God had sworn with an oath to him, that he would set one of his family upon his throne; he foreseeing this spoke of the resurrection of the Christ, that neither was he left in Hades, nor did his flesh see corruption.

"This Jesus did God raise up, whereof we all are witnesses. Therefore being by the right hand of God exalted, and having received of the Father the promise of the Holy Spirit, he hath poured forth this, which ye see and hear.

For David ascended not into the heavens: but he said himself:

"'The Lord said unto my Lord,
Sit thou on my right hand,
Till I make thine enemies the footstool of thy feet.'

"Therefore let all the house of Israel know assuredly, that God hath made that same Jesus, whom ye have crucified, both Lord and Christ."

Thousands Respond to Peter's Message

Now when they heard this, they were pricked in their heart, and said to Peter and the rest of the apostles, "Brethren, what shall we do?"

Then Peter said to them: "Repent, and be baptized every one of you in the name of Jesus Christ for the remission of your sins; and ye shall receive the gift of the Holy Spirit. For the promise is to you, and to your children, and to all that are afar off, even as many as the Lord our God shall call unto him." And with many other words he testified and exhorted them, saying, "Save yourselves from this crooked generation."

Then they that received his word were baptized: and the same day there were added to them about three thousand souls. And they continued steadfastly in the apostles' doctrine and fellowship, in the breaking of bread and the prayers. And fear came upon every soul; and many wonders and signs were done by the apostles. And all that believed were together, and had all things common; and they sold their possessions and goods, and divided them among all, according as any man had need. And day by day, continuing steadfastly with one accord in the temple, and breaking bread at home, they took their food with gladness and singleness of heart, praising God, and having favor with all the people. And the Lord added to them day by day those that were being saved.

Peter at the Gate Beautiful

Now Peter and John were going up into the temple[3] at the hour of prayer, being the ninth hour.

PETER AND JOHN HEAL THE LAME MAN
From a drawing by Raphael

And a certain man that was lame from his birth was carried, whom they laid daily at the gate of the temple which is called Beautiful, to ask alms of those who went into the temple. This man, seeing Peter and John about to go into the temple, asked to receive an alms. And Peter, fastening his eyes upon him, with John, said, "Look on us."

And he gave heed to them, expecting to receive something from them. But Peter said, "Silver and gold have I none; but what I have, that give I thee. In the name of Jesus Christ of Nazareth, walk!"

And he took him by the right hand, and raised him up: and immediately his feet and his ankle bones received strength. And, leaping up, he stood, and began to walk; and he entered with them into the temple, walking, and leaping, and praising God.

And all the people saw him walking and praising God: and knowing that it was he who sat for alms at the Beautiful Gate of the temple, they were filled with wonder and amazement at that which had happened to him.

And as the lame man who was healed held Peter and John, all the people ran together to them in the porch that is called Solomon's, greatly wondering.

THE FIRST SHADOW OF PERSECUTION

Peter and His Associates Are Warned to be Silent

And as they spoke to the people, the priests and the captain of the temple and the Sadducees came upon them, being greatly troubled because they taught the people, and proclaimed in Jesus the resurrection from the dead. And they laid hands on them, and put them in prison unto the morrow: for it was now eventide. But many of them that heard the word believed; and the number of the men came to be about five thousand.

Peter Answers the Challenge of the Authorities

And it came to pass on the morrow, that their rulers and elders and scribes were gathered together in Jerusalem; and Annas the high priest was there, and Caiaphas, and John, and Alexander, and as many as were of the kindred of the high priest. And when they had set them in the midst, they asked, "By what power, or in what name, have ye done this?"

Then Peter, filled with the Holy Spirit, said to them: "Ye rulers of the people, and elders of Israel, if we this day are examined concerning a good deed done to a lame man, by what means he is made whole; be it known to you all, and to all the people of Israel, that in the name of Jesus Christ of Nazareth, whom ye crucified, whom God raised from the

JOHN AND PETER
From a painting by Albrecht Dürer

dead, even in him doth this man stand here before you whole. He is the stone which was set at nought of you the builders, which hath become the head of the corner. And in none other is there salvation: for there is none other name under heaven given among men, whereby we must be saved."

The Religious Leaders Are Perplexed

Now when they saw the boldness of Peter and John, and perceived that they were unlearned and ignorant men, they marveled; and they took knowledge of them, that they had been with Jesus. And seeing the man who was healed standing with them, they could say nothing against it.

But when they had commanded them to go aside out of the council, they conferred among themselves, saying: "What shall we do to these men? that a notable miracle hath been wrought through them, is manifest to all that dwell in Jerusalem; and we cannot deny it. But that it spread no further among the people, let us threaten them, that they speak henceforth to no man in this name."

And they called them, and commanded them not to speak at all nor teach in the name of Jesus.

The Christian Disciples Rejoice

But Peter and John answered and said to them, "Whether it is right in the sight of God to hearken to you rather than to God, judge ye: for we cannot but speak the things which we saw and heard."

So when they had further threatened them, they let them go, not finding how they might punish them, because of the people; for all men glorified God for that which was done. For the man was more than forty years old, on whom this miracle of healing was wrought.

Being let go, they went to their own company, and reported all that the chief priests and the elders had said to them. And when they heard it, they lifted up their voice to

God with one accord, and said: "O Lord, thou that madest the heaven and the earth and the sea, and all that in them is: who by the Holy Spirit, by the mouth of our father David thy servant, saidst:

"'Why did the Gentiles rage,
And the peoples imagine vain things?
The kings of the earth set themselves in array,
And the rulers were gathered together
Against the Lord, and against his Anointed':

for of a truth in this city against thy holy Servant Jesus, whom thou anointedst, both Herod and Pontius Pilate, with the Gentiles and the peoples of Israel, were gathered together, to do whatsoever thy hand and thy counsel foreordained to come to pass. And now, Lord, behold their threatenings; and grant to thy servants, that with all boldness they may speak thy word, while thou stretchest forth thy hand to heal; and that signs and wonders may be done through the name of thy holy Servant Jesus."

And when they had prayed, the place was shaken wherein they were gathered together; and they were all filled with the Holy Spirit, and they spoke the word of God with boldness.

THE FELLOWSHIP OF THE BELIEVERS

They Hold Their Property in Common

And the multitude of those who believed were of one heart and of one soul; and not one of them said that anything of the things which he possessed was his own; but they had all things common.[4]

And with great power gave the apostles their witness of the resurrection of the Lord Jesus; and great grace was upon them all.

For neither was there among them any that lacked; for as many as were possessors of lands or houses sold them, and brought the prices of the things that were sold, and laid them at the apostles' feet: and distribution was made to each, according as any one had need. And Joseph, who by the apostles was surnamed Barnabas (The son of consolation), a Levite, and of the country of Cyprus, having land, sold it, and brought the money, and laid it at the apostles' feet.

Ananias and Sapphira Withhold a Part

But a certain man named Ananias, with Sapphira his wife, sold a possession, and kept back part of the price, his wife also knowing about it, and brought a certain part, and laid it at the apostles' feet.

But Peter said: "Ananias, why hath Satan filled thy heart to lie to the Holy Spirit, and to keep back part of the price of the land? While it remained, was it not thine own? and after it was sold, was it not in thine own power? Why hast thou conceived this thing in thy heart? thou hast not lied to men, but to God."

And Ananias hearing these words fell down and gave up his spirit; and great fear came upon all them that heard it. And the young men rose, and wrapped him round, and they carried him out and buried him.

It was about the space of three hours after, when his wife, not knowing what was done, came in. And Peter said to her, "Tell me whether ye sold the land for so much."

And she said, "Yea, for so much."

Then Peter said to her, "How is it that ye have agreed together to tempt the Spirit of the Lord? behold, the feet of those who have buried thy husband are at the door, and shall carry thee out."

Then she fell down immediately at his feet, and gave up her spirit: and the young men came in and found her dead, and they carried her out and buried her by her husband.

And great fear came upon all the church, and upon as many as heard these things.

IMPRISONMENT AND RELEASE OF THE APOSTLES

Works of Healing Attract the Multitude

And by the hands of the apostles were many signs and wonders wrought among the people.

And they were all with one accord in Solomon's porch. And of the rest dared no man join himself to them; but the people magnified them.

And believers were the more added to the Lord, multitudes both of men and women; insomuch that they even brought forth the sick into the streets, and laid them on beds and couches, that at the least the shadow of Peter passing by might overshadow some of them.

There also came together the multitude from the cities round about Jerusalem, bringing sick folks, and those who were vexed with unclean spirits; and they were healed every one.

The Apostles Are Delivered from Prison at Night

Then the high priest rose up, and all they that were with him (which is the sect of the Sadducees), and were filled with jealousy, and laid hands on the apostles, and put them in the common prison.

But an angel of the Lord by night opened the prison doors, and brought them forth, and said, "Go, stand and speak in the temple to the people all the words of this Life."

And when they heard this, they entered into the temple early in the morning, and taught.

But the high priest came, and they that were with him, and called the council together, and all the senate of the children of Israel, and sent to the prison house to have them brought. But the officers that came found them not in the prison; and they returned, and told, saying, "The prison house we found shut in all safety, and the keepers standing at the doors: but when we had opened, we found no man within."

Now when the captain of the temple and the chief priests heard these things, they were much perplexed concerning them whereunto this would grow.

Then came one and told them, saying, "Behold, the men whom ye put in the prison are in the temple, standing and teaching the people."

Then went the captain with the officers, and brought them, but without violence; for they feared the people, lest they should be stoned.

The Apostles Affirm Their Loyalty to Christ

When they had brought them, they set them before the council: and the high priest asked them, saying, "Did not we strictly command you that ye should not teach in this name? and behold, ye have filled Jerusalem with your doctrine, and intend to bring this man's blood upon us."

But Peter and the other apostles answered and said: "We ought to obey God rather than men. The God of our fathers raised up Jesus, whom ye slew, hanging him on a tree. Him did God exalt with his right hand to be a Prince and a Saviour, to give repentance to Israel, and forgiveness of sins. And we are witnesses of these things; and so is the Holy Spirit, whom God hath given to them that obey him."

When they heard that, they were cut to the heart, and were minded to slay them.

Gamaliel Defends the Christians Before the Council at Jerusalem

But there stood up one in the council, a Pharisee, named Gamaliel, a doctor of the law, honored among all the people, and commanded to put the apostles forth a little while. And he said to them: "Ye men of Israel, take heed to yourselves as touching these men, what ye are about to do. For before these days rose up Theudas, boasting himself to be somebody; to whom a number of men, about four hundred, joined themselves; who was slain; and all, as many as obeyed him, were scattered, and brought to nought. After this man rose up Judas of Galilee in the days of the enrolment, and drew away many people after him: he also perished; and all, even as many as obeyed him, were dispersed.

"And now I say to you, Refrain from these men, and let them alone; for if this counsel or this work is of men, it will come to nought; but if it is of God, ye cannot overthrow it; lest haply ye be found even to be fighting against God."

And to him they agreed; and when they had called the apostles to them, they beat them and commanded them not to speak in the name of Jesus, and let them go.

They therefore departed from the presence of the council, rejoicing that they were counted worthy to suffer dishonor for his name. And daily, in the temple, and at home, they ceased not to teach and to preach Jesus as the Christ.

THE FIRST CHRISTIAN MARTYR

Stephen Becomes One of the Administrators of the Common Fund

In these days, when the number of the disciples was multiplying, there arose a murmuring of the Grecian Jews against the Hebrews, because their widows were neglected in the daily ministration.

Then the twelve called the multitude of the disciples to them, and said: "It is not fit that we should leave the word of God, and serve tables. Wherefore, brethren, look ye out from among you seven men of good report, full of the Holy Spirit and of wisdom, whom we may appoint over this business. But we will continue steadfastly in prayer, and in the ministry of the word."

SAINT STEPHEN'S GATE, JERUSALEM

This gate in the eastern wall of Jerusalem leads out to Olivet and Bethany. Its plainness is somewhat relieved by the curious heraldic sculptures on the walls on either side and by the stumps of columns built into the wall above. It is named in honor of the first Christian martyr, for, according to tradition, the stoning of Stephen took place outside this gate. But we should rather look for the authentic site somewhere beyond the Damascus Gate, where now stands the great Basilica of Saint Stephen.

And the saying pleased the whole multitude. And they chose Stephen, a man full of faith and of the Holy Spirit, and Philip, and Prochorus, and Nicanor, and Timon, and Parmenas, and Nicolaüs, a proselyte of Antioch; whom they

THE CONDEMNATION OF STEPHEN
From a painting by Cerase Fracassini

set before the apostles: and when they had prayed, they laid their hands on them. And the word of God increased; and the number of the disciples multiplied in Jerusalem greatly; and a great company of the priests were obedient to the faith.

Stephen Proves Himself a Powerful Witness

And Stephen, full of grace and power, wrought great wonders and signs among the people. But there arose certain of them that were of the synagogue called the synagogue of the Libertines, and of the Cyrenians, and of the Alexandrians, and of them of Cilicia and of Asia, disputing with Stephen. And they were not able to withstand the wisdom and the Spirit by which he spoke. Then they bribed men, who said, "We have heard him speak blasphemous words against Moses, and against God."

And they stirred up the people, and the elders, and the scribes, and came upon him, and seized him, and brought him into the council, and set up false witnesses, who said,

"This man ceaseth not to speak words against this holy place, and the law: for we have heard him say, that this Jesus of Nazareth shall destroy this place, and shall change the customs which Moses delivered to us."

THE MARTYRDOM OF STEPHEN
From a painting by Giovanni Mariani

And all that sat in the council, fastening their eyes on him, saw his face as it had been the face of an angel.

Then said the high priest, "Are these things so?"

Stephen Is Killed by a Mob

We give here only the last portion of Stephen's defense. He began his defense with a careful account, from the beginning, of the ways by which God had revealed himself to the forefathers. When he showed how deaf to every prophetic word his hearers had always been, and especially to the message of Jesus, they lost all self-control. The accusation which made them furious, and brought upon him the attack of the mob, was as follows:

"Ye stiff-necked and unregenerate in heart and ears, ye do always resist the Holy Spirit: as your fathers did, so do ye. Which one of the prophets did not your fathers persecute? and they killed them that showed beforehand of the coming of the Righteous One; of whom ye have now become betrayers and murderers; ye who received the law as it was ordained by angels, and have not kept it."

When they heard these things, they were cut to the heart, and they raged against him. But he, being full of the Holy Spirit, looked up steadfastly into heaven, and saw the glory of God, and Jesus standing on the right hand of God, and he said, "Behold, I see the heavens opened, and the Son of man standing on the right hand of God."

Then they cried out with a loud voice, and stopped their ears, and rushed upon him with one accord; and they cast him out of the city, and stoned him: and the witnesses laid down their garments at the feet of a young man whose name was Saul. And they stoned Stephen, as he was calling upon God, and saying, "Lord Jesus, receive my spirit!"

And he kneeled down, and cried with a loud voice, "Lord, lay not this sin to their charge." When he had said this, he fell asleep. And Saul was consenting to his death.

And there arose on that day a great persecution against the church which was in Jerusalem; and they were all scattered abroad throughout the regions of Judea and Samaria, except the apostles.

And devout men carried Stephen to his burial, and made great lamentation over him.

As for Saul, he laid waste the church, entering into every house, and dragging out men and women committed them to prison.

EXPERIENCES OF THE APOSTLES IN SAMARIA

The Preaching of Philip Is Received with Joy

Therefore they that were scattered abroad went everywhere preaching the word. And Philip went down to the city of Samaria, and proclaimed to them the Christ. And the people with one accord gave heed to those things which Philip spoke, when they heard, and saw the miracles which he did. For unclean spirits, crying with a loud voice, came out of many that were possessed with them: and many that

ST. STEPHEN
From a painting by Sir John Millais

were palsied, and that were lame, were healed. And there was great joy in that city.

Simon the Magician Is Confounded

But there was a certain man, called Simon, who before this in the city used sorcery, and amazed the people of Samaria, claiming that he was some great one; to whom they all gave heed, from the least to the greatest, saying, "This man is that power of God which is called Great." And they gave heed to him, because for a long time he had amazed them with his sorceries.

But when they believed Philip preaching good tidings concerning the kingdom of God, and the name of Jesus Christ, they were baptized, both men and women. Then Simon himself believed also: and when he was baptized, he continued with Philip; and was amazed, beholding the miracles and signs which were done.

Now when the apostles who were at Jerusalem heard that Samaria had received the word of God, they sent to them Peter and John; who, when they had come down, prayed for them, that they might receive the Holy Spirit; for as yet it had fallen upon none of them: only they had been baptized into the name of the Lord Jesus. Then laid they their hands on them, and they received the Holy Spirit.

Simon's Bribe Is Refused

Now when Simon saw that through the laying on of the apostles' hands the Holy Spirit was given, he offered them money, saying, "Give me also this power, that on whomsoever I lay my hands, he may receive the Holy Spirit."

But Peter said to him: "Thy silver perish with thee, because thou hast thought that the gift of God may be purchased with money. Thou hast neither part nor lot in this matter: for thy heart is not right in the sight of God. Repent therefore of this thy wickedness, and pray God, if perhaps the thought of thy heart may be forgiven thee. For I perceive that thou art in the gall of bitterness and in the bond of iniquity."

Then answered Simon and said, "Pray ye to the Lord for me, that none of the things which ye have spoken come upon me."

And they, when they had testified and preached the word of the Lord, returned to Jerusalem, and preached the gospel to many villages of the Samaritans.

STEPHEN AND SAUL

Stephen, who died while I stood by consenting,
Wrought in his death the making of a life,
Bruised one hard heart to thought of swift repenting,
Fitted one fighter for a nobler strife.

Stephen, the Saint, triumphant and forgiving,
Prayed while the hot blows beat him to the earth.
Was that a dying? Rather it was living!
Through his soul's travail my soul came to birth.

Stephen, the Martyr, full of faith and fearless,
Smiled when his bruised lips could no longer pray,
Smiled with a courage undismayed and peerless,
Smiled! — and that smile is with me, night and day.

Oh, was it I that stood there, all consenting?
I at whose feet the young men's clothes were laid?
Was it my will that wrought that hot tormenting?
My heart that boasted over Stephen, dead?

Yes, it was I; and sore to me the telling.
Yes, it was I; and thought of it has been
God's potent spur my whole soul's might compelling
These outer darknesses for Him to win.
— *John Oxenham*

From "Bees in Amber"
Copyright by The American Tract Society

EXPANSION AND PERSECUTION

PHILIP AND THE COURTIER OF ETHIOPIA

The Ethiopian Is Eager to Know the Truth

AN angel of the Lord spoke to Philip, saying, "Arise, and go toward the south to the way that goeth down from Jerusalem to Gaza: the same is desert."

Then he arose and went. And, behold, a man of Ethiopia, an officer of great authority under Candace, queen of the Ethiopians, who had the charge of all her treasure, and had come to Jerusalem to worship, was returning, and sitting in his chariot was reading Isaiah the prophet. Then the Spirit said to Philip, "Go near, and join thyself to this chariot."

And Philip ran to him, and heard him reading the prophet Isaiah, and said, "Understandest thou what thou readest?"

And he said, "How can I, except some one shall guide me?" And he besought Philip to come up and sit with him.

Now the place of the scripture which he was reading was this:

"He was led as a sheep to the slaughter;
And as a lamb before his shearer is dumb,
So he openeth not his mouth:
In his humiliation his judgment [justice to him] was taken
 away;
And his generation who shall declare?
For his life is taken from the earth."

And the officer said to Philip, "I pray thee, of whom speaketh the prophet this? of himself, or of some other?"

Then Philip opened his mouth, and beginning from this passage of scripture, preached to him Jesus.

VIEW OF ROME, SAINT PETER'S CATHEDRAL IN THE DISTANCE

The Ethiopian Believes that Christ Is the Son of God and Is Baptized

As they went on their way, they came to a certain water; and the officer said, "See, here is water; what doth hinder me to be baptized?"

And Philip said, "If thou believest with all thy heart, thou mayest."

He answered and said, "I believe that Jesus Christ is the Son of God."

And he commanded the chariot to stand still; and they both went down into the water, both Philip and the officer; and he baptized him.

When they came up out of the water, the Spirit of the Lord caught away Philip, and the officer saw him no more; and he went on his way rejoicing.

But Philip was found at Azotus: and passing through he preached the gospel to all the cities, till he came to Cæsarea.

Then the church throughout all Judea and Galilee and Samaria had peace, being built up; and, walking in the fear of the Lord and in the comfort of the Holy Spirit, was multiplied.

THE EFFECTIVE MINISTRY OF PETER

Æneas Is Healed

It came to pass, as Peter went throughout all parts, he came down also to the saints who dwelt at Lydda. There he found a certain man named Æneas, who had kept his bed eight years; for he was palsied.

Peter said to him, "Æneas, Jesus Christ maketh thee whole: arise, and make thy bed." And straightway he arose.

And all that dwelt at Lydda and Sharon saw him, and turned to the Lord.

LYDDA, GENERAL VIEW

Lydda is a most ancient city. It is mentioned by Thothmes III of Egypt (1500 B.C.) in his list of towns captured in Palestine. All the conquerors through the ages have taken it. The place is of interest to Christians because here Peter healed Æneas; and it lives in legend because, since the sixth century, Saint George, the patron saint of England, has been called a native of the town. To his memory the Crusaders built the huge church which still stands, though now transformed into a mosque.

Dorcas Is Brought Back to Life

Now there was at Joppa a certain disciple named Tabitha (Dorcas): this woman was full of good works and deeds of charity which she did.

And it came to pass in those days, that she fell sick, and died: and when they had washed her, they laid her in an upper chamber.

And as Lydda was nigh to Joppa, the disciples, hearing that Peter was there, sent to him two men, desiring him that he would not delay to come to them.

Then Peter arose and went with them. And when he had come, they brought him into the upper chamber: and all the widows stood by him weeping, and showing the coats and

EXPANSION AND PERSECUTION 31

ALMSDEEDS OF DORCAS
From an engraving by William C. Dobson

garments which Dorcas made, while she was with them. But Peter put them all forth, and kneeled down, and prayed; and turning to the body, he said, "Tabitha, arise."

And she opened her eyes; and when she saw Peter, she sat up. And he gave her his hand, and lifted her up; and when he had called the disciples and widows, he presented her alive. And it became known throughout all Joppa; and many believed on the Lord.

THE MEETING OF PETER AND CORNELIUS

Cornelius the Centurion Has a Vision

It came to pass, that Peter abode many days in Joppa, with one Simon a tanner.

THE TRADITIONAL HOUSE OF SIMON THE TANNER
High up above the sea stands this little stone building. Tanners are still found in the neighborhood. From the roof, as of old, there is a glorious view of the sea and of the ledges that form the insignificant harbor. Joppa deserves to live in Christian memory because it is the place where Peter first learned to transcend the limits of Judaism and become fully Christian.

Now there was a certain man in Cæsarea called Cornelius, a centurion of the company called the Italian company, a devout man, and one who feared God with all his house, who gave much alms to the people, and prayed to God always. He saw in a vision, about the ninth hour of the day, an angel of God coming in to him, and saying to him, "Cornelius!"

When he looked on him, he was afraid, and said, "What is it, Lord?"

And he said to him, "Thy prayers and thine alms have gone up for a memorial before God. And now send men to Joppa, and bring one Simon, whose surname is Peter: he lodgeth with one Simon a tanner, whose house is by the seaside: he shall tell thee what thou oughtest to do."

And when the angel who spoke to Cornelius had departed, he called two of his household servants, and a devout soldier of his bodyguard; and when he had told all these things to them, he sent them to Joppa.

Peter also Has a Vision

On the morrow, as they went on their journey, and drew nigh to the city, Peter went up upon the housetop to pray, about the sixth hour; and he became very hungry, and desired to eat; but while they made ready, he fell into a trance; and he saw heaven opened, and a certain vessel descending to him, as it were a great sheet, let down by four corners upon the earth: wherein were all manner of four-footed beasts and creeping things of the earth and birds of the air.

And there came a voice to him, saying, "Rise, Peter; kill and eat."

But Peter said, "Not so, Lord; for I have never eaten anything that is common and unclean."

And the voice came to him again the second time, "What God hath cleansed, that call not thou common."

This was done three times; and the vessel was received up again into heaven.

Peter Goes to Cornelius

Now while Peter was much perplexed as to what the vision which he had seen might mean, behold, the men who were sent by Cornelius, having made inquiry for Simon's house, stood before the gate, and called and asked whether Simon, who was surnamed Peter, were lodging there. And while Peter thought on the vision, the Spirit said to him, "Behold, three men seek thee. Arise therefore, and get thee down, and go with them, nothing doubting: for I have sent them."

Then Peter went down to the men who were sent to him from Cornelius, and said, "Behold, I am he whom ye seek: what is the reason wherefore ye have come?"

And they said, "Cornelius a centurion, a righteous man, and one that feareth God, and well reported of by all the nation of the Jews, was warned from God by a holy angel to send for thee to come to his house, and to hear words from thee."

Then he called them in and lodged them.

And on the morrow Peter went away with them, and certain brethren from Joppa accompanied him. And on the morrow they entered into Cæsarea.

The Two Find that God Has Brought Them Together

And Cornelius was waiting for them, having called together his kinsmen and near friends. And as Peter was coming in, Cornelius met him, and fell down at his feet, and worshiped him. But Peter raised him up, saying, "Stand up; I myself also am a man."

As he talked with him, he went in, and found many that had come together. And he said to them: "Ye know how it is an unlawful thing for a man that is a Jew to keep company or come to one of another nation; and yet God hath

THE RUINS OF CÆSAREA

Little now remains to aid the fancy in a restoration of this once attractive metropolis, which owed its origin to Herod the Great. Its decay has been as complete as its rise was sudden. In the short span of twelve years, Herod transformed a mere landing place on the Mediterranean into an important port on the highway between Tyre and Egypt. He named it in honor of Augustus Cæsar, and made it the headquarters of Roman rule for Judea. Cæsarea had a large harbor, protected by a mole; a system of drainage whereby tides were utilized to flush the streets; two aqueducts, one of them eight miles long; a hippodrome, a theater, many sumptuous palaces, and, dominating all, a temple to Augustus raised on a platform and visible far out at sea. The completion of all this magnificence was celebrated by games and entertainments that cost a fabulous sum.

Christianity early gained a foothold here. Cæsarea was the home of "Philip the evangelist" and his "four virgin daughters who prophesied." Here lived Cornelius, the first Gentile member of the Christian church; and here Peter and Paul visited fellow-believers. Such was the strength of the new church here that, upon the fall of Jerusalem, Cæsarea became the spiritual capital of Christianity in Palestine.

showed me that I should not call any man common or unclean. Therefore I came to you without doubting, when I was sent for. I ask therefore with what intent ye have sent for me."

And Cornelius said: "Four days ago, until this hour, I was keeping the ninth hour of prayer in my house; and behold, a man stood before me in bright apparel, and said, 'Cornelius, thy prayer is heard, and thine alms are had in remembrance in the sight of God. Send therefore to Joppa, and call hither Simon, whose surname is Peter; he lodgeth in the house of Simon a tanner, by the seaside: who, when he cometh, shall speak to thee.' Immediately therefore I

PETER AT THE HOUSE OF CORNELIUS
From a painting by Bernard Fabritius

sent to thee; and thou hast well done that thou hast come. Now therefore we are all here present in the sight of God, to hear all things that have been commanded thee of God."

Peter Explains the Gospel

Then Peter opened his mouth, and said: "Of a truth I perceive that God is no respecter of persons; but in every nation he that feareth him, and worketh righteousness, is acceptable to him. The word which God sent to the children of Israel, preaching good tidings of peace by Jesus Christ (he is Lord of all) — that saying ye yourselves know, which was spread abroad throughout all Judea, beginning from Galilee, after the baptism which John preached; how God anointed Jesus of Nazareth with the Holy Spirit and with power; how he went about doing good, and healing all that were oppressed of the devil; for God was with him.

"And we are witnesses of all things which he did both in the land of the Jews, and in Jerusalem; whom also they slew, hanging him on a tree. Him God raised up the third day, and showed him, not to all the people, but to witnesses chosen before of God, even to us, who ate and drank with him after he rose from the dead.

"And he charged us to preach to the people, and to testify that this is he who is ordained of God to be the Judge of the living and the dead. To him bear all the prophets witness, that through his name whosoever believeth on him shall receive remission of sins."

The Spirit Comes upon Gentile as well as Jew

While Peter yet spoke these words, the Holy Spirit fell on all those who heard the word. And the Jews who believed were astonished, as many as came with Peter, because on the Gentiles also was poured out the gift of the Holy Spirit. For they heard them speak with tongues, and magnify God.

Then answered Peter, "Can any man forbid the water, that these should not be baptized, who have received the Holy Spirit as well as we?" And he commanded them to be baptized in the name of the Lord.

Then prayed they him to tarry certain days.

The Apostles Realize the Wider Reach of the Gospel

Now the apostles and the brethren who were in Judea heard that the Gentiles also had received the word of God. And when Peter had come up to Jerusalem, the Jews con-

THE APOSTLES' SPRING ON THE ROAD TO JERICHO

tended with him, saying, "Thou wentest in to the Gentiles, and didst eat with them."

But Peter began, and expounded the matter to them in order.

When they heard these things, they held their peace, and glorified God, saying, "Then hath God granted to the Gentiles also repentance unto life."

Now they that were scattered abroad after the trouble that arose about Stephen traveled as far as Phœnicia, and Cyprus, and Antioch, speaking the word to none save only to Jews. But there were some of them, men of Cyprus and Cyrene, who, when they came to Antioch, spoke to the Greeks also, preaching the Lord Jesus. And the hand of the Lord was with them; and a great number believed and turned to the Lord.

THE GOSPEL IN ANTIOCH

The First Messenger to be Sent Outside the Holy Land

And the report concerning them came to the ears of the church which was in Jerusalem: and they sent forth Barnabas as far as Antioch; who, when he came, and saw the grace of God, was glad; and he exhorted them all, that with purpose of heart they would cleave to the Lord; for he was a good man, and full of the Holy Spirit and of faith: and many were added unto the Lord.

And the disciples were called Christians first in Antioch.

Relief Is Sent to Famine-stricken Judea

Now in these days came prophets from Jerusalem to Antioch. And there stood up one of them named Agabus, and signified by the Spirit that there should be a great famine throughout all the world: which came to pass in the days of Claudius.

SAINT JAMES THE ELDER
From a painting by Rubens

Then the disciples, every man according to his ability, determined to send relief to the brethren who dwelt in Judea. This also they did.

THE STORM OF PERSECUTION BREAKS

Peter Is Imprisoned

Now about that time Herod the king stretched forth his hands to afflict certain of the church. And he killed James the brother of John with the sword. And because he saw it pleased the Jews, he proceeded to seize Peter also. And those were the days of unleavened bread. And when he had taken him, he put him in prison, and delivered him to four squads of soldiers to guard him; intending after the passover to bring him forth to the people. Peter therefore was kept in prison; but prayer was made without ceasing by the church to God for him.

When Herod was about to bring him forth, the same night Peter was sleeping between two soldiers, bound with two chains; and guards before the door kept the prison.

Peter Is Wonderfully Delivered

And behold, an angel of the Lord stood by him, and a light shone in the cell: and he smote Peter on the side, and awoke him, saying, "Rise up quickly!"

And his chains fell off from his hands. And the angel said to him, "Gird thyself, and bind on thy sandals." And so he did.

Then he said to him, "Cast thy garment about thee, and follow me."

And he went out, and followed him; and he knew not that it was true which was done by the angel, but thought he saw a vision.

When they were past the first and the second guard, they came to the iron gate that leadeth into the city, which opened to them of its own accord: and they went out, and passed on through one street; and straightway the angel departed from him.

When Peter had come to himself, he said, "Now I know of a truth, that the Lord hath sent his angel and delivered me out of the hand of Herod, and from all the expectation of the people of the Jews."

And when he had considered the thing, he came to the house of Mary the mother of John whose surname was Mark, where many were gathered together praying.

And as Peter knocked at the door of the gate, a maid came to answer, named Rhoda. And when she knew Peter's voice, she opened not the gate for gladness, but ran in, and told how Peter stood before the gate. And they said to her, "Thou art mad." But she confidently affirmed that it was even so. And they said, "It is his angel!"

But Peter continued knocking; and when they had opened the door and saw him, they were astonished. But he, beckoning to them with the hand to hold their peace, declared to them how the Lord had brought him out of the prison. And he said, "Go tell these things to James, and to the brethren." And he departed, and went to another place.

SAINT PETER IN PRISON
From a painting by Rembrandt

Now as soon as it was day, there was no small stir among the soldiers, what had become of Peter. And when Herod had

THE RELEASE OF SAINT PETER
From a fresco by Raphael

This is one of the famous frescoes in the so-called Raphael Stanze, or series of audience chambers in the palace of the Vatican, Rome. Behind the grating one sees the soldiers sleeping at their post, the confused and half-awake Peter, and the vigorous angel, robed in celestial light, who is to lead him forth from his dungeon.

sought for him, and found him not, he examined the guards, and commanded that they should be put to death.

And Peter went down from Judea to Cæsarea, and tarried there.

From this time, Peter does a less conspicuous work. He leaves the leadership of the church in Jerusalem to James, the brother of the Lord; and the leadership of the world-wide church is assumed by Paul. Later, we have a glimpse of him conferring with Paul about the burning question regarding the method by which foreigners should be admitted to the church. One of the letters of Paul mentions Peter's traveling about with his wife proclaiming the Gospel. There is an early tradition that he became the head of the church in Rome, and was crucified there. Among the companions of Peter was John Mark, and it is believed that he received from Peter many personal reminiscences of Jesus, which cause the Gospel of Mark to be regarded as, in important respects, "Peter's Gospel." Our last word from Peter is in the message found in the Epistle of Peter.

THE CHURCH OF "QUO VADIS" NEAR ROME

This church is a memorial to the tradition that Peter, in fleeing from Rome during the period of persecution under the Emperor Nero, met Christ at this spot and asked, "Quo vadis, Domine?" (Whither goest thou, Lord?) Christ replied that he was going to Rome to be crucified again. Peter, rebuked and repentant, turned back, and eventually suffered martyrdom by crucifixion.

Peter's Last Message

Christ also suffered for you, leaving you an example, that ye should follow in his steps: who did no sin, neither was guile found in his mouth: who, when he was reviled, reviled not again; when he suffered, threatened not; but committed himself to him that judgeth righteously: who his own self bore our sins in his body upon the tree, that we, having died unto sins, might live unto righteousness; by whose stripes ye were healed. For ye were going astray like sheep; but are now returned to the Shepherd and Bishop of your souls.

The elders who are among you I exhort, who am a fellow-elder, and a witness of the sufferings of Christ, and also a partaker of the glory that shall be revealed: tend the flock of God which is among you, exercising the oversight thereof, not by constraint, but willingly; not for filthy lucre, but of a ready mind; neither as lording it over the charge allotted to you, but making yourselves examples to the flock. And when the chief Shepherd shall be manifested, ye shall receive the crown of glory that fadeth not away.[5]

QUO VADIS?

Peter, outworn,
And menaced by the sword,
Shook off the dust of Rome;
And, as he fled,
Met one, with eager face,
Hastening cityward,
And, to his vast amaze,
It was the Lord.

"Lord, whither goest thou?"
He cried, importunate;
And Christ replied,
"Peter, I suffer loss.
I go to take thy place,
To bear thy cross."

Then Peter bowed his head,
Discomforted;
There, at the Master's feet,
Found grace complete,
And courage, and new faith,
And turned, with him,
To death.

— *John Oxenham*

From "Bees in Amber"
Copyright by The American Tract Society

©*Underwood & Underwood*

PAUL'S GATE, TARSUS

This gate is part of an ancient monument, the nature of which is quite obscure; no one knows who built it, when it was built, or why. It is sufficiently large, however, to have served some important purpose. The picture emphasizes the former greatness of the home of the Apostle to the Gentiles. In reward for its assistance during the civil wars of Rome, Tarsus was made a free city by Augustus, and was governed by its own laws and magistrates.

PAUL AND THE WORLD-WIDE CHURCH

PAUL AND THE WORLD-WIDE CHURCH

WHEN we read of Simon Peter, we are impressed by the fact that he would never have come to prominence or great usefulness if he had not had contact with Jesus of Nazareth. Paul of Tarsus, on the contrary, was one who under any circumstances was destined to become a leader and a man of power. His ability, his training, his energy, and his utter devotion to the cause in which he believed, might have made him the most noted scholar of his race, or a revolutionist against Rome, or, if he had worked in harmony with the imperial authorities, a notable politician or statesman.

In his prime, however, there came to him the sudden revelation of Christ that changed the entire course of his life. He thereupon began his work as evangelist to his own people in foreign lands; but, meeting opposition and rejection, he was led to preach the Gospel among the mixed races of Asia Minor, Macedonia, and Greece. His work was well planned. Accompanied by young disciples whom he trained to succeed him in local leadership, he went along the main highways of travel preaching his message. He sought the Jewish synagogues, where there was at first a free forum; and when he was driven from these, he used any place where men gathered or could be brought together. His plan was to remain in important centers until he built up a church organization, which should become the Christian headquarters of a whole district. To such places he returned to confirm his disciples. To communities which he could not immediately visit, he sent marvelous letters, in which he set forth the ideals and rules by which they should order their lives. Besides being overseer of all these churches, he organized and collected their benevolences, disciplined their unworthy members, and was, as far as possible, their devoted pastor.

This tremendous work was done in spite of great obstacles. The man who carried it on was in infirm health, suffering from some "thorn in the flesh" that hampered him and caused him anguish.

He worked amid all the perils and discomforts of travel in ancient days — in shipwreck, cold, hunger, and loneliness: moreover, in order to obtain a livelihood, he was obliged at times to engage in a humble occupation. He was confronted by constant misunderstandings on the part of lesser men at the head of affairs in the mother church, and by the active hostility of others among his own countrymen. He was the object of continual persecution, which brought upon him extreme physical sufferings and other penalties, both legal and illegal.

"Without the cheer of sister or of daughter,
　　Without the stay of father or of son,
Lone on the land and homeless on the water,
　　Passed he in patience till his work was done."

Not only did Paul become the father of organized Christendom; he was also the father of Christian thought. From him, through Augustine and Calvin and Luther, came down those central doctrines that have had and still have greatest influence in the formulated thought of the churches. His hasty messages were gathered into the ordered thinking of Christian scholars. Preaching is still largely an endeavor to interpret the message of Paul.

The man whose influence has been and still is so mighty possessed a magnetic and lovable personality. Though traditionally of inferior presence, he seems to have had an electric effect upon his companions. There are outbursts of deep and tender affection in his letters which prove that he had a great heart as well as a great mind.

The passion of his life was Jesus Christ, whom he had never seen in the flesh. To him, he said, to live was Christ.

Of the facts of the earthly life of Jesus he says almost nothing: it was rather Christ, the Redeemer, the Risen Lord, who won and held every thought and endeavor of his being.

The story that follows is planned to include not only the narrative in the Book of Acts, but to interweave in its proper place each reference to his own life which Paul made in his letters. By this plan, it is possible to know more of his early experiences and of his last days than is given in the writings of his faithful companion, Luke.

PAUL

Emancipator of Early Christianity and Its Chief Apostle

THE witnesses who were about to stone Stephen "laid down their garments," we are told, "at the feet of a young man whose name was Saul." This was Saul of Tarsus, better known as the Apostle Paul.

He and his associates had been unable "to resist the wisdom and the Spirit" with which Stephen had spoken. They therefore had brought him to speedy trial and condemnation, on charges of blasphemy against Moses and God; and Paul, standing by, witnessed the execution, fully consenting to it.

But Stephen scored a double victory on that day. In meeting death so triumphantly in defense of his newly-found faith in Christ, he was, first of all, victorious over himself. Then, he was victorious over Paul, whom he had already confuted in argument. In his dying manifestation of the Christ-spirit, he took the first conquering step into the soul of Paul. Never thereafter was the latter able to forget the power of that picture—the kneeling saint praying for the forgiveness of the men who were even then stoning him to death.

It was not long after that Paul yielded himself completely to the very Christ for whom Stephen had on that memorable day laid down his life. His conversion was effected finally by a dramatic, a miraculous episode.

Sensing clearly the danger to Judaism involved in any serious spread of that new spirit and teaching, he had set out on a definite course of persecution, determined to beat down the heresy wherever it raised its head. He learned that it was asserting itself in Damascus; he at once sought and obtained from the high priest letters to the synagogues of Damascus, authorizing him to arrest any whom he might find there following after this new Way, whether they were men or women, and to bring them bound to Jerusalem for trial.

What his thoughts were along that journey, who shall tell? Perhaps he was pondering those strange assertions of Stephen and his companions, that the recently crucified Jesus was indeed the promised Messiah, that God had raised him from the dead, that he would soon return to usher in the Kingdom, and that through repentance and faith in him remission of sins could be had, and also the empowering gift of the Holy Spirit. If this were true, what a wonderful release it would be from the impossible exactions of the Mosaic Law, under which Paul was even then groaning in dissatisfaction and distress of soul! The thought of it increased to an agony his sense of bondage. He tells us in his letter to the Romans that he cried within himself, "O wretched man that I am! who shall deliver me from the body of this death?" But, on the other hand, how absurd it was to be told to look to a dead Messiah for all this; and a crucified one, at that! True, they said he was risen; but what evidence was there of that, apart from the statements of these deluded men? If only Jesus were alive, and not dead, how easily the whole matter could be settled!

Then it happened — the miracle of centuries, second only, perhaps, to the Resurrection of Jesus in importance! Jesus himself appeared to him, subdued his spirit, won his allegiance, and led him out of his bondage into the liberty of the Gospel of grace. The account of that experience needs to be read in the very words of Paul. Of one thing it assured him beyond every possible shadow of doubt — Jesus was alive! And with that revelation came also his commission — "a chosen vessel unto me, to bear my name before the Gentiles and kings, and the children of Israel."

What wonder that it drove him into solitude, even as the baptismal experience of Jesus had driven him into the wilderness! Perhaps, as some writers suggest, Paul went into the region of Sinai, and there, near the place where God through Moses had transmitted his Law to Israel, thought out the implications of this new revelation both for the Jews and for the Gentiles.

At any rate, when he returned from his seclusion in Arabia, he seems to have had well in hand the essential features of what he was compelled later to emphasize as his gospel. The Law had served its purpose: it had been a schoolmaster to Israel to bring her to Christ. Jesus by his blameless life and unmerited death had become the world's all-sufficient atonement. Salvation now was gained, not by keeping the Law, but through faith in him.

This was Paul's own emancipation from Judaism, and he became, under God, the liberator of early Christianity, disentangling it from the trammels of Jewish legalism, carrying it with all-enduring zeal to the leading centers of the Roman world, and setting it forward on its world-conquering way.

No sentimental romance was his career, but an epic of apostolic labors and heroisms. Read his own account and hear the veteran tell of conflicts endured in a strenuous, battle-shocked life. How it thrills and shames us!

And his zealous, powerful life reached its climax in the glory of martyrdom. We first met him witnessing the stoning of Stephen; we last see him in a Roman prison awaiting his own execution, exclaiming: "I have fought a good fight, I have finished my course, I have kept the faith. Henceforth there is laid up for me a crown of righteousness, which the Lord, the righteous judge, shall give me at that day; and not to me only, but to all them also that love his appearing."

PAUL
From a painting by Raphael

PAUL'S EARLY LIFE

PREPARATION FOR HIS LIFE WORK

The Jews probably kept by themselves in Tarsus, and Paul's religious training when a boy came from the leaders of the local synagogue. When he became a young man, he was sent to Jerusalem, where he was the student of the great and broad-minded Gamaliel.

The Jewish custom was that every boy, whether destined for a profession or not, should learn a trade, so as to be able under all circumstances to support himself. Paul learned one of the local trades, that of making tents from goats' hair. In his defense of himself to the people of Jerusalem, spoken on the castle stairs, Paul referred to his early life as follows:

He Tells His Own Story

"I AM a Jew, born in Tarsus, a city of Cilicia, but brought up in this city [Jerusalem], at the feet of Gamaliel, instructed according to the strict manner of the law of our fathers, being zealous for God, even as ye all are this day: and I persecuted this Way to the death, binding and delivering into prisons both men and women."[6]

On another occasion Paul said:

"Though I myself might have confidence even in the flesh: if any other man thinketh to have confidence in the flesh, I yet more: consecrated the eighth day, of the stock of Israel, of the tribe of Benjamin, a Hebrew of Hebrews; as touching the law, a Pharisee; as touching zeal, persecuting the church; as touching the righteousness which is in the law, found blameless.

"Howbeit what things were gain to me, these have I counted loss for Christ. Yea verily, and I count all things to be loss for the excellency of the knowledge of Christ Jesus my Lord: for whom I suffered the loss of all things, and do count them but refuse, that I may gain Christ, and be found in him, not having a righteousness of mine own, even that

GENERAL VIEW OF TARSUS

Paul could hardly say today that he was "a citizen of no mean city." Tarsus is large, but mean. It bears all the earmarks of Turkish domination. Hardly a fragment of its ancient splendor remains above ground. The harbor has silted up; the river which brought sea-going ships to the very center of the town is now useless for navigation; the forums, the theaters, the baths, the temples, and the great Stoic university, have completely vanished. One institution of learning still exists, and it is housed in the large buildings in the foreground of the picture—Saint Paul's College, manned by American missionaries, who teach the religion of the Apostle Paul and follow his inspiring example in spite of war, massacre, typhus, and the complete substitution of Turkish inhabitants for Armenian and Greek. The snow-capped Taurus mountains that Paul so often climbed still look down upon the Plain of Tarsus from their silent station in the north.

which is of the law, but that which is through faith in Christ, the righteousness which is of God by faith: that I may know him, and the power of his resurrection, and the fellowship of his sufferings, and die even as he died; if by any means I may attain unto the resurrection from the dead. Not that I have already obtained, or am already made perfect: but I press on, if so be that I may apprehend that for which also I was apprehended by Christ Jesus.

"Brethren, I count not myself yet to have apprehended: but one thing I do, forgetting the things which are behind, and stretching forward to the things which are before, I press on toward the goal unto the prize of the high calling of God in Christ Jesus."

STREET SCENE IN TARSUS

Not all of Tarsus is as shabby as this picture would indicate. It has paved streets, substantial bazaars, and a few public buildings. Yet there is nothing in the city to recall the days of its splendor, when the Roman general Antony made it his headquarters and the Egyptian queen Cleopatra rode up the Cydnus in her gilded barge to captivate the great Roman. Tarsus is now the center of an agricultural district, the main interests of which are the raising of fruit and the keeping of sheep.

Again, Paul wrote:

"I thank him that enabled me, even Christ Jesus our Lord, because he counted me faithful, appointing me to his service; though I was before a blasphemer, and a persecutor, and injurious; but I obtained mercy, because I did it ignorantly in unbelief; and the grace of our Lord abounded exceedingly with faith and love which is in Christ Jesus. This is a faithful saying, and worthy of all acceptation, that Christ Jesus came into the world to save sinners; of whom I am chief: howbeit for this cause I obtained mercy, that in me as chief might Jesus Christ show forth all his longsuffering, for an example of them that should thereafter believe on him to life everlasting."

Paul's Conversion as Described by the Author of the Book of Acts

HE AT FIRST PERSECUTES THE CHURCH

The Jews cast Stephen out of the city, and stoned him: and the witnesses laid down their garments at the feet of a young man whose name was Saul. And Saul was consenting to his death.

And there arose on that day a great persecution against the church which was in Jerusalem; and they were all scattered abroad throughout the regions of Judea and Samaria, except the apostles.

As for Saul, he laid waste the church, entering into every house, and dragging out men and women committed them to prison.

HE BECOMES A CHRISTIAN

Saul, yet breathing threatening and slaughter against the disciples of the Lord, went to the high priest, and asked of him letters to Damascus to the synagogues, that if he found any that were of the Way, whether they were men or women, he might bring them bound to Jerusalem.

As he journeyed, he came near Damascus: and suddenly there shone round about him a light out of heaven: and he fell upon the earth, and heard a voice saying to him, "Saul, Saul, why persecutest thou me?"

And he said, "Who art thou, Lord?"

Then the Lord said, "I am Jesus whom thou persecutest: it is hard for thee to kick against the goads."

And he trembling and astonished said, "Lord, what wilt thou have me to do?"

THE SO-CALLED HOUSE OF ANANIAS, DAMASCUS

The priest in the center of the picture is about to enter the door that leads down into a little chapel under the open court. This chapel is said to occupy the site of the house of Ananias. Worship is held here regularly in accordance with the Western rite, for the chapel is in charge of Franciscan monks.

The Lord said to him, "Rise, and go into the city, and it shall be told thee what thou must do."

And the men who journeyed with him stood speechless, hearing a voice, but seeing no man. So Saul rose from the earth; and when his eyes were opened, he saw nothing; and they led him by the hand, and brought him into Damascus. And he was three days without sight, and neither ate nor drank.

Now there was a certain disciple at Damascus, named Ananias; and to him the Lord said in a vision, "Ananias!"

And he said, "Behold, I am here, Lord."

The Lord said to him, "Rise, and go into the street which is called Straight, and inquire in the house of Judas for one called Saul, of Tarsus; for behold, he prayeth; and he hath seen in a vision a man named Ananias coming in, and putting his hand on him, that he might receive his sight."

But Ananias answered, "Lord, I have heard from many of this man, how much evil he hath done to thy saints at Jerusalem; and here he hath authority from the chief priests to bind all that call upon thy name."

But the Lord said to him, "Go thy way; for he is a chosen vessel unto me, to bear my name before the Gentiles and kings, and the children of Israel; for I will show him how great things he must suffer for my name's sake."

And Ananias went his way, and entered into the house; and putting his hands on him, said, "Brother Saul, the Lord, even Jesus, who appeared to thee in the way which thou camest, hath sent me, that thou mayest receive thy sight, and be filled with the Holy Spirit."

And immediately there fell from his eyes as it were scales, and he received his sight; and he rose, and was baptized. And when he had received food, he was strengthened.

PAUL'S ACTIVE MINISTRY BEGUN

The Christians Are Suspicious of Paul

Then was Saul certain days with the disciples who were at Damascus. And immediately he proclaimed Christ in the synagogues, that he is the Son of God.

But all that heard him were amazed, and said, "Is not this that man who in Jerusalem made havoc of those who called on the name of Jesus? and he came hither for this intent, that he might bring them bound before the chief priests."

But Saul increased the more in strength, and put to confusion the Jews who dwelt at Damascus, proving that this is the Christ.

After many days, the Jews took counsel together to kill him; but their plot became known to Saul. And they watched

PAUL'S GATE, DAMASCUS

This gate is truly authentic, for it is in a part of the city wall that was here in Paul's day. Through the gate you may see the beginning of the "street called Straight." The first turn on the right leads you to the house of Ananias, where Paul received his sight and was baptized after his remarkable experience on the way to the city.

THE TRADITIONAL PLACE OF PAUL'S ESCAPE, DAMASCUS

the gates day and night to kill him. But his friends took him by night, and let him down through the wall, lowering him in a basket.

And when Saul came to Jerusalem, he tried to join himself to the disciples; but they were all afraid of him, and believed not that he was a disciple. But Barnabas took him, and brought him to the apostles, and declared to them how he had seen the Lord in the way, and that he had spoken to him, and how he had preached boldly at Damascus in the name of Jesus.

And he was with them coming in and going out at Jerusalem, preaching boldly in the name of the Lord: and he spoke and disputed against the Grecian Jews. But they went about to kill him. And when the brethren knew it, they brought him down to Cæsarea, and sent him forth to Tarsus.

Paul's Own Explanation of His Attitude and Purposes

his declaration of his position

I make known to you, brethren, that the gospel which was preached by me is not according to man; for I neither received it from man, nor was I taught it, but I received it through revelation of Jesus Christ.

For ye have heard of my manner of life in time past in the Jews' religion, how that beyond measure I persecuted the church of God, and made havoc of it: and I advanced in the Jews' religion beyond many of mine own age among my countrymen, being more exceedingly zealous for the traditions of my fathers.

THE TRADITIONAL PLACE OF PAUL'S ESCAPE, DAMASCUS

When Paul escaped from Damascus the town was a flourishing city, surrounded, no doubt, by a strong wall built in the well-known substantial Roman fashion. Since that day, wars have devastated the East, and Damascus has suffered repeatedly from siege and capture and destructive fires. The lower stratum of this wall is built of old material, perhaps of the Roman age, but the structure itself can not be more than four hundred years old.

But when it pleased God, who set me apart from my birth, and called me through his grace, to reveal his Son in me, that I might preach him among the Gentiles; straightway I conferred not with flesh and blood: neither went I up to Jerusalem to those who were apostles before me: but I went into Arabia; and returned again to Damascus.

Then after three years I went up to Jerusalem to visit Cephas [Peter], and abode with him fifteen days. But other of the apostles saw I none, save James the Lord's brother.

Afterwards I came into the regions of Syria and Cilicia; and was unknown by face to the churches of Judea which were in Christ: but they had heard only that he who persecuted us in times past now preacheth the faith of which he once made havoc; and they glorified God in me.

HIS CONVICTIONS CONCERNING HIS LIFE MISSION

The grace was given me of God, that I should be a minister of Jesus Christ to the Gentiles, ministering the gospel of God, that the offering up of the Gentiles might be made acceptable, being sanctified by the Holy Spirit. I have therefore my glorying in Jesus Christ in those things which pertain to God. For I will not dare to speak of any things save those which Christ wrought through me, for the obedience of the Gentiles, by word and deed, in the power of signs and wonders, in the power of the Holy Spirit; so that from Jerusalem, and round about even to Illyricum, I have fully preached the gospel of Christ. Yea, so have I striven to preach the gospel, not where Christ was already named, lest I should build upon another man's foundation; but, as it is written:

"They shall see, to whom no tidings of him came,
And they who have not heard shall understand."

To me, who am less than the least of all saints, was this grace given, to preach among the Gentiles the unsearchable riches of Christ; and to make all men see what is the dispensation of the mystery which for ages hath been hid in God, who created all things; to the intent that now to the principalities and the powers in the heavenly places might be made known through the church the manifold wisdom of God, according to the eternal purpose which he purposed in Christ Jesus our Lord.

Though I was free from all men, yet I brought myself under bondage to all, that I might gain the more. To the Jews I became as a Jew, that I might gain Jews; to them that are under the law, as under the law, not being myself under the law, that I might gain them that are under the law; to them that are without law, as without law, not being without law to God, but under law to Christ, that I might gain them that are without law. To the weak I became weak, that I might gain the weak: I have become all things to all men, that I may by all means save some. And I do all things for the gospel's sake, that I may be a joint partaker thereof.

I have learned, in whatsoever state I am, therein to be content. I know how to be abased, and I know also how to abound. In everything and in all things I have learned the secret both to be filled and to be hungry, both to abound and to be in want. I can do all things through Christ who strengtheneth me.

THE MASTER LIBRARY

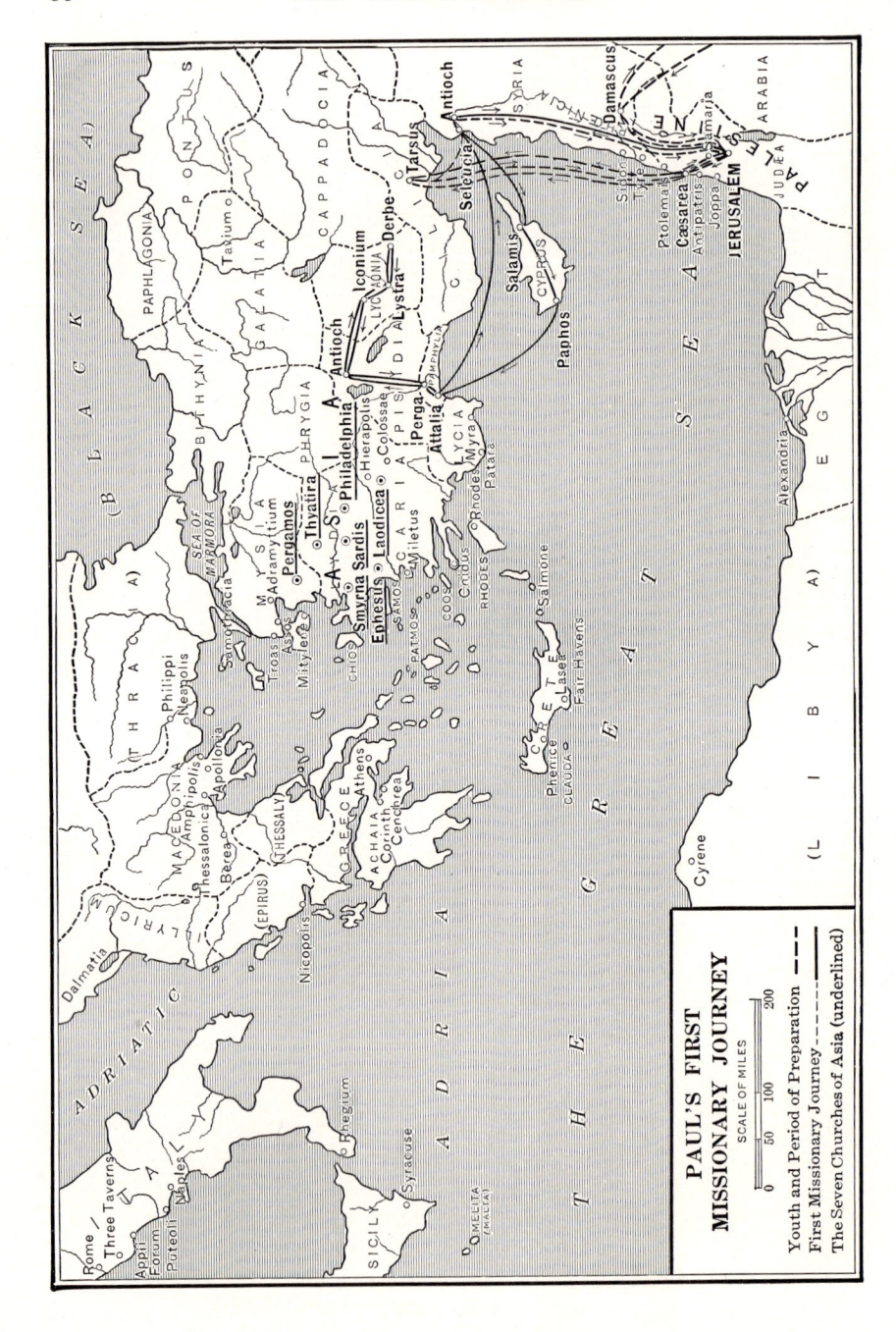

PAUL'S FIRST MISSIONARY JOURNEY

SCALE OF MILES
0   50   100   200

Youth and Period of Preparation ━━━
First Missionary Journey ━ ━ ━
The Seven Churches of Asia (underlined)

PAUL'S EARLY LIFE

PAUL'S YOUTH AND PERIOD OF PREPARATION

Tarsus, Cilicia
  Birth. A Roman citizen
  Schooling at synagogue
  Learns trade of tentmaker
Jerusalem, Judea
  Educated under Gamaliel
Tarsus, Cilicia
  Lives here during ministry of Jesus
Jerusalem, Judea
  Rabbi of Cilician Hellenists
  Member of Sanhedrin
  Consented to Stephen's death
  Persecuted the Christians
Damascus, Syria
  Conversion
  Baptism
  Preaches in the synagogue
Arabia
  Retirement
Damascus, Syria
  Life is threatened
  Forced to flee
Jerusalem, Judea
  Received by the Apostles
  Vision of Christ in the Temple
  Forced to flee
Tarsus, Cilicia (via Cæsarea)
  Suffers shipwreck
  Persecuted by Romans and Jews
Antioch, Syria
  With Barnabas founds Gentile church
Jerusalem, Judea
  Brings contributions for relief
  James killed by Herod
  Peter imprisoned and delivered
Antioch, Syria
  Joined by John Mark
  Called to the Gentiles

FIRST MISSIONARY JOURNEY AND COUNCIL AT JERUSALEM

Seleucia (Port of Antioch)
  Embarks with Barnabas and Mark
Salamis, Cyprus
  Preaches in the synagogues
Paphos, Cyprus
  Elymas the Sorcerer struck blind
  Sergius Paulus converted
  Now known as Paul, not Saul
Perga, Pamphylia (via Attalia)
  Mark returns to Jerusalem
  Paul stricken with fever
Antioch, Pisidia
  Preaches to Jews and Gentiles
  Expelled from the city
Iconium, Lycaonia
  Many converted in synagogue
  Forced to flee
Lystra, Lycaonia
  Is worshiped and later stoned
Derbe, Lycaonia
  Preaches and gains many disciples
Lystra, Iconium, Antioch
  Confirms disciples and appoints elders
  Timothy becomes his disciple
Perga, Pamphylia
  Preaches
Attalia
Antioch, Syria
  Reports his work to the church
  Traveled 1400 miles in two years
  Dispute over Gentiles
Jerusalem, Judea (via Phœnicia and Samaria)
  The Council at Jerusalem
  Joined by Silas
Antioch, Syria
  Reports action of the Council

ANTIOCH IN SYRIA

Antioch was founded about 300 B.C. by Seleucus, one of the generals of Alexander, who, on the death of his master, divided the world between himself and three others. The city was named after the founder's father, Antiochus—a name that became one of sinister omen to the Jews because of their sufferings at the hands of a later member of the family, Antiochus Epiphanes. The city had a splendid situation. It lay on the slopes of a lofty mountain. At its foot ran the navigable river Orontes fourteen miles to the sea, where a splendid harbor sheltered the fleets of all nations. Antioch thus became a terminal for the caravan roads that stretched eastward and southward. It became rich and prosperous. Successive kings adorned

(Continued at bottom of opposite page)

FIRST MISSIONARY JOURNEY OF PAUL

THE OUTWARD VOYAGE

Paul and Barnabas Undertake a New Campaign

BARNABAS and Saul returned from Jerusalem, when they had fulfilled their ministration, and took with them John, whose surname was Mark.

Now there were, in the church that was at Antioch, certain prophets and teachers, Barnabas, and Symeon that was called Niger, and Lucius of Cyrene, and Manaen the foster brother of Herod the tetrarch, and Saul.

As they ministered to the Lord, and fasted, the Holy Spirit said, "Separate me Barnabas and Saul for the work whereunto I have called them." Then, when they had fasted and prayed and laid their hands on them, they sent them away.

---

it magnificently, until in the days of Paul it ranked third in importance among the cities of the empire. Straight across it from east to west ran a splendid corso with double colonnades, so that in wet weather the populace could walk from one end of the city to the other under cover. The promenade was adorned with trees, flowers, fountains, and statues.

Politically, Antioch became free when the Roman general Pompey pacified the East. Julius Cæsar built here a splendid basilica, and gave the city a new aqueduct, a theater, and public baths. Augustus, Agrippa, Herod the Great, and Tiberius also embellished it. When Paul came here at the invitation of Barnabas it had over five hundred thousand inhabitants, and was called "the Queen of the East." With all its magnificence, however, it was an exceedingly wicked city. According to the testimony of antiquity, it was one of the foulest and most depraved in the world. The Grove of Daphne, five miles out of the city, became such an infamous place, through its shrines of Venus and Isis, its theaters, baths and dancing saloons, that soldiers who visited it were dismissed from the imperial service.

Though Jews formed a large portion of the population, the Christian church that sprang up in the city was more largely Gentile than Jewish. It was quite natural, therefore, that Antioch should speedily become the center of missionary activity among the Gentiles, and should number among its members the greatest missionary of all—the Apostle Paul himself.

The earthquakes, wars, and pestilences have all but destroyed this famous city. From Byzantine times the story of Antioch has been a long tragedy, until now barely six thousand Turkish inhabitants huddle among the ruins.

ELYMAS STRICKEN BLIND
From a painting by Raphael

They Sail to the Island of Cyprus

So they, being sent forth by the Holy Spirit,[7] departed to Seleucia; and from thence they sailed to Cyprus.[8] And when they were at Salamis, they proclaimed the word of God in the synagogues of the Jews; and they had also John as their attendant.

And when they had gone through the whole island to Paphos, they found a certain sorcerer, a false prophet, a Jew, whose name was Bar-Jesus; who was with the proconsul, Sergius Paulus, a man of understanding. The same called to him Barnabas and Saul, and sought to hear the word of God. But Elymas the sorcerer (for so is his name by interpretation) withstood them, seeking to turn aside the proconsul from the faith.

Then Saul, who was also called Paul, filled with the Holy Spirit, fastened his eyes on him, and said: "O full of all guile and all villainy, thou son of the devil, thou enemy of all righteousness, wilt thou not cease to pervert the right ways of the Lord? And now, behold, the hand of the Lord is upon thee, and thou shalt be blind, not seeing the sun for a season."

And immediately there fell on him a mist and a darkness; and he went about seeking some to lead him by the hand.

Then the proconsul, when he saw what was done, believed, being astonished at the teaching of the Lord.

Paul Is Welcomed at Antioch in Pisidia

Now Paul and his company set sail from Paphos, and came to Perga in Pamphylia. And John [Mark] departed from them, and returned to Jerusalem.

But when they departed from Perga, they came to Antioch in Pisidia; and they went into the synagogue on the sabbath day, and sat down. And after the reading of the law and the prophets the rulers of the synagogue sent to them, saying, "Brethren, if ye have any word of exhortation for the people, say on."

Paul's Address at Antioch

HE SUMMARIZES THE EVENTS LEADING UP TO THE ADVENT OF CHRIST

Then Paul stood up, and beckoning with his hand said:

"Men of Israel, and ye that fear God, hearken. The God of this people Israel chose our fathers, and exalted the people when they dwelt as strangers in the land of Egypt, and with a high arm led he them forth out of it.

"And for about the time of forty years he bore with them in the wilderness. And when he had destroyed seven nations in the land of Canaan, he gave them their land for an inheritance, for about four hundred and fifty years: and after that he gave them judges until Samuel the prophet.

"Afterwards they asked for a king; and God gave to them Saul the son of Kish, a man of the tribe of Benjamin, for the space of forty years. And when he had removed him, he raised up David to be their king; to whom also he bore witness, and said, 'I have found David the son of Jesse, a man after mine own heart, who shall fulfil all my will.'

"Of this man's family hath God, according to his promise, raised to Israel a Saviour, Jesus; when John had first preached before his coming the baptism of repentance to all the people of Israel.

"And as John was finishing his work, he said, 'Whom think ye that I am? I am not he. But behold, there cometh one after me, the shoes of whose feet I am not worthy to unloose.'

HE BRIEFLY TELLS THE STORY OF JESUS

"Brethren, children of the race of Abraham, and those among you who fear God, to us is the word of this salvation sent. For they that dwell at Jerusalem, and their rulers, because they knew him not, nor yet the voices of the prophets which are read every sabbath day, fulfilled them in condemning him. And though they found no cause of death in him, yet desired they Pilate that he should be slain. And when they had fulfilled all that was written of him, they took him down from the tree, and laid him in a tomb.

"But God raised him from the dead; and he was seen for many days by them that came up with him from Galilee to Jerusalem, who are now his witnesses to the people.

HE PREACHES FORGIVENESS OF SINS

"Now we declare to you glad tidings of the promise made to the fathers, how that God hath fulfilled the same to our children, in that he raised up Jesus; as also it is written in the second psalm, 'Thou art my Son; this day have I begotten thee.' And as concerning that he raised him from the dead, now no more to return to corruption, he said on this wise, 'I will give you the sure mercies of David.' Wherefore he saith also in another psalm, 'Thou wilt not suffer thy Holy One to see corruption.' For David, after he had in his own generation served the counsel of God, fell asleep, and was laid unto his fathers, and saw corruption; but he whom God raised again saw no corruption.

"Be it known to you therefore, brethren, that through this man is proclaimed to you remission of sins; and by him all that believe are justified from all things, from which ye could not be justified by the law of Moses. Beware therefore, lest that come upon you, which is spoken in the prophets:

"'Behold, ye despisers,
And wonder, and perish;
For I work a work in your days,
A work which ye shall in no wise believe,
If one declare it unto you.'"

Paul's Message Is Received by Some and Rejected by Others

When the Jews had gone out of the synagogue, the Gentiles besought that these words might be spoken to them the next sabbath.

Now when the congregation broke up, many of the Jews and of the devout proselytes followed Paul and Barnabas; who, speaking to them, urged them to continue in the grace of God. And the next sabbath almost the whole city came together to hear the word of God. But when the Jews saw the multitudes, they were filled with jealousy, and contradicted the things which were spoken by Paul, and blasphemed.

The Apostles Turn to the Gentiles

Then Paul and Barnabas spoke out boldly, and said: "It was necessary that the word of God should first be spoken to you. But seeing ye put it from you, and judge

"LO, WE TURN TO THE GENTILES"
From a painting by Frederick Shields

yourselves unworthy of everlasting life, lo, we turn to the Gentiles. For so hath the Lord commanded us, saying:

"'I have set thee for a light of the Gentiles,
That thou shouldst be for salvation unto the ends of the earth.'"

And when the Gentiles heard this, they were glad, and glorified the word of the Lord; and as many as were ordained to eternal life believed. And the word of the Lord was spread abroad throughout all the region. But the Jews urged on the devout women of honorable estate, and the chief men of the city, and stirred up a persecution against Paul and Barnabas, and expelled them out of their borders. But they shook off the dust of their feet against them, and came to Iconium. And the disciples were filled with joy and with the Holy Spirit.

The People of Iconium Are Stirred to Violence

It came to pass in Iconium[9] that they entered together into the synagogue of the Jews, and so spoke that a great multitude both of Jews and of Greeks believed. But the unbelieving Jews stirred up the Gentiles, and made them hostile to the brethren.

Long time therefore they tarried there speaking boldly in the Lord, who bore witness to the word of his grace, and granted signs and wonders to be done by their hands.

But the multitude of the city was divided; and part held with the Jews, and part with the apostles. And when there was made an attempt, both of the Gentiles and of the Jews with their rulers, to treat them shamefully, and to stone them, they became aware of it, and fled to Lystra and Derbe, cities of Lycaonia, and to the region that lieth round about; and there they preached the gospel.

Paul and Barnabas Are Hailed as Gods

At this point, just as Paul makes one of his first approaches to a Gentile community upon this first missionary journey, it is interesting to inquire regarding his personal appearance. A book about Paul, that goes back ultimately to a document of the first century, states that he was "bald-headed, bow-legged, strongly built, a man small in size, with meeting eyebrows, with a rather large nose; full of grace, for at times he looked like a man, and at times he had the face of an angel." This striking description, which suggests a really human and personal charm, is that which has been adopted by Christian art. It also explains the impression that he made at Lystra, for if Barnabas was mistaken for Jupiter because of his dignity and nobility of bearing, Paul may have been thought to be Mercury because of his liveliness and eloquence.

At Lystra there sat a certain man, powerless in his feet, a cripple from his birth, who never had walked. The same heard Paul speaking: who, fastening his eyes upon him, and perceiving that he had faith to be healed, said with a loud voice, "Stand upright on thy feet!" And he leaped up and walked.

PAUL IS WORSHIPED AT LYSTRA
From a painting by Raphael

And when the people saw what Paul had done, they lifted up their voice, saying in the speech of Lycaonia, "The gods have come down to us in the likeness of men!"

And they called Barnabas, Jupiter; and Paul, Mercury, because he was the chief speaker. Then the priest of Jupiter, whose temple was before the city, brought oxen and garlands to the gates, and would have done sacrifice with the multitudes.

But when the apostles, Barnabas and Paul, heard of it, they rent their garments, and ran in among the people, crying out and saying: "Sirs, why do ye these things? We also are men of like passions with you, and bring you good tidings, that ye should turn from these vain things to the living God, who made the heaven and the earth and the sea, and all things that are therein: who in times past suffered all nations to walk in their own ways. Nevertheless he left not himself without witness, in that he did good, and gave you

BUST OF JUPITER
From the Vatican Museum, Rome

This is one of the famous representations of Father Zeus, the chief of the Greek divinities, whom the Romans identified with their own Jupiter. The abundant hair and beard indicate maturity and strength, the well-developed forehead shows intellectuality, and the kindly face suggests those qualities of fatherhood which the ancients desired to find in their chief divinity.

from heaven rains and fruitful seasons, filling your hearts with food and gladness."

Even with these sayings scarce restrained they the multitudes from doing sacrifice to them.

THE RIVER ORONTES AT ANTIOCH IN SYRIA
Courtesy of Professor G. L. Robinson, D.D.

The Orontes is the chief river of Syria. It rises in the lofty plain between Lebanon and Anti-Lebanon, flows northward through a valley that was famous for its civilization in the days of Abraham and even earlier, then turning abruptly westward it breaks through the mountains and descends past Antioch to the sea. In Paul's day, the river was not navigable for seagoing ships. The vast trade of Antioch had therefore to pass through the port of Seleucia, where the river enters the Mediterranean.

THE RETURN VOYAGE

Paul Narrowly Escapes Death

But there came thither certain Jews from Antioch and Iconium: and having persuaded the people, they stoned Paul, and dragged him out of the city, supposing that he was dead.

Howbeit, as the disciples stood round about him, he rose up, and came into the city; and the next day he departed with Barnabas to Derbe. When they had preached the gospel to that city, and had made many disciples, they returned again to Lystra, and to Iconium, and to Antioch, confirming the souls of the disciples, exhorting them to continue in the faith, and that "we must through much tribulation enter into the kingdom of God." And when they had appointed for them elders in every church, and had prayed with fasting, they commended them to the Lord, on whom they believed.

And after they had passed throughout Pisidia, they came to Pamphylia. And when they had spoken the word in Perga, they went down to Attalia; and thence they sailed to Antioch, from whence they had been committed to the grace of God for the work which they had fulfilled. And when they had come, and had gathered the church together, they told all that God had done with them, and how he had opened a door of faith to the Gentiles.

And they abode a long time with the disciples.

Must the Gentile Christians Become Jews?

The success of Paul and Barnabas now brought up a discussion at Jerusalem between Paul and Peter and the other Christians gathered there as to the terms under which Gentiles should be admitted to the churches.

Certain men who came down from Judea taught the brethren, and said, "Except ye keep the custom of Moses, ye cannot be saved." And when Paul and Barnabas had no little disagreement and questioning with them, they determined that Paul and Barnabas, and certain other of them, should go up to Jerusalem to the apostles and elders about this question.

They therefore, being brought on their way by the church, passed through Phœnicia and Samaria, declaring the conversion of the Gentiles: and they caused great joy to all the brethren. When they had come to Jerusalem, they were received by the church and the apostles and the elders, and they rehearsed all the things that God had done with them.

But there rose up certain of the sect of the Pharisees who believed, saying, "It is needful to command them to keep the custom and the law of Moses."

And the apostles and the elders came together to consider of this matter.

Peter Gives His Opinion

When there had been much disputing, Peter rose up and said to them: "Brethren, ye know how that a good while ago God made choice among you, that the Gentiles by my mouth should hear the word of the gospel, and believe. And God, who knoweth the heart, bore them witness, giving them the Holy Spirit, even as he did to us; and he made no distinction between us and them, purifying their hearts by faith. Now therefore why tempt ye God, that ye should put a yoke upon the neck of the disciples, which neither our fathers nor we were able to bear? But we believe that through the grace of the Lord Jesus Christ we shall be saved, even as they."

Then all the multitude kept silence; and they hearkened to Barnabas and Paul as they told what signs and wonders God had wrought among the Gentiles by them.

James Agrees with Peter

After they had ceased speaking, James answered, saying: "Brethren, hearken to me: Symeon [Peter] hath rehearsed how God at the first visited the Gentiles, to take out of them a people for his name. And to this agree the words of the prophets; as it is written:

"'After this I will return,
 And will build again the tabernacle of David, which hath fallen down;
 And I will build again the ruins thereof,
 And I will set it up:
 That the residue of men may seek after the Lord,
 And all the Gentiles, upon whom my name is called,
 Saith the Lord, who maketh all these things known from the beginning of the world.'

Wherefore my judgment is, that we trouble not those who from among the Gentiles turn to God; but that we write to them, that they abstain from the pollutions of idols, and from uncleanness, and from what is strangled, and from blood. For Moses from generations of old hath in every city them that preach him, being read in the synagogues every sabbath day."

A Message Is Sent to the Gentiles

Then pleased it the apostles and elders, with the whole church, to send chosen men of their own company to Antioch with Paul and Barnabas; namely, Judas called Barsabbas, and Silas, chief men among the brethren.

And they wrote letters by them after this manner:

"The apostles and the elders, brethren, to the brethren who are of the Gentiles in Antioch and Syria and Cilicia, greeting:—

"Forasmuch as we have heard that certain men who went out from us have troubled you with words, vexing your souls; to whom we gave no commandment; it seemed good to us, having come to one accord, to send chosen men to you with our beloved Barnabas and Paul, men that have hazarded their lives for the name of our Lord Jesus Christ. We have sent therefore Judas and Silas, who shall also tell you the same things by word of mouth.

"For it seemed good to the Holy Spirit, and to us, to lay upon you no greater burden than these necessary things: that ye abstain from things sacrificed to idols, and from blood, and from things strangled, and from uncleanness; from which if ye keep yourselves, it shall be well with you. Fare ye well."

A Brotherly Delegation Comes to Antioch

So when they were dismissed, they came to Antioch; and when they had gathered the multitude together, they delivered the epistle. And when they had read it, they rejoiced for the consolation it afforded. And Judas and Silas, being prophets also themselves, exhorted the brethren with many words, and confirmed them. And after they had spent some time there, they were dismissed in peace from the brethren to those that had sent them forth.

Notwithstanding it pleased Silas to abide there still.

Paul also and Barnabas tarried in Antioch, teaching and preaching the word of the Lord, with many others also.

Paul's Own Account of the Controversy Concerning the Gentiles

In his letter to the Galatians, Paul thus describes the outcome of the controversy concerning the admission of Gentiles to the Christian churches which took place during one of his visits to Jerusalem:

After the space of fourteen years I went up again to Jerusalem with Barnabas, and took Titus with me also. And I went up by revelation, and laid before them the gospel which I preach among the Gentiles, but privately before those who were of repute, lest by any means I should be running, or had run, in vain.

But false brethren were privily brought in, who came in privily to spy out our liberty which we have in Christ Jesus, that they might bring us into bondage: to whom we gave place in the way of subjection, no, not for an hour; that the truth of the gospel might continue with you. But from those who were reputed to be somewhat (whatsoever they were, it maketh no matter to me: God accepteth not man's person) — they, I say, who were of repute imparted nothing to me. But on the contrary, when they saw that the gospel to the Gentiles was committed to me, as the gospel to the Jews was to Peter (for he that wrought for Peter unto the apostleship to the Jews wrought for me also to the Gentiles); and when James, Cephas, and John, who were reputed to be pillars, perceived the grace that was given to me, they gave to me and Barnabas the right hands of fellowship, that we should go to the Gentiles, and they to the Jews. Only they would that we should remember the poor; which very thing I was also zealous to do.

THE APOSTLE PAUL
From a painting by Rembrandt

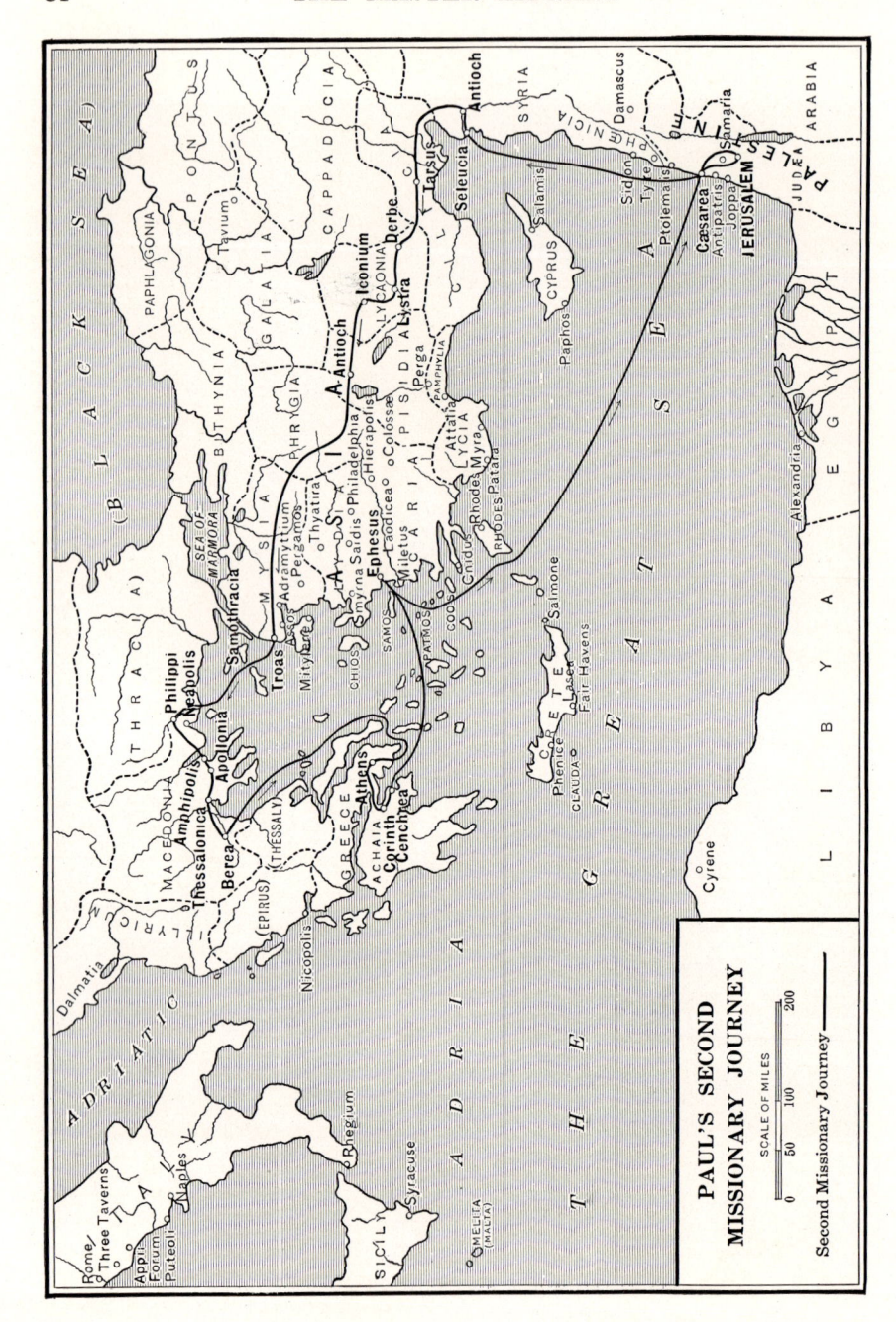

PAUL'S SECOND MISSIONARY JOURNEY

PAUL'S SECOND MISSIONARY JOURNEY

Antioch, Syria
  Travels through Cilicia with Silas
  Barnabas and Mark sail for Cyprus

Derbe and Lystra, Lycaonia
  Delivers decrees of the Jerusalem Council to the churches
  Joined by Timothy at Lystra

Troas, Mysia (via Iconium and Antioch)
  Vision of the man from Macedonia
  Joined by Luke

Philippi, Macedonia (via Samothracia and Neapolis)
  Conversion of Lydia
  Conversion of clairvoyant girl
  Imprisoned with Silas
  Great earthquake
  Conversion of the jailor
  Release and departure

Thessalonica, Macedonia (via Amphipolis, Apollonia)
  Preaches in the synagogue
  Many Gentiles converted
  A stay of several months
  Works at his trade
  Jews mob the house of Jason, Paul's host
  Charged with treason against the Roman emperor
  Forced to give bonds
  Released from court
  Departs by night under escort

Berea, Macedonia
  Hospitably received
  Preaches successfully
  Stays several weeks
  Thessalonian Jews stir up the people
  Forced to flee
  Timothy and Silas remain

Athens, Achaia
  The address on Mars' Hill
  Conversion of Dionysius the Areopagite

Corinth, Achaia
  Stays a year and a half
  Lodges at the home of Aquila and Priscilla
  Works at his trade
  Preaches in the synagogue
  Silas and Timothy arrive with gifts from the Philippians
  Jews begin opposition
  Paul compelled to cease preaching in the synagogue
  Preaches in home of Titus Justus
  Ruler of the synagogue converted
  Writes Thessalonians I and II
  Incurs hostility of Jews
  Brought before the Roman Proconsul, Gallio
  Cleared of the charge of violating the law; accusers driven from the judgment seat
  Sails with Aquila and Priscilla

Ephesus, Lydia (via Cenchrea)
  Preaches in the synagogue
  Urged to stay
  Promises to return
  Leaves Aquila and Priscilla in charge

Jerusalem (via Cæsarea)
  Salutes the mother church
  Probably attends the Passover

Antioch (via Cæsarea and Seleucia)
  Had traveled over 2000 miles in three years
  Founded many strategic churches
  Possibly wrote Galatians

SAINT MARK

From a painting by Rubens

This idealized portrait depicts the student who wrote the earliest, the briefest, and the clearest of the biographies of Jesus that have come down to us. In the background on the right, lowers the lion which in Christian art always represents this Evangelist.

SECOND MISSIONARY JOURNEY OF PAUL

THE FIRST STAGE OF THE JOURNEY

Antioch to Troas

Timothy Becomes Paul's Companion

SOME days after, Paul said to Barnabas, "Let us return now and visit our brethren in every city where we proclaimed the word of the Lord, and see how they fare."

And Barnabas was minded to take with them John also, who was called Mark. But Paul thought it not good to take with them him who withdrew from them from Pamphylia, and went not with them to the work. And the contention was so sharp between them that they parted asunder one from the other, and Barnabas took Mark with him, and sailed away to Cyprus; but Paul chose Silas, and departed, being commended by the brethren to the grace of God. And he went through Syria and Cilicia, confirming the churches.

Then came he to Derbe and Lystra. And behold, a certain disciple was there, named Timothy, the son of a Jewess who believed; but his father was a Greek. The same was well reported of by the brethren that were at Lystra and Iconium. Him would Paul have to go forth with him.

And as they went through the cities, they delivered them the decrees to keep which had been ordained of the apostles and elders that were at Jerusalem.

And so were the churches strengthened in the faith, and increased in number daily.

Now they went through the region of Phrygia and Galatia, having been forbidden by the Holy Spirit to speak the word in Asia [Minor]; and when they had come over against Mysia,

THE TROJAN PLAIN

When Paul was in Troas, he may well have paid a visit to the neighboring plain and the ancient mound which concealed the citadel of King Priam. In the foreground are some of the remains of that famous hillock on which ten successive cities have been built. Achilles, Hector, and all the heroes of the Iliad, fought on this plain. On the shore of the Hellespont yonder to the right, the Greeks drew up their ships. Behind Tenedos, just off the picture to the left, the Greek fleet waited for Ulysses and his companions of the wooden horse to open the gates and signal for their return. Seven hundred years later another warrior passed this way: the youthful Alexander stopped at Troy on his way to conquer the world.

Paul may have heard of these heroes, but his interests were in a different realm. He looked beyond the strait and the sea to the land where the man of Macedon was beckoning to him.

The low-lying peninsula between the strait and the sky is tragic Gallipoli, where in the Great World War thousands of the young men of the British Empire laid down their lives.

they attempted to go into Bithynia; but the Spirit suffered them not; and passing by Mysia, they came down to Troas.

A Cry for Help Comes from Macedonia

And a vision appeared to Paul in the night. There stood a man of Macedonia,[10] and prayed him, saying, "Come over into Macedonia, and help us."

After he had seen the vision, immediately we endeavored to go into Macedonia, concluding that God had called us to preach the gospel to them.

At this point in the Book of Acts, the introduction of the word "we" suggests that the author himself, Luke, had now joined Paul, and that what follows is largely a record from his own diary.

THE SECOND STAGE OF THE JOURNEY
Troas to Corinth

Lydia Shows Her Hospitality

Setting sail therefore from Troas, we came with a straight course to Samothrace, and the next day to Neapolis; and from thence to Philippi,[11] which is the chief city of that part of Macedonia, a Roman colony: and we were in that city tarrying certain days.

And on the sabbath day we went out of the city by a riverside, where we supposed there was a place of prayer; and we sat down, and spoke to the women who had come together. And a certain woman named Lydia, a seller of purple, of the city of Thyatira, one who worshiped God, heard us: whose heart the Lord opened, to give heed to the things which were spoken by Paul. And when she was baptized, and her household, she besought us, saying, "If ye have judged me to be faithful to the Lord, come into my house, and abide there." And she persuaded us.

Paul and Silas Are Imprisoned

And it came to pass, as we went to prayer, that a certain maid, possessed with a spirit of divination, met us, who brought her masters much gain by soothsaying. The same followed Paul and us, and cried out, saying, "These men are servants of the Most High God, who proclaim to you the way of salvation."

And this she did for many days. But Paul, being troubled, turned and said to the spirit, "I charge thee in the name of Jesus Christ to come out of her."

And he came out that very hour.

But when her masters saw that the hope of their gain was gone, they laid hold of Paul and Silas, and drew them into the market place before the rulers. And they brought them

THE NARROWEST PART OF THE BOSPORUS

to the magistrates, saying, "These men, being Jews, do exceedingly trouble our city, and set forth customs which it is not lawful for us to receive, neither to observe, being Romans."

And the multitude rose up together against them: and the magistrates tore their garments off them, and commanded to beat them with rods. And when they had laid many stripes upon them, they cast them into prison, charging the jailor to keep them safely: who, having received such a charge, cast them into the inner prison, and made their feet fast in the stocks.

The Release of Paul and Silas

About midnight Paul and Silas were praying and singing hymns to God, and the prisoners were listening to them; and suddenly there was a great earthquake, so that the foundations of the prison were shaken. And immediately all the doors were opened; and every one's bands were loosed. And the jailor, awaking out of his sleep and seeing the prison doors open, drew his sword, and was about to kill himself, supposing that the prisoners had escaped.

But Paul cried with a loud voice, saying, "Do thyself no harm: for we are all here."

THE NARROWEST PART OF THE BOSPORUS

Paul's crossing from Asia to Europe was almost epic in its simplicity and its significance. It marked the beginning of the great conquest. A religion from the East invaded the West. The whole course of history was destined thenceforth to be different. As one stands in this picture on the Asiatic shore of the Bosporus one looks across to Europe. The two continents here come face to face, and at this point passage from one to the other is comparatively easy. Across these straits Asia once advanced to conquest, when the armies of Darius and Xerxes attempted the subjugation of Greece. Similarly in the third century B.C., Europe, in the person of Alexander, crossed not far from here to invade Asia. Asia again, in the person of Mohammed II and his Turks, crossed to subjugate Europe in the fifteenth century, A.D. The castle yonder ascending the steep hill was built by this Turk to command the straits.

And now, with better aims, America is present at this great crossroads, for the buildings on the left belong to Robert College, and represent the gift of the West to balance the debt it owes to Saint Paul. Indeed, America has crossed the Bosporus, for on the Asiatic heights in the foreground now stands Constantinople College, America's gift to the young women of Turkey. The messengers to and fro are the shuttles and the centuries are the threads in the great loom of Time on which the pattern of history is being woven.

Then he called for lights, and sprang in, and, trembling for fear, fell down before Paul and Silas, and brought them out, and said, "Sirs, what must I do to be saved?"

And they said, "Believe on the Lord Jesus, and thou shalt be saved, and thy household."

And they spoke to him the word of the Lord, and to all that were in his house. And he took them the same hour of the night, and washed their stripes; and was baptized, he and all his, immediately. And he brought them up into his house, and set food before them, and rejoiced greatly, with all his house, having believed in God.

But when it was day, the magistrates sent the police, saying, "Let those men go." And the jailor reported the words to Paul, saying, "The magistrates have sent to let you go: now therefore come forth, and go in peace."

But Paul said to them, "They have beaten us publicly, uncondemned, men who are Romans, and have cast us into prison; and now do they cast us out secretly? nay verily; let them come themselves and bring us out."

And the police told these words to the magistrates; and they feared, when they heard that they were Romans. And they came and besought them; and when they had brought them out, they asked them to depart out of the city. And they went out of the prison, and entered into the house of Lydia; and when they had seen the brethren, they comforted them, and departed.[12]

Perils Are Encountered at Thessalonica

Now when they had passed through Amphipolis and Apollonia, they came to Thessalonica,[13] where was a synagogue of the Jews: and Paul, as his custom was, went in to them, and for three sabbath days reasoned with them from the scriptures, arguing that it behooved the Christ to suffer, and to rise again from the dead; and that "this Jesus, whom, I proclaim to you, is the Christ."

And some of them believed, and joined themselves to Paul and Silas; and of the devout Greeks a great multitude, and of the chief women not a few. But the Jews who believed not, being moved with jealousy, took to them certain vile fellows of the rabble, and gathering a crowd, set all the city in an uproar; and assaulting the house of Jason, they sought to bring them out to the people. When they found them not, they dragged Jason and certain brethren before the rulers of the city, crying, "These men who have turned the world upside down have come hither also; whom Jason hath received: and these all act contrary to the decrees of Cæsar, saying that there is another king, one Jesus."

And they troubled the multitude and the rulers of the city, when they heard these things. And when they had taken bail from Jason and the rest, they let them go.

Paul's Own Reference to His Visit to the Thessalonians

We were gentle among you, even as when a nurse cherisheth her own children. Even so, being affectionately desirous of you, we were well pleased to impart to you, not the gospel of God only, but also our own souls, because ye had become very dear to us. For ye remember, brethren, our labor and toil: laboring at our trade[14] night and day, that we might not become a burden to any of you, we preached to you the gospel of God.

And ye became imitators of us, and of the Lord, having received the word in much affliction, with joy of the Holy Spirit; so that ye became an example to all that believe in Macedonia and Achaia [Greece]. For from you hath sounded forth the word of the Lord, not only in Macedonia and Achaia, but also in every place your faith toward God hath gone forth; so that we need not to speak anything. For they

ATHENS

themselves report what manner of entering in we had to you; and how ye turned to God from idols, to serve the living and true God.

For ye yourselves, brethren, know our entering in to you, that it hath not been found vain; but having suffered before and been shamefully treated, as ye know, at Philippi, we grew bold in our God to speak to you the gospel of God in much conflict.

For this cause also thank we God without ceasing, that, when ye received from us the word of the message, even the word of God, ye accepted it, not as the word of men, but, as it is in truth, the word of God, which also worketh in you that believe.

For ye, brethren, became imitators of the churches of God which are in Judea in Christ Jesus: for ye also suffered the same things from your own countrymen, even as they did from the Jews; who both killed the Lord Jesus and the prophets, and have persecuted us.

Paul Reaches Athens

And the brethren [at Thessalonica] immediately sent away Paul and Silas by night to Berea[15]: who coming thither went into the synagogue of the Jews. These were more noble than those in Thessalonica, in that they received the word with all readiness of mind, and searched the scriptures daily, to see

---

ATHENS

This is what Paul saw when he came to Athens: the gray slopes of Hymettus bounding the plain on the right; the sturdy rock of the Acropolis, bearing on its summit a wondrous crown of temples; the flat rock in the center of the picture, where he was destined to preach his memorable sermon; the sharp hill of Lykabettus bounding the city on the northeast; and, in the distance, grand old Pentelicus, the white patch on its side showing the quarries from which comes the priceless marble. Though the modern city lies almost wholly north of the Acropolis (to the left), in Paul's day it quite surrounded it. No doubt Paul ascended the very hill from which we view this scene, to hear some of the famous orators of Athens as they addressed the assembly that gathered there. But today Mars' Hill is less famed for its Pnyx and its orators than it is as the scene of Paul's sermon when he was invited to expound "this new doctrine" to the inquisitive Athenians, who "spent their time in nothing else, but either to tell or to hear some new thing."

MARS' HILL, ATHENS

You are looking northwest from the slope of the Acropolis. In front of you is the rough rock known as Areopagus, or the hill of Ares (Mars). The cave in the detached rock to the right is traditionally the haunt of the Furies, who waited upon murderers. This precinct was consecrated to the trial of persons accused of capital crimes because the god Ares was here first summoned to answer for the murder of Halirrhothios. That incident marks the transition in the Greek race from the barbaric custom of blood revenge to the civilized method of trial by law. Mars' Hill is therefore an important milestone in the moral development of man.

In the hollow to the right of the hill was the ancient Agora of Athens, in which the actual law court of the Areopagus was held. As Paul pleaded his case in this ancient court, he stood in full view of the traditional site of the beginning of Greek law, as well as in view of the crowning glory of Greek religion—the Parthenon.

whether these things were so. Therefore many of them believed; also of the Greek women of honorable estate, and of men, not a few.

But when the Jews of Thessalonica had knowledge that the word of God was proclaimed by Paul at Berea also, they came thither likewise, and stirred up the people. And then immediately the brethren sent forth Paul to go as far as to the sea; but Silas and Timothy abode there still. And they that conducted Paul brought him to Athens[16]; and receiving a commandment to Silas and Timothy to come to him with all speed, they departed.

Paul Studies the Beliefs of the Athenians

Now while Paul waited for them at Athens, his spirit was stirred in him, when he saw the city full of idols. Therefore reasoned he in the synagogue with the Jews and the devout persons, and in the market place daily with them that met with him.

Then certain philosophers of the Epicureans,[17] and of the Stoics,[18] encountered him. And some said, "What would this babbler say?": others, "He seemeth to be a teacher of strange gods"; because he preached Jesus and the resurrection.

And they took him, and brought him to the Areopagus, saying, "May we know what this new doctrine, whereof thou speakest, is? For thou bringest certain strange things to our ears: we would know therefore what these things mean." (Now all the Athenians and the strangers sojourning there spent their time in nothing else, but either to tell or to hear some new thing.)

The Address on Mars' Hill

Then Paul stood in the midst of Mars' Hill, and said: "Ye men of Athens, I perceive that in all things ye are very religious. For as I passed along, and observed the objects of your worship, I found also an altar with this inscription: To an Unknown God. What therefore ye worship in ignorance, this set I forth to you. The God that made the world and all things therein, he, being Lord of heaven and earth, dwelleth not in temples made with hands; neither is he served by men's hands, as though he needed anything, seeing he himself giveth to all life, and breath, and all things; and

PAUL PREACHING AT ATHENS
From a painting by Raphael

he made of one people every nation of men to dwell on all the face of the earth, having determined their appointed seasons, and the bounds of their habitation; that they should seek the Lord, if haply they might feel after him, and find him, though he is not far from each one of us: for in him we live, and move, and have our being; as certain even of your own poets have said,[19] 'For we are also his offspring.' Being then the offspring of God, we ought not to think that the Godhead is like gold, or silver, or stone, graven by art and man's device. The times of ignorance therefore God overlooked; but now he commandeth all men everywhere to repent; because he hath appointed a day in which he will judge the world in righteousness by the man whom he hath ordained. And of this he hath given assurance to all men, in that he hath raised him from the dead."

TEMPLE OF VICTORIOUS ATHENA, ATHENS

If Paul came up onto the rock of the Areopagus, this little temple looked down upon him from the corner of the Acropolis. It is a gem of architecture, built by the Athenians in memory of Athena's help in beating back the Persians. It has seen hard usage; the Turks once destroyed it and built it into a fortification wall fifty feet below. But patient scholars have found most of the stones and have put them back. In Paul's day its beauty was unspoiled. It was this temple among others that the apostle had in mind when he referred to "the objects of your worship," seen by him on the way to court.

Now when they heard of the resurrection of the dead, some mocked; but others said, "We will hear thee again concerning this matter."

So Paul departed from among them.[20] Howbeit certain men were drawn to him, and believed: among whom also was Dionysius the Areopagite, and a woman named Damaris, and others with them.

THE PARTHENON AT ATHENS

He Preaches in the Commercial City of Corinth

After these things Paul departed from Athens, and came to Corinth. There he found a certain Jew named Aquila, born in Pontus, lately come from Italy, with his wife Priscilla, because Claudius had commanded all Jews to depart from Rome. He became acquainted with them; and because he was of the same trade, he abode with them, and they worked together; for by occupation they were tentmakers. And he reasoned in the synagogue every sabbath, and persuaded the Jews and the Greeks.

But when Silas and Timothy came down from Macedonia, Paul gave attention to preaching, testifying to the Jews that Jesus was the Christ. And when they opposed themselves, and blasphemed, he shook out his raiment, and said to them, "Your blood be upon your own heads; I am clean: from henceforth I will go to the Gentiles."

And he departed thence, and went into the house of a certain man named Titus Justus, one that worshiped God, whose house was close by the synagogue. And Crispus, the ruler of the synagogue, believed on the Lord with all his house; and many of the Corinthians hearing believed, and were baptized. Then spoke the Lord to Paul in the night by a vision, "Be not afraid, but speak, and hold not thy peace:

THE PARTHENON AT ATHENS

Paul was so intent on spiritual things that he may not have taken time to visit what to him was a heathen temple. If this was the case, he missed seeing the most beautiful building in the world. In his day the Parthenon was perfect. Its white columns and delicately ornamented roof stood out in dazzling brilliancy against the blue sky. In the pediments were the sculptured stories of Athena's birth and her contest with Poseidon. Around the walls ran the celebrated frieze sculptured by Phidias, representing a procession of Athenian youths and maidens going to present their annual offering to Athena. This temple was the supreme gift of Greek genius to the goddess who represented their ideal. Its perfection has been at once the delight and despair of all succeeding artists. For centuries through war's vicissitudes it stood intact. Even when the Turks conquered Greece and turned the Parthenon into a mosque, they did not otherwise touch the building than by erecting a minaret. The present mournful ruin is the result of an explosion in the year 1688, when a German gunner in the employ of the Venetian Republic sent a hot shot through the roof into the powder which the Turks were storing in this priceless building.

© *Underwood & Underwool*

EXCAVATIONS AT CORINTH

Corinth, like Panama, is situated on an isthmus. It drew its wealth from the trade that passed by. Like Panama, too, it has its canal. The Corinthian canal was begun by Nero in the very year that Paul came to Corinth, but it was not completed till 1893. The ancient city had all the characteristics one might expect to find in such a location—a large floating population of sailors and traveling salesmen, and a large slave population employed in loading and unloading ships and in hauling them across the isthmus on a made track. The city was exceedingly wicked, not only because of the nature of its population, but also because of the presence of the famous Temple of Venus, the immoralities of which were notorious throughout the empire.

American excavators have unearthed this old city of Paul's day. The pool in the foreground is the Spring of Pyrene, where, in the myth, Bellerophon succeeded in catching and bridling the winged horse Pegasus. Not a hundred yards from this spot was found a little Jewish synagogue. For the lintel of its door the builders used a second-hand piece of carved marble. The carved side was turned inward, and on the other side was rudely engraved the phrase, "Synagogue of the Jews." This piece of marble is preserved in the Corinth Museum.

Fire and the ravages of a succession of wars reduced ancient Corinth to a complete ruin. The modern city was destroyed by an earthquake in the year 1858, and was rebuilt at a more convenient location on the Gulf of Corinth.

for I am with thee, and no man shall attack thee to hurt thee: for I have many people in this city."

And he dwelt there a year and six months, teaching the word of God among them.

Paul's Comment on His Visit to Corinth

I, brethren, when I came to you, came not with excellency of speech or of wisdom, proclaiming to you the testimony of God. For I determined not to know anything among you, save Jesus Christ, and him crucified. And I was with you in weakness, and in fear, and in much trembling. And my speech and my preaching were not in persuasive words of wisdom, but in demonstration of the Spirit and of power: that your faith should not stand in the wisdom of men, but in the power of God.

I think God hath set forth us the apostles last of all, as men doomed to death: for we are made a spectacle to the world, both to angels and men. We are fools for Christ's sake, but ye are wise in Christ; we are weak, but ye are strong; ye are honored, but we are despised. Even to this present hour we both hunger, and thirst, and are naked, and are buffeted, and have no certain dwelling place; and we labor, working with our own hands: being reviled, we bless; being persecuted, we endure; being defamed, we entreat: we are made as the filth of the world, the offscouring of all things, even until now.

THE THIRD STAGE OF THE JOURNEY

Corinth to Antioch

Paul Is Brought Before the Proconsul

When Gallio was proconsul of Achaia, the Jews rose up with one accord against Paul, and brought him to the judgment seat, saying, "This fellow persuadeth men to worship God contrary to the law."

TURKISH CASTLE ON THE SITE OF EPHESUS

Proud Ephesus is no more. Wars and pestilence depopulated the ancient city. The little stream of Cayster silted up the harbor, the currents of traffic were diverted, the houses fell to ruin, and the Turks finished the destruction. They felt it necessary, however, to garrison the spot, and to build their fortress they used the beautiful marble blocks of the church of Saint John the Divine which had been built there in memory of the beloved disciple. But the builders of this church had taken these same stones from the theater, the stadium, and the great Temple of Diana of the Ephesians. The crumbling walls in this picture are therefore an epitome of the city's history and its successive loyalties to three religions.

But when Paul was about to open his mouth, Gallio said to the Jews, "If indeed it were a matter of crime or of wicked villainy, O ye Jews, it would be reasonable that I should bear with you; but if they are questions about words and names and your own law, look to it yourselves; I am not minded to be a judge of such matters."

And he drove them from the judgment seat. Then all the Greeks took Sosthenes, the ruler of the synagogue, and beat him before the judgment seat. But Gallio cared for none of these things.

He Reasons with the Jews at Ephesus

And Paul, after this, tarried there yet a good while, and then took his leave of the brethren, and sailed thence for

Syria, and with him Priscilla and Aquila; having shorn his head in Cenchreæ; for he had a vow. And they came to Ephesus, and he left them there; but he himself entered into the synagogue, and reasoned with the Jews. When they asked him to stay a longer time with them, he consented not; but bade them farewell, saying, "I will return again to you, if God will." And he set sail from Ephesus.[21]

And when he had landed at Cæsarea, he went up to Jerusalem and saluted the church, and went down to Antioch.

Paul Rebukes the Galatian Christians

Hardly had Paul left Galatia at the beginning of his second missionary journey when his converts there became perverted by Jewish ideas brought in by false brethren from Jerusalem. While at Antioch, Paul learned of this disaffection, and was obliged to write to them firmly and convincingly about the simplicity and true freedom of the Christian life.

O foolish Galatians, who hath bewitched you, before whose eyes Jesus Christ was openly set forth crucified? This only would I learn from you, Received ye the Spirit by the works of the law, or by the hearing of faith? Are ye so foolish? having begun in the Spirit, are ye now perfected in the flesh?

Before faith came, we were kept in ward under the law. Wherefore the law was our schoolmaster to bring us to Christ, that we might be justified by faith. But now that faith hath come, we are no longer under a schoolmaster. For ye are all sons of God, through faith, in Christ Jesus. For as many of you as were baptized into Christ put on Christ.

And if ye are Christ's, then are ye Abraham's true descendants, heirs according to promise.

Wherefore thou art no longer a bondservant, but a son; and if a son, then an heir through God.

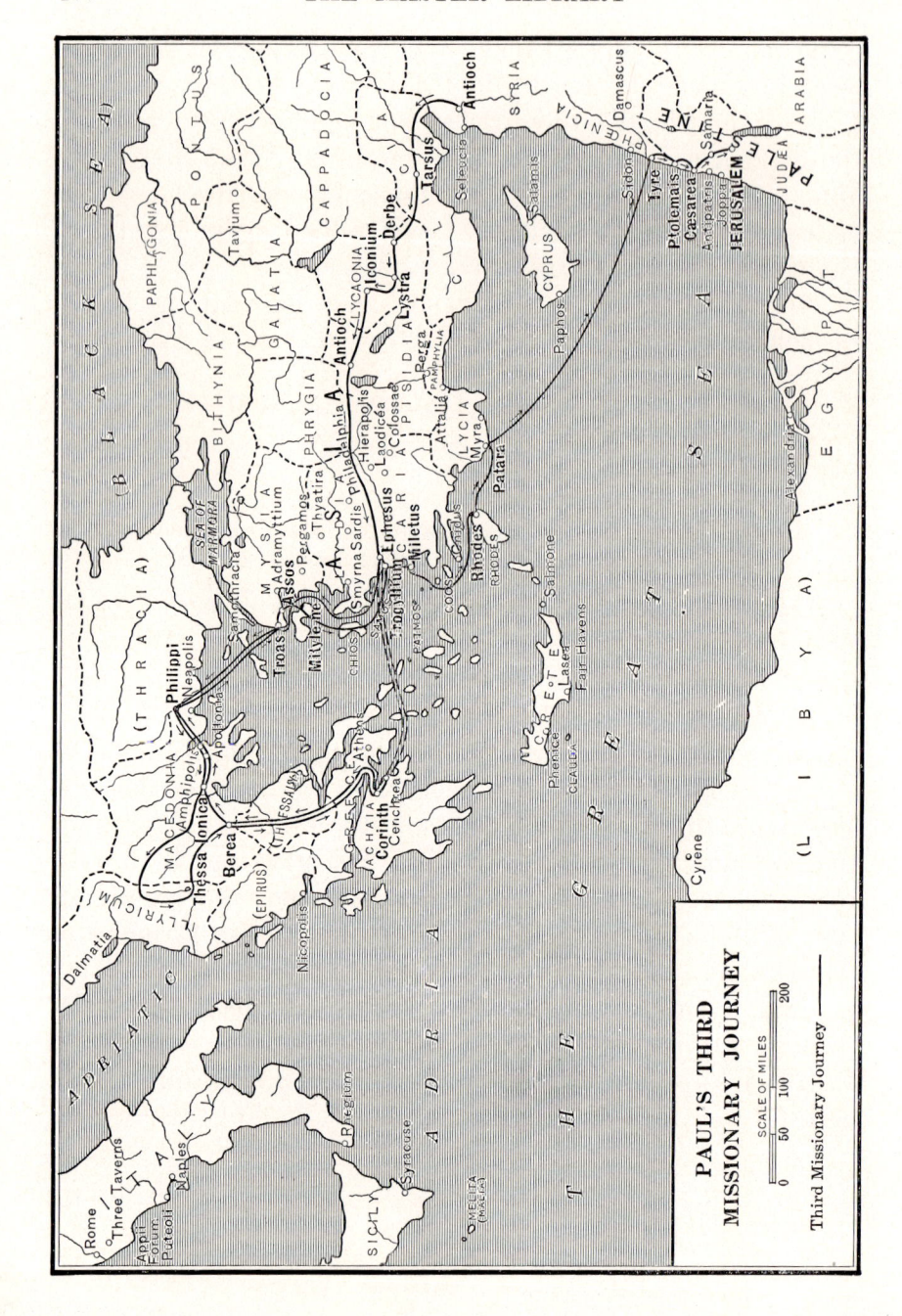

PAUL'S THIRD MISSIONARY JOURNEY

THE THIRD MISSIONARY JOURNEY

Antioch, Syria
  Sets forth with Timothy and probably Titus

Phrygia and Galatia
  Visited the churches
  Collection for poor of Judea

Ephesus, Lydia
  Rebaptized the disciples of John
  Preached in synagogue and in school of Tyrannus
  Performed miracles of healing
  Jewish exorcists defeated
  Books of magic burned
  Short visit to Corinth and return
  Letter (now lost) written to Corinth
  Planned to visit Macedonia, Achaia, Judea, Rome
  Sent Timothy and Erastus into Macedonia
  Received messengers and visitors from Corinth
  Wrote I Corinthians
  Titus sent to Corinth to inquire effect of I Corinthians and make collection for Jerusalem poor
  Had stayed three years and evangelized Asia
  Driven out by the riot of the imagemakers

Troas, Mysia
  Disappointed not to meet Titus

Philippi, Macedonia
  Joined by Timothy and Titus
  Preached throughout Macedonia
  Wrote II Corinthians

Illyricum
  Short tour. Plans to visit Spain

Corinth, Achaia
  Stayed three months, with Luke
  Probably wrote Galatians
  Wrote Epistle to Romans; carried by Phœbe
  Planned visit to Rome and Spain after going to Jerusalem with alms for the church
  Tried to sail for Syria
  A plot against his life
  Went by land through Macedonia

Philippi, Macedonia
  Kept the Passover with Luke
  Other companions proceeded in advance to Troas

Troas, Mysia
  Met his companions and abode seven days
  Preached to the disciples
  Eutychus is restored
  Paul went by foot, and his friends by ship to

Assos, Mysia
  They embark for

Miletus (via Mitylene, Chios, Samos, Trogyllium)
  Address to Ephesian elders
  Forebodings of danger at Jerusalem

Tyre, Phœnicia (via Cos, Rhodes, and Patara)
  Stayed seven days with the Christians
  Warned not to go to Jerusalem

Cæsarea (via Ptolemais)
  Stayed with Philip many days
  Prophecy of Agabus—Paul to be imprisoned

Jerusalem, Judea
  Abode with Mnason of Cyprus
  Paul "ready not to be bound only, but also to die"

©Underwood & Underwood

ANTIOCH IN ASIA MINOR

This town is in the plateau of Asia Minor, high above the sea. On or near this spot was the Antioch of Paul's day, the Roman town in the province of Pisidia in which Latin was the ordinary tongue. Paul visited it four times, and founded there the church mentioned in the Epistle to the Galatians.

THIRD MISSIONARY JOURNEY OF PAUL

THE FIRST STAGE OF THE JOURNEY

Antioch to Ephesus

Paul Encourages a Missionary Spirit

AFTER he had spent some time there [at Antioch], he departed, and went through the region of Galatia[22] and Phrygia in order, strengthening all the disciples.

One thing that Paul was anxious about at this time was the binding of these foreign Christians to the mother church by encouraging them to take offerings for needy believers in Jerusalem. In a letter to the Corinthians he refers to the matter as follows:

Now concerning the collection for the saints, as I gave order to the churches of Galatia, so also do ye. Upon the first day of the week let every one of you lay by him in store, as God hath prospered him, that no collections be made when I come. And when I come, whomsoever ye shall approve, them will I send with letters to carry your bounty to Jerusalem.

An Able Helper Joins the Apostles

Now a certain Jew named Apollos, born at Alexandria,[23] an eloquent man, and mighty in the scriptures, came to Ephesus. This man had been instructed in the way of the Lord; and being fervent in spirit, he spoke and taught diligently the things concerning Jesus, knowing only the baptism of John. He began to speak boldly in the synagogue. But when Aquila and Priscilla heard him, they took him unto them, and expounded to him the way of God more accurately. And when he was minded to pass into Achaia, the brethren encouraged him, and wrote to the disciples to receive

THE MAGICIANS BURN THEIR BOOKS
From a drawing by Isings

"Many of them also that practiced magical arts brought their books together and burned them in the sight of all; and they counted the price of them, and found it fifty thousand pieces of silver."

him; and, when he had come, he helped them much who had believed through grace; for he powerfully confuted the Jews, and that publicly, showing by the scriptures that Jesus was the Christ.

The People at Ephesus Are Mightily Stirred

And it came to pass, that, while Apollos was at Corinth, Paul having passed through the upper country came to Ephesus; and finding certain disciples, he said to them, "Have ye received the Holy Spirit since ye believed?"

They said to him, "We have not so much as heard whether there is a Holy Spirit."

And he said, "Into what then were ye baptized?"

They said, "Into John's baptism."

Then Paul said, "John baptized with the baptism of repentance, saying to the people that they should believe on him that should come after him, that is, on Jesus."

When they heard this, they were baptized into the name of the Lord Jesus. And when Paul had laid his hands upon them, the Holy Spirit came on them; and they spoke with tongues, and prophesied. And they were in all about twelve men.

And he went into the synagogue, and spoke boldly for the space of three months, reasoning and persuading as to the things concerning the kingdom of God. But when some were hardened and disobedient, speaking evil of the Way before the multitude, he departed from them, and separated the disciples, reasoning daily in the school of Tyrannus. And this continued for the space of two years; so that all they that dwelt in Asia heard the word of the Lord Jesus, both Jews and Greeks.

And God wrought special miracles by the hands of Paul: insomuch that from his body were carried away to the sick handkerchiefs or aprons, and the diseases departed from them, and the evil spirits went out of them.

RUINS OF EPHESUS

You are standing on the top row of seats in the great theater. The architectural fragment hints at the original beauty of this structure, built in the late Roman days on the very site of the theater of Paul's day. Here is where the town clerk "appeased the people." The straight rows of stones leading away from you toward the center of the picture on the right mark one of the ancient colonnaded streets of the city. The cluster of ruins on the right is partly Roman baths and partly the Byzantine church of Ephesus in which the Third Ecumenical Council was held.

The plain beyond represents the ancient harbor. Beyond the headlands lies the Ægean. The theater has been recently excavated so that all the seats are visible. The school of Tyrannus, where Paul taught, is off the picture to the left, and the Temple of Diana is a mile or more behind us.

Paul labored in Ephesus for nearly three years, and in this city John and some of the other Apostles made their headquarters. Its great Temple of Diana was destroyed by the invading Goths, 263 A.D.

Many that believed came, and confessed, and declared their deeds.

Many of them also that practiced magical arts brought their books together and burned them in the sight of all; and they counted the price of them, and found it fifty thousand pieces of silver.

So mightily grew the word of God and prevailed.

After these things were ended, Paul purposed in the spirit, when he had passed through Macedonia and Achaia, to go to Jerusalem, saying, "After I have been there, I must also see Rome."

And having sent into Macedonia two of them that ministered to him, Timothy and Erastus, he himself stayed in Asia for a while.

THE SILVERSMITHS OF EPHESUS ARE AROUSED

A RIOT BREAKS OUT

About that time there arose no small stir concerning the Way. For a certain man named Demetrius, a silversmith, who made silver shrines of Diana, brought no little business to the craftsmen; whom he called together, with the workmen of like occupation, and said: "Sirs, ye know that by this business we have our wealth. Moreover ye see and hear, that not alone at Ephesus, but almost throughout all Asia, this Paul hath persuaded and turned away many people, saying that they are no gods, which are made with hands: so that not only is there danger that this our trade come into disrepute; but also that the temple of the great goddess Diana be made of no account, and that she should even be deposed from her magnificence, whom all Asia and the world worshipeth."

When they heard this, they were filled with wrath, and cried out, saying, "Great is Diana of the Ephesians!" And the whole city was filled with the confusion: and having seized Gaius and Aristarchus, men of Macedonia, Paul's companions in travel, they rushed with one accord into the theater. And when Paul would have entered in to the people, the disciples suffered him not. And certain also of the chief officers of Asia, who were his friends, sent to him, and besought him not to venture into the theater. Some therefore cried one thing, and some another; for the assembly was in confusion; and the larger part knew not wherefore they had come together.

And they drew Alexander out of the multitude, the Jews putting him forward. And Alexander beckoned with the hand, and would have made his defense to the people. But when they perceived that he was a Jew, all with one voice about the space of two hours cried out, "Great is Diana of the Ephesians!"

THE RIOT IS QUELLED

When the town clerk had quieted the people, he said: "Ye men of Ephesus, what man is there who knoweth not that the city of the Ephesians is temple-keeper of the great goddess Diana, and of the image which fell down from Jupiter? Seeing then that these things cannot be denied, ye ought to be quiet, and to do nothing rashly. For ye have brought hither these men, who are neither robbers of churches nor blasphemers of our goddess.

"Wherefore if Demetrius, and the craftsmen who are with him, have a matter against any man, the courts are open, and there are proconsuls: let them accuse one another. But if ye seek anything about other matters, it shall be settled in the regular assembly. For indeed we are in danger of being accused concerning this day's riot, there being no cause for it: and we shall not be able to give account of this concourse."

And when he had thus spoken, he dismissed the assembly.

After the uproar had ceased, Paul called to him the disciples, and embraced them, and departed to go into Macedonia.

THE SECOND STAGE OF THE JOURNEY
Ephesus to Corinth

Paul Departs from Ephesus

Paul had been at Ephesus three years. While here, he performed heroic labors and met with signal successes, endured many privations and encountered great perils. After a mob rose against him, he decided to leave Ephesus for Macedonia. Paul says of this second visit to Macedonia:

When I came to Troas to preach Christ's gospel and a door was opened to me of the Lord, I had no rest in my spirit, because I found not Titus my brother; but taking leave of them, I went from thence into Macedonia.

When we came into Macedonia [to Philippi] our flesh had no rest, but we were troubled on every side; without were fightings, within were fears. Nevertheless God, that comforteth the lowly, comforted us by the coming of Titus.

Paul Writes to the Christians at Corinth
HE EXHORTS THEM AGAINST IDOL-WORSHIP

Soon after his first visit to Corinth, a visit made in the course of his second missionary journey, Paul was distressed to learn of the worldliness and even the immorality of some Corinthian church members. He seems to have written them letters from Ephesus and from Macedonia. Eventually, Titus was able to reassure him as to conditions in Corinth, and his last letter is less stern and more joyous than the earlier ones.

Be not unequally yoked with unbelievers: for what fellowship hath righteousness with unrighteousness? or what communion hath light with darkness? And what concord hath Christ with Belial? or what portion hath a believer with an unbeliever? And what agreement hath a temple of God with idols? for we are a temple of the living God; even as God said:

"I will dwell in them, and walk in them;
I will be their God, and they shall be my people."

Wherefore, "Come ye out from among them, and be ye separate," saith the Lord,

> "And touch no unclean thing;
> And I will receive you,
> And I will be to you a Father,
> And ye shall be to me sons and daughters."

Having therefore these promises, beloved, let us cleanse ourselves from all defilement of flesh and spirit, perfecting holiness in the fear of God.

GLORIFY GOD IN BODY AND IN SPIRIT

Know ye not that your bodies are members of Christ? He that is joined to the Lord is one spirit. Or know ye not that your body is a temple of the Holy Spirit which is in you, which ye have from God? and ye are not your own; for ye were bought with a price: glorify God therefore in your body.

I will come to you shortly, if the Lord will; and I will know, not the word of those who are puffed up, but the power. For the kingdom of God is not in word, but in power. What will ye? shall I come to you with a rod, or in love and a spirit of gentleness?

PAUL EXPRESSES HIS AFFECTION

This is the third time I am coming to you. I have said beforehand, and I do say beforehand (as when I was present the second time, so now, being absent) to them that heretofore have sinned, and to all the rest, that, if I come again, I will not spare. Examine yourselves, whether ye are in the faith; prove your own selves.

Now I pray to God that ye do no evil; not that we may appear approved, but that ye may do that which is honorable, even though we be as reprobate. For this cause I write these things while absent, that I may not when present deal sharply, according to the authority which the Lord gave me for building up, and not for casting down.

Out of much affliction and anguish of heart I wrote to you with many tears; not that ye should be grieved, but that ye might know the love which I have more abundantly to you. For to this end also did I write, that I might know the proof of you, whether ye are obedient in all things.

HE SENDS A MESSAGE OF COMFORT

He that comforteth the lowly, even God, comforted us by the coming of Titus; and not by his coming only, but by the comfort wherewith he was comforted in you, while he told us your longing, your mourning, your zeal for me; so that I rejoiced yet more. For though I made you sorry with my epistle, I do not regret it: though I did regret it (for I see that that epistle made you sorry, though but for a season), I now rejoice, not that ye were made sorry, but that ye were made sorry unto repentance; for ye were made sorry after a godly sort, that ye might suffer loss by us in nothing. For godly sorrow worketh repentance unto salvation, a repentance which bringeth no regret: but the sorrow of the world worketh death.

For behold, what earnest care it wrought in you, yea what clearing of yourselves, yea what indignation, yea what fear, yea what longing, yea what zeal, yea what avenging! In everything ye approved yourselves to be pure in the matter.[24]

PAUL PREACHES AS FAR WEST AS ILLYRICUM

Illyricum was a mountain province on the Adriatic, north of Macedonia, and looking toward Italy. The boundaries of this Roman province were not always the same, but shifted at different times. While its exact location and limits in the time of Paul cannot be definitely determined, it covered practically the same territory as that now occupied by the modern countries of Montenegro, Herzegovina, Croatia, and possibly Bosnia and Albania.

From Jerusalem, and round about even to Illyricum, I have fully preached the gospel of Christ.

Three Months Are Spent in Greece

And when he had gone through those parts, and had given them much exhortation, he came into Greece. And he spent three months there [at Corinth].

> It was at Corinth that Paul wrote his letter to the Romans. At that time he had not yet visited Rome; but his intention, formed while he was at Ephesus, to do so at some later date, is thus recorded: "Paul purposed in the spirit, when he had passed through Macedonia and Achaia, to go to Jerusalem, saying, 'After I have been there, I must also see Rome.'"

A Greeting to the Christians at Rome

> The following are Paul's greetings to the church at Rome. The main part of this letter, Paul's masterpiece, is found in this volume in the section entitled "Christian Thought."

I would not have you ignorant, brethren, that oftentimes I purposed to come to you (but was hindered hitherto), that I might have some fruit in you also, even as among other Gentiles. I am debtor both to Greeks and to Barbarians, both to the wise and to the unwise. So, as much as in me is, I am ready to preach the gospel to you that are at Rome also.

I was hindered these many times from coming to you; but now, having no more any place in these regions, and having these many years a longing to come to you, whensoever I go to Spain (for I hope to see you in my journey, and to be brought on my way thitherward by you, if first in some measure I shall have been satisfied with your company) — but now, I say, I go to Jerusalem, ministering to the saints. For it hath been the good pleasure of Macedonia and Achaia to make a certain contribution for the poor among the saints who are at Jerusalem. When therefore I have accomplished this, and have sealed to them this fruit, I will go on by you to Spain. And I know that, when I come to you, I shall come in the fulness of the blessing of Christ.

Now I beseech you, brethren, by our Lord Jesus Christ, and by the love of the Spirit, that ye strive together with me in your prayers to God for me; that I may be delivered from them that are disobedient in Judea, and that my ministration which I have for Jerusalem may be acceptable to the saints; that I may come to you in joy through the will of God, and together with you find rest. Now the God of peace be with you all. Amen.

Paul's Reference to His Hardships and Sufferings

PERILS AND PRIVATIONS

From Paul's letters we take these statements, which include mention of many exciting and perilous experiences not recorded in the account in the Book of Acts.

Of the Jews five times received I forty stripes less one. Thrice was I beaten with rods, once was I stoned, thrice I suffered shipwreck, a night and a day have I been in the deep; in journeyings often, in perils of rivers, in perils of robbers, in perils from my own countrymen, in perils from the Gentiles, in perils in the city, in perils in the wilderness, in perils in the sea, in perils among false brethren; in labor and travail, in watchings often, in hunger and thirst, in fastings often, in cold and nakedness. Besides those things that are outside, there is that which presseth upon me daily, anxiety for all the churches. In Damascus the governor under Aretas the king guarded the city of the Damascenes in order to take me; and through a window was I let down in a basket by the wall, and escaped his hands.

THE SPIRITUAL TRIUMPH OF PAUL

I know a man in Christ, fourteen years ago (whether in the body, I know not; or whether out of the body, I know not; God knoweth), such a one caught up even to the third heaven. And I know such a man (whether in the body, or apart from the body, I know not; God knoweth), how that he was caught up into Paradise, and heard unspeakable words, which it is not lawful for a man to utter. On behalf of such a one will I glory: but on mine own behalf I will not glory, save in my weaknesses. And lest I should be exalted overmuch by reason of the exceeding greatness of the revelations, there was given to me a thorn in the flesh, a messenger of Satan to buffet me, lest I should be exalted overmuch.

Concerning this thing I besought the Lord thrice, that it might depart from me. But he hath said to me:

"My grace is sufficient for thee:
For my power is made perfect in weakness."

THE RAPTURE OF PAUL
From a painting by Zampieri

The word "rapture" is here used in the original Greek sense of being snatched up. It may be applied literally—in which case the soul of Paul was snatched up into the Third Heaven; or figuratively—in which case his spirit was so entranced with a vision of heaven that he was virtually "absent from the body." The artist has in a way translated both meanings of the word. The visible ascension of Paul portrays his experience as best it may be represented in a literal sense. On the other hand, the expression of ecstasy on the Apostle's face suggests the spiritual exaltation that filled his soul.

Most gladly therefore will I rather glory in my weaknesses, that the power of Christ may rest upon me. Therefore I take pleasure in weaknesses, in injuries, in necessities, in persecutions, in distresses, for Christ's sake: for when I am weak, then am I strong.

PAUL AFFIRMS HIS LOYALTY TO CHRIST

In all things commending ourselves, as ministers of God, in much patience, in afflictions, in necessities, in distresses, in stripes, in imprisonments, in tumults, in labors, in watchings, in fastings: in pureness, in knowledge, in longsuffering, in kindness, in the Holy Spirit, in love unfeigned, in the word of truth, in the power of God; by the armor of righteousness on the right hand and on the left, by glory and dishonor, by evil report and good report; as deceivers, and yet true; as unknown, and yet well known; as dying, and behold, we live; as chastened, and not killed; as sorrowful, yet always rejoicing; as poor, yet making many rich; as having nothing, and yet possessing all things.

Henceforth let no man trouble me; for I bear branded on my body the marks of Jesus.

THE THIRD STAGE OF THE JOURNEY

Corinth to Jerusalem

EPHESUS IS REVISITED

When a plot was laid against Paul by the Jews, as he was about to set sail for Syria, he determined to return through Macedonia. And there accompanied him as far as Asia, Sopater of Berea; and of the Thessalonians, Aristarchus and Secundus; and Gaius of Derbe, and Timothy; and of Asia, Tychicus and Trophimus. But these had gone before, and were waiting for us at Troas. And we sailed away from Philippi after the days of unleavened bread, and came to them to Troas in five days; where we abode seven days.

THE GATEWAY OF EPHESUS

Although the ancient gateway and flanking towers long ago fell into decay, and were reconstructed so roughly that many of the stones are not in their former position, enough of the original gate is left to indicate the magnificence of the Ephesus known to Saint Paul.

Upon the first day of the week, when we were gathered together to break bread, Paul discoursed with them, intending to depart on the morrow; and continued his speech until midnight. And there were many lights in the upper chamber, where they had gathered together. And there sat in the window a certain young man named Eutychus, borne down with deep sleep; and as Paul discoursed yet longer, being borne down by his sleep he fell down from the third story, and was taken up dead. And Paul went down, and fell on him, and embracing him, said, "Make ye no ado; for his life is in him."

When he therefore came up again, and had broken the bread, and eaten, and talked with them a long while, even till break of day, so he departed. And they brought the young man alive, and were not a little comforted.

And we, going before to the ship, set sail for Assos, there intending to take in Paul; for so had he appointed, planning himself to go by land.

And when he met with us at Assos, we took him in, and came to Mitylene. And we sailed thence, and came the next day over against Chios; and the next day we touched at Samos; and tarried at Trogyllium; and the next day we came to Miletus. For Paul had determined to sail past Ephesus, that he might not have to spend time in Asia; for he was hastening, if it were possible for him, to be at Jerusalem the day of Pentecost.

The Ephesians Bid Paul a Touching Farewell

From Miletus he sent to Ephesus, and called to him the elders of the church. And when they had come to him, he said to them: "Ye yourselves know, from the first day that I set foot in Asia, after what manner I was with you all the time, serving the Lord with all lowliness of mind, and with tears, and with trials which befell me by the plots of the Jews; how I shrank not from declaring unto you anything that was profitable, and teaching you publicly, from house to house, testifying both to Jews, and also to Greeks, repentance toward God, and faith toward our Lord Jesus Christ.

"And now, behold, I go bound in the spirit to Jerusalem, not knowing the things that shall befall me there: save that the Holy Spirit testifieth to me in every city, saying that bonds and afflictions await me. But I hold not my life of any account, as dear to myself, so that I may accomplish my course, and the ministry which I received from the Lord Jesus, to testify the gospel of the grace of God.

"And now, behold, I know that ye all, among whom I went about preaching the kingdom, shall see my face no more. Wherefore I testify to you this day, that I am pure from the blood of all men. For I shrank not from declaring to you the whole counsel of God.

"Take heed to yourselves, and to all the flock, in which the Holy Spirit hath made you bishops, to feed the church of God, which he purchased with his own blood. I know that after my departing grievous wolves shall enter in among you, not sparing the flock; and from among your own selves shall men arise, speaking perverse things, to draw away the disciples after them. Wherefore watch ye, remembering that by the space of three years I ceased not to admonish every one night and day with tears.

"And now, brethren, I commend you to God, and to the word of his grace, which is able to build you up, and to give you the inheritance among all those who are sanctified.

"I coveted no man's silver, or gold, or apparel. Ye yourselves know, that these hands ministered to my necessities, and to them that were with me. In all things I gave you an example, that so laboring ye ought to help the weak, and to remember the words of the Lord Jesus, how he said, 'It is more blessed to give than to receive.'"

When he had thus spoken, he kneeled down, and prayed with them all. And they all wept bitterly, and fell on Paul's neck, and kissed him, sorrowing most of all for the word which he had spoken, that they should behold his face no more. And they accompanied him to the ship.

Agabus Foretells the Imprisonment of Paul

When it came to pass, that we had parted from them, and had set sail, we came with a straight course to Cos, and the day following to Rhodes, and from thence to Patara; and having found a ship crossing over to Phœnicia, we went aboard, and set sail. And when we had come in sight of Cyprus, we left it on the left hand, and sailed to Syria, and landed at Tyre: for there the ship was to unload her cargo. And having found the disciples, we tarried there seven days. These said to Paul through the Spirit, that he should not go up to Jerusalem. And when it came to pass that we had accomplished the days, we departed and went on our journey; and they all, with wives and children, accompanied us on our way, till we were out of the city: and kneeling down on the beach, we prayed, and bade each other farewell. And we went on board the ship; but they returned home again.

PAUL AND THE DISCIPLES AT TYRE
From a drawing by Jenny Wylie
"And kneeling down on the beach, we prayed, and bade each other farewell."

When we had finished the voyage from Tyre, we arrived at Ptolemais, and we saluted the brethren, and abode with them one day. And the next day we that were of Paul's company departed, and came to Cæsarea; and we entered into the house of Philip the evangelist, who was one of the seven, and abode with him. Now this man had four daughters, who prophesied.

As we tarried there many days, there came down from Judea a certain prophet, named Agabus. And coming to us, and taking Paul's girdle, he bound his own hands and feet, and said, "Thus saith the Holy Spirit, 'So shall the Jews at Jerusalem bind the man that owneth this girdle, and shall deliver him into the hands of the Gentiles.'"

When we heard these things, both we, and they of that place, besought him not to go up to Jerusalem.

Then Paul answered, "What do ye, weeping and breaking my heart? for I am ready not to be bound only, but also to die at Jerusalem for the name of the Lord Jesus."

And when he would not be persuaded, we ceased, saying, "The will of the Lord be done."

After these days we went up to Jerusalem. There went with us also certain of the disciples from Cæsarea, bringing with them one Mnason of Cyprus, an early disciple, with whom we should lodge.

PAUL'S EXPERIENCES AT JERUSALEM

THE CONSPIRACY AGAINST PAUL

Paul Makes a Report on His Mission

WHEN we came to Jerusalem, the brethren received us gladly.

The day following Paul went with us to James; and all the elders were present. And when he had saluted them, he declared one by one the things which God had wrought among the Gentiles by his ministry.

When they heard it, they glorified the Lord, and said to him, "Thou seest, brother, how many thousands of Jews there are who believe; and they are all zealous for the law; and they have been informed concerning thee, that thou teachest all the Jews who are among the Gentiles to forsake Moses, and not to walk after the customs."

The council advised Paul to conciliate the Jewish Christians of Jerusalem, who thought that he was persuading Jews not to keep the Mosaic Law. Paul assented to this request and gave evidence of his sincerity by paying the Temple charges for four men who had taken a vow to perform one of the Temple rites, and by performing the rite himself.

The Jews Bring Forth Accusations

Then the Jews who were from Asia [Paul's enemies], when they saw him in the temple, stirred up all the people, and laid hands on him, crying out, "Men of Israel, help! This is the man who teacheth all men everywhere against the people, and the law, and this place. And, moreover, he brought Greeks also into the temple, and hath defiled this holy place." For they had before seen with him in the city Trophimus the Ephesian, whom they supposed that Paul had brought into the temple.

PAUL RESCUED FROM THE MULTITUDE
From a drawing by Gustave Doré

"And when he came upon the stairs, he was borne by the soldiers on account of the violence of the crowd."

And all the city was moved, and the people ran together: and they laid hold on Paul, and dragged him out of the temple; and forthwith the doors were shut.

And as they were seeking to kill him, tidings came up to the chief captain of the garrison, that all Jerusalem was in confusion. And forthwith he took soldiers and centurions, and ran down to them: and when they saw the chief captain and the soldiers, they left off beating Paul.

A Roman Officer Rescues Paul

Then the chief captain came near, and took him, and commanded him to be bound with two chains; and inquired who he was, and what he had done. And some shouted one thing, some another, among the crowd. When the captain could not know the truth for the uproar, he commanded him to be brought into the castle. And when he came upon the stairs,[25] he was borne by the soldiers on account of the violence of the crowd; for the multitude of the people followed after, crying out, "Away with him!"

And as Paul was about to be brought into the castle, he said to the chief captain, "May I speak to thee?"

He said, "Dost thou know Greek? Art thou not then the Egyptian, who before these days stirred up to sedition and led out into the wilderness the four thousand men of the Assassins?" But Paul said, "I am a Jew, of Tarsus in Cilicia, a citizen of no mean city: and, I beseech thee, give me leave to speak to the people."

When the officer gave him leave, Paul stood on the stairs, and beckoned with the hand to the people. And when they were all silent, he spoke to them in the Hebrew language.

Paul Makes His Defense in Jerusalem

Paul told the story of his birth, youth, and conversion, which has already been related, and then delivered the message that had been given him at Damascus by Ananias.

"Ananias, a devout man according to the law, well reported by all the Jews that dwelt at Damascus, came to me, and standing by me, said to me, 'Brother Saul, receive thy sight.' And the same hour I looked up and saw him.

"And he said: 'The God of our fathers hath appointed thee, to know his will, and to see the Righteous One, and to hear a voice from his mouth. For thou shalt be a witness for him to all men of what thou hast seen and heard. And now why tarriest thou? arise, and be baptized, and wash away thy sins, calling on the name of the Lord.'

"Now it came to pass, that, when I had returned to Jerusalem, and while I prayed in the temple, I fell into a trance; and saw the Lord saying to me, 'Make haste, and get thee quickly out of Jerusalem; because they will not receive of thee testimony concerning me.'

"And I said, 'Lord, they themselves know that I imprisoned and beat in every synagogue them that believed on thee; and when the blood of thy martyr Stephen was shed, I also was standing by, and consenting to his death, and kept the garments of them that slew him.'

"He said to me, 'Depart: for I will send thee forth far hence to the Gentiles.'"

A CITIZEN OF THE EMPIRE CLAIMS HIS RIGHTS

They gave him audience unto this word, and they lifted up their voices, and said, "Away with such a fellow from the earth: for it is not fit that he should live!"

And as they cried out, and threw off their garments, and cast dust into the air, the chief captain commanded him to be brought into the castle, bidding that he should be examined by scourging; that he might know for what cause they so shouted against him.

When they had tied him up with the thongs, Paul said to the centurion that stood by, "Is it lawful for you to scourge a man that is a Roman, and uncondemned?"

When the centurion heard it, he went and told the chief captain, saying, "Take heed what thou doest; for this man is a Roman."

Then the chief captain came, and said to him, "Tell me, art thou a Roman?"

He said, "Yea."

And the chief captain answered, "With a great sum obtained I this freedom."

And Paul said, "But I was free born."

Then they that were about to examine him straightway departed from him; and the chief captain also was afraid, when he knew that he was a Roman, and because he had bound him.

On the morrow, desiring to know why he was accused of the Jews, he loosed him, and commanded the chief priests and all the council to come together, and brought Paul down, and set him before them.

Paul Defends Himself Before the Sanhedrin

And Paul, looking steadfastly on the council, said, "Brethren, I have lived in all good conscience before God until this day." And the high priest Ananias commanded them that stood by him to smite him on the mouth.

Then said Paul to him, "God shall smite thee, thou whited wall; and sittest thou to judge me according to the law, and commandest me to be smitten, contrary to the law?"

And they that stood by said, "Revilest thou God's high priest?"

Then Paul said, "I knew not, brethren, that he was high priest; for it is written, 'Thou shalt not speak evil of a ruler of thy people.'"

But when Paul perceived that the one part were Sadducees, and the other Pharisees, he cried out in the council, "Brethren, I am a Pharisee, a son of Pharisees: touching the hope and resurrection of the dead I am called in question."

And when he had so said, there arose a dissension between the Pharisees and the Sadducees; and the assembly was divided. (For the Sadducees say that there is no resurrection, neither angel, nor spirit; but the Pharisees believe both.) And there arose a great clamor; and some of the scribes that were of the Pharisees stood up, and strove, saying, "We find no evil in this man; and what if a spirit hath spoken to him, or an angel?"

When there arose a great dissension, the chief captain, fearing lest Paul should be torn in pieces by them, commanded the soldiers to go down, and take him by force from among them, and bring him into the castle. And the night following the Lord stood by him, and said, "Be of good cheer: for as thou hast testified concerning me at Jerusalem, so must thou bear witness also at Rome."

The Jews Conspire to Murder Paul

When it was day, the Jews banded together, and bound themselves by an oath, saying that they would neither eat nor drink till they had killed Paul. And they were more than forty who made this conspiracy. And they came to the chief priests and the elders, and said: "We have bound ourselves by a great oath, to taste nothing until we have killed Paul. Now therefore do ye with the council request the chief captain to bring him down to you, as though ye would judge of his case more exactly: and we, before he comes near, are ready to kill him."

But Paul's sister's son heard of their lying in wait, and he came and entered into the castle, and told Paul.

Then Paul called to him one of the centurions, and said, "Take this young man to the chief captain; for he hath something to tell him."

So he took him, and brought him to the chief captain, and said, "Paul the prisoner called me to him, and asked me to take this young man to thee, who hath something to say to thee."

Then the chief captain took him by the hand, and going aside asked him privately, "What hast thou to tell me?"

And he said: "The Jews have agreed to ask thee to bring down Paul tomorrow into the council, as though they would inquire somewhat more exactly concerning him. Do not thou yield to them; for there lie in wait for him of them more than forty men, who have bound themselves by an oath, neither to eat nor to drink till they have killed him; and now are they ready, looking for a promise from thee."

Paul Secures Another Respite

So the chief captain let the young man go, charging him, "Tell no man that thou hast informed me of this."

Then he called to him two of the centurions, and said: "Make ready two hundred soldiers to go as far as Cæsarea, and horsemen threescore and ten, and spearmen two hundred, at the third hour of the night." And he bade them provide a beast for Paul to ride on, and bring him safe to Felix the governor. And he wrote a letter after this form:

"Claudius Lysias to the Most Excellent Governor Felix, greeting:—

"This man was seized by the Jews, and was about to be slain by them: when I came upon them with the soldiers, and rescued him, having learned that he was a Roman. And desiring to know why they accused him, I brought him down to their council: whom I found to be accused about questions of their law, but to have nothing laid to his charge worthy of death or of bonds. And when it was told me that there would be a plot against the man, I sent him to thee forthwith, charging his accusers also to say before thee what they had against him."

So the soldiers, as it was commanded them, took Paul, and brought him by night to Antipatris. But on the morrow they left the horsemen to go with him, and returned to the

THE HARBOR OF CÆSAREA

Cæsarea was one of the triumphs of Herod the Great. Seeing that Palestine was in dire need of a harbor, he constructed vast breakwaters two hundred feet wide at a point on the coast where there were a few ledges that might be used as a basis. The breakwaters were built of tremendous stones, sunk in the sea sometimes to a depth of twenty fathoms, and forming a complete protection from the prevailing winds. He then built a superb city, and made it the most important one of Palestine. Its public buildings were of marble, and were adorned with costly pillars from foreign quarries, as the relics now in the Piazzetta in Venice testify. There were the usual colonnaded street and agora, a temple, a theater, an amphitheater, and a palace. The great hippodrome had seats for twenty thousand spectators. Herod named the city Cæsarea in honor of Augustus Cæsar, his imperial patron. Later, Cæsarea became the residence of all the Roman procurators. In its dungeons Paul was a prisoner for two years. Today the city has wholly vanished.

castle: and they, when they came to Cæsarea, and delivered the letter to the governor, presented Paul also before him.

When he had read it, he asked of what province he was. And when he understood that he was of Cilicia, "I will hear thy cause," said he, "when thine accusers have also come." And he commanded him to be kept in Herod's palace.

The Defense Before Felix

After five days the high priest Ananias came down with certain elders, and a lawyer to plead their case, one Tertullus; and they informed the governor against Paul.

And when he was called, Tertullus began to accuse him, saying: "Seeing that by thee we enjoy much peace, and that by thy care evils are corrected for this nation, we accept it in all ways, and in all places, most excellent Felix,[26] with all thankfulness.

"But that I be not further tedious to thee, I pray thee to hear us of thy clemency a few words. For we have found this man a pestilent fellow, and a mover of insurrections among all the Jews throughout the world, and a ringleader of the sect of the Nazarenes: who moreover attempted to profane the temple: on whom also we laid hold: from whom thou wilt be able, by examining him thyself, to take knowledge of all these things, whereof we accuse him."

And the Jews also joined in the charge, saying that these things were so.

Then Paul, after the governor had beckoned to him to speak, answered:

"Forasmuch as I know that thou hast been of many years a judge to this nation, I cheerfully make my defense: seeing that thou canst take knowledge, that it is not more than twelve days since I went up to Jerusalem to worship. And neither in the temple did they find me disputing with any man, or stirring up a crowd, nor in the synagogue, nor in the city. Neither can they prove to thee the things whereof they now accuse me.

"But this I confess to thee, that after the Way which they call a sect, so serve I the God of our fathers, believing all things which are according to the law, and which are written in the prophets; having hope toward God, which these also themselves look for, that there shall be a resurrection both of the just and the unjust. Herein I also strive to have a conscience void of offense toward God and men always.

"Now after many years I came to bring alms to my nation, and offerings: amidst which they found me purified in the temple, with no crowd, nor yet with tumult: but there were certain Jews from Asia — who ought to have been here before thee, and to make accusation, if they had aught against me. Or else let these men themselves say, what wrongdoing they found, when I stood before the council, except it be for this one utterance, that I cried standing among them, 'Touching the resurrection of the dead I am called in question before you this day.'"

But Felix, having more exact knowledge concerning the Way, deferred them, saying, "When Lysias the chief captain shall come down, I will determine your matter."

And he gave order to the centurion that Paul should be kept in charge, and should have indulgence; and not to forbid any of his friends to minister to him.

After certain days, Felix came with Drusilla, his wife, who was a Jewess, and sent for Paul, and heard him concerning the faith in Christ Jesus.

As he reasoned of righteousness, and temperance, and the judgment to come, Felix was terrified, and answered, "Go thy way for this time; when I have a convenient season, I will call thee to me." He hoped moreover that money would be given him by Paul: wherefore he sent for him the oftener, and communed with him. But after two years Felix was succeeded by Porcius Festus[27]; and desiring to gain favor with the Jews, Felix left Paul in bonds.

Paul Appeals to Cæsar

Festus, therefore, having come into the province, after three days went up from Cæsarea to Jerusalem. Then the chief priests and the principal men of the Jews informed him against Paul; and they besought him, asking as a favor, that he would send for him to Jerusalem, laying a plot to kill him on the way.

But Festus answered, that Paul was kept at Cæsarea, and that he himself was about to depart thither shortly. "Let them therefore," said he, "who are influential among you, go down with me, and, if there is anything amiss in the man, let them accuse him."

And when he had tarried among them not more than eight or ten days, he went down to Cæsarea; and the next day, sitting on the judgment seat, he commanded Paul to be brought.

When he came, the Jews who had come down from Jerusalem stood round about him, bringing against him many and grievous charges, which they could not prove; while Paul said in his defense, "Neither against the law of the Jews, nor against the temple, nor against Cæsar, have I sinned at all."

But Festus, desiring to gain favor with the Jews, answered Paul, and said, "Wilt thou go up to Jerusalem, and there be judged of these things before me?"

Then said Paul: "I am standing before Cæsar's judgment seat, where I ought to be judged: to the Jews have I done no wrong, as thou also very well knowest. If then I am a wrongdoer, and have committed anything worthy of death, I refuse not to die; but if none of those things is true, whereof these accuse me, no man can give me up to them. I appeal to Cæsar."[28]

King Agrippa Arrives at Cæsarea

Then Festus, when he had conferred with the council, answered, "Thou hast appealed to Cæsar: to Cæsar shalt thou go."

Now when certain days had passed, Agrippa the king and Bernice came to Cæsarea, and saluted Festus. And as they tarried there many days, Festus laid Paul's case before the king, saying: "There is a certain man left a prisoner by Felix; about whom, when I was at Jerusalem, the chief priests and the elders of the Jews informed me, asking for sentence against him. To whom I answered, 'It is not the custom of the Romans to give up any man, before he who is accused have the accusers face to face, and have had opportunity to make his defense concerning the matter laid against him.' Therefore, when they came together here, I made no delay, but on the morrow I sat on the judgment seat, and commanded the man to be brought forth.

Concerning whom, when the accusers stood up, they brought no charge of such evil things as I supposed; but had certain questions against him of their own religion, and of one Jesus, who was dead, whom Paul affirmed to be alive. And I, being perplexed how to inquire concerning these things, asked him whether he would go to Jerusalem, and there be judged of these matters. But when Paul had appealed to be kept for the decision of the emperor, I commanded him to be kept till I might send him to Cæsar."

Then Agrippa said to Festus, "I also could wish to hear the man myself."

"Tomorrow," said he, "thou shalt hear him."

So on the morrow, when Agrippa had come, and Bernice, with great pomp, and they had entered into the audience room, with the chief captains, and the principal men of the city, at the command of Festus Paul was brought in.

And Festus said: "King Agrippa, and all men who are here present with us, ye see this man, about whom all the multitude of the Jews made suit to me, both at Jerusalem and here, crying that he ought not to live any longer. But I found that he had committed nothing worthy of death, and as he himself appealed to the emperor, I determined to send him. Of whom I have no certain thing to write to my lord. Wherefore I have brought him forth before you, and especially before thee, King Agrippa, that, after examination, I may have something to write. For it seemeth to me unreasonable, in sending a prisoner, not to signify the charges against him."

Paul Defends Himself Before Agrippa

Agrippa said to Paul, "Thou art permitted to speak for thyself."

Then Paul stretched forth his hand, and made his defense: "I think myself happy, King Agrippa, that I am to make my defense before thee this day touching all the things whereof I am accused by the Jews: especially because thou art expert in all customs and questions which are among the Jews: wherefore I beseech thee to hear me patiently.

"My manner of life then from my youth up, which was from the beginning among mine own nation, and at Jerusalem, know all the Jews; who knew me from the beginning, if they are willing to testify, how that after the strictest sect of our religion I lived a Pharisee. And now I stand here to be judged for the hope of the promise made by God to our fathers; to which promise our twelve tribes, earnestly serving God day and night, hope to attain. And concerning this hope, O King Agrippa, I am accused by the Jews.

"Why is it judged incredible with you, that God should raise the dead?

"I verily thought myself, that I ought to do many things contrary to the name of Jesus of Nazareth. And this I also did in Jerusalem: and I both shut up many of the saints in prison, having received authority from the chief priests; and when they were put to death, I gave my vote against them. And punishing them oftentimes in every synagogue, I strove to make them blaspheme; and being exceedingly mad against them, I persecuted them even to foreign cities.

"Whereupon as I journeyed to Damascus with authority and commission from the chief priests, at midday, O king, I saw on the way a light from heaven, above the brightness of the sun, shining round about me and them that journeyed with me. And when we had all fallen to the earth, I heard a voice saying to me in the Hebrew language, 'Saul, Saul, why persecutest thou me? it is hard for thee to kick against the goad.' And I said, 'Who art thou, Lord?' And the Lord said, 'I am Jesus whom thou persecutest. But rise, and stand upon thy feet; for to this end I have appeared to thee, to appoint thee a minister and a witness both of the things wherein thou hast seen me, and of the things wherein I will appear to thee: delivering thee from the people, and from the Gentiles, to whom I send thee, to open their eyes, that they may turn from darkness to light, and from the power of Satan to God; that they may receive forgiveness of sins, and an inheritance among them that are sanctified by faith in me.'

PAUL BEFORE FESTUS
From a painting by Rudolph Trache

"Whereupon, O King Agrippa, I was not disobedient to the heavenly vision, but declared both to them of Damascus, and at Jerusalem, and throughout all the land of Judea, and also to the Gentiles, that they should repent and turn to God, doing works worthy of repentance. For this cause the Jews seized me in the temple, and tried to kill me.

"Having therefore obtained the help that is from God, I stand unto this day, testifying both to small and great; saying nothing but what the prophets and Moses have said should come; how that the Christ must suffer, and how that he first by the resurrection of the dead should proclaim light both to the [Jewish] people and to the Gentiles."

King Agrippa Is Deeply Moved

But as he thus made his defense, Festus said with a loud voice, "Paul, thou art mad! Thy much learning doth make thee mad."

But he said: "I am not mad, most excellent Festus; but speak forth words of truth and soberness. For the king knoweth of these things, unto whom also I speak freely. For I am persuaded that none of these things is hidden from him; for this hath not been done in a corner. King Agrippa, believest thou the prophets? I know that thou believest."

Then Agrippa said to Paul, "Almost thou persuadest me to be a Christian."

And Paul said, "I would to God, that not only thou, but also all that hear me this day, were both almost, and altogether, such as I am, except these bonds."

When he had thus spoken, the king rose up, and the governor, and Bernice, and they that sat with them. And when they had with drawn, they spoke one to another, saying, "This man doeth nothing worthy of death or of bonds."

And Agrippa said to Festus, "This man might have been set at liberty, if he had not appealed to Cæsar."

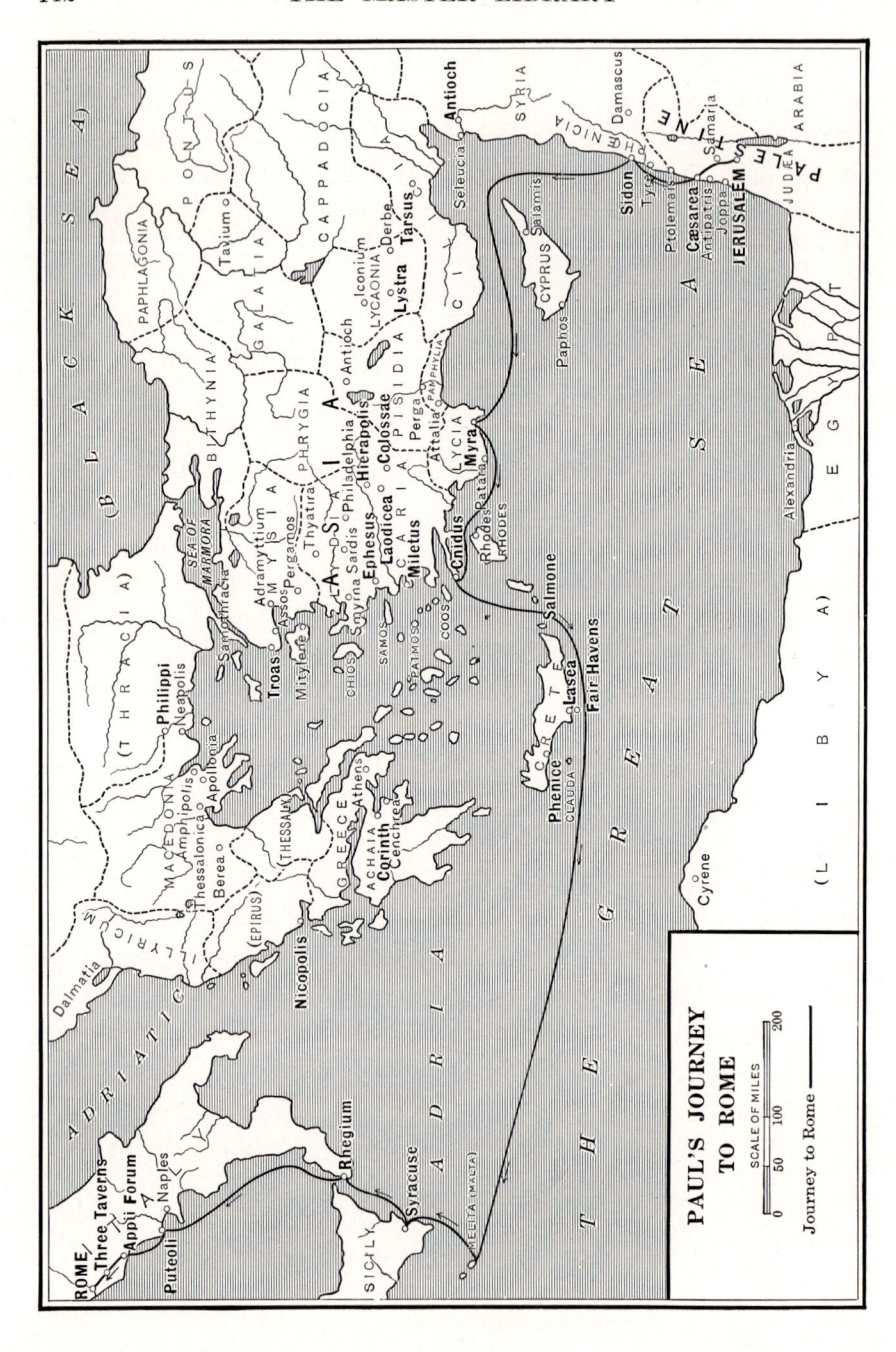

PAUL'S JOURNEY TO ROME

PAUL'S JOURNEY TO ROME

Jerusalem, Judea
  Reports to Apostles and elders
  Conforms to Jewish ritual by vow in Temple
  Assaulted in Temple by Jews
  Rescued by Roman soldiery
  Speech from the castle stairs
  Speech before the Sanhedrin
  Conspiracy to kill Paul discovered by Romans
  Night journey to Cæsarea, under guard
Cæsarea, Judea (via Antipatris)
  Trial before Felix
  Judgment postponed
  Sermon before Felix and Drusilla
  Trial before Festus
  Appeals to Cæsar
  Defense before King Agrippa
  Sent to Rome, attended by Luke and Aristarchus
Sidon, Phœnicia
  Allowed to land and see friends
Myra, Lycia
  Changed to vessel bound for Italy
Cnidus, Caria
  Changed course; unfavorable winds
Fair Havens (via Salmone)
Clauda, an island near Crete
  Storm of fourteen days
Melita (Malta), island near Sicily
  Shipwreck and escape
  Performs miracles, healing many
  Stays three months
Syracuse, Sicily
  Stays three days
Rhegium, Italy
  Stops one day
Puteoli, Italy
  Stays seven days with Christians

Appii Forum and *Three Taverns*, Italy
  Met by brethren
Rome, Italy
  Imprisoned but allowed to preach
  Meets the chief Jews of Rome
  Lives guarded two years in own house
  During imprisonment visited by friends and former companions
  Wrote Epistles to Colossians and Ephesians: delivered by Tychicus
  Wrote letter to Philemon; delivered by Onesimus
  Epaphroditus brings gifts from Philippians: delivers Epistle to Philippians
  Tried and acquitted

CONJECTURAL TRAVELS

Colossæ, *Laodicea*, and *Hierapolis*, in Caria; *Spain* and *Gaul*

AUTHENTIC TRAVELS

Miletus, Caria; *Ephesus*, Lydia; *Troas*, Mysia; *Philippi*, Macedonia; *Corinth*, Achaia; *Nicopolis*, Epirus; *Crete*
  Wrote I Timothy and Titus
Rome, Italy
  Great fire; Christians blamed
  Paul imprisoned as an evil-doer
  Treated more harshly than before
  Deserted by all but Luke
  First hearing before Roman magistrate
  Allowed defense; temporarily acquitted
  Held for new trial
  Wrote II Timothy
  Executed on Ostian Way

THE ISLAND OF MALTA

In the Book of Acts, Malta is called Melita. The place has never been of consequence except for strategic purposes. In the Middle Ages the Knights of Malta held the island as a watchtower against the Saracen. Great Britain today holds it as a naval base to guard the narrow passes by which steamers approach Port Said. The principal square in the town of Malta is named after Paul, and the cathedral which faces it is built upon the traditional site of the house where Paul was entertained.

PAUL'S JOURNEY TO ROME

SHIPWRECK AND SUFFERING

Paul Starts as a Prisoner for Rome

WHEN it was determined that we should sail for Italy, they delivered Paul and certain other prisoners to one named Julius, a centurion of the Augustan band. And embarking in a ship of Adramyttium, which was about to sail to ports on the coasts of Asia, we put to sea, Aristarchus, a Macedonian of Thessalonica, being with us.

The next day we touched at Sidon: and Julius treated Paul courteously, and gave him leave to go to his friends and refresh himself. When we had put to sea from thence, we sailed under the lee of Cyprus, because the winds were contrary.

When we had sailed across the sea which is off Cilicia and Pamphylia, we came to Myra, a city of Lycia. And there the centurion found a ship of Alexandria sailing for Italy; and he put us therein.

When we had sailed slowly many days, and had come with difficulty over against Cnidus, the wind not further suffering us, we sailed under the lee of Crete,[29] over against Salmone; and with difficulty coasting along it we came to a place which is called Fair Havens; nigh whereunto was the city of Lasea.

Paul Is Shipwrecked in Winter

When much time was spent, and when sailing was now dangerous, because the winter was near, Paul warned them, and said to them, "Sirs, I perceive that this voyage will be with injury and much loss, not only of the lading and the ship, but also of our lives."

But the centurion gave more heed to the master, and to the owner of the ship, than to those things which were spoken by Paul. And because the haven was not commodious to winter in, the larger part advised to put to sea from thence, if by any means they could reach Phœnix, and winter there; which is a haven of Crete, looking northeast and southeast.

And when the south wind blew softly, supposing that they had obtained their purpose, they weighed anchor, and sailed along Crete, close inshore. But not long after there beat down from it a tempestuous wind, which is called Euraquilo; and when the ship was caught, and could not face the wind, we gave way to it, and were driven.

And running under the lee of a small island called Clauda, we were able, with difficulty, to secure the boat: and when they had hoisted it up, they used ropes, undergirding the ship; and, fearing lest they should be cast upon the Syrtis, they lowered the gear, and so were driven.

And as we labored exceedingly with the storm, the next day they began to throw the freight overboard; and the third day they cast out with their own hands the tackling of the ship.

Paul Cheers His Companions

When neither sun nor stars shone upon us for many days, and no small tempest lay on us, all hope that we should be saved was now taken away.

And when they had been long without food, then Paul stood forth in the midst of them, and said: "Sirs, ye should have hearkened to me, and not have set sail from Crete, and have gotten this harm and loss. But now I exhort you to be of good cheer: for there shall be no loss of life among you, but only of the ship. For there stood by me this night an angel of the God whose I am, whom also I serve, saying, 'Fear not, Paul; thou must stand before Cæsar: and lo, God hath granted thee all them that sail with thee.' Wherefore, sirs, be of good cheer: for I believe God, that it shall be even so as it hath been spoken to me. Howbeit we must be cast upon a certain island."

PAUL'S SHIP ON THE FIFTEENTH DAY

Paul's voyage from Cæsarea to Italy was accomplished in three ships, the first a coasting merchantman, and the second and third, liners in the grain trade. The coasting vessel took him from Cæsarea to Myra, a city on the southern coast of Asia Minor. There he found an Alexandrian grain ship sailing for Italy. It seems strange to us moderns, that the Mediterranean was closed to traffic from November to March every year. The winter storms were too much even for the big merchantmen of those days. Paul knew this, and warned the captain. The above picture shows the ship anchored by the stern off a place called today Saint Paul's Bay, on the coast of Malta. In the background is Salmonetta Island "where two seas meet." The illustration shows the cables by which the ship has been undergirded in the middle, and the anchor lines from the stern. It shows the rudder bands being loosened and the small sail hoisted in the bow so that they may make for the inlet between the rocks. The plan to save the ship was not successful; she struck a reef and broke up.

But when the fourteenth night had come, as we were driven to and fro in the sea of Adria, about midnight the sailors surmised that they were drawing near to land; and they sounded, and found twenty fathoms; and when they had gone a little farther, they sounded again, and found fifteen fathoms. Then fearing lest we should be cast ashore on rocky ground, they let go four anchors from the stern, and wished for the day.

And as the sailors were seeking to flee out of the ship, and had lowered the boat into the sea, pretending that they would lay out anchors from the bow, Paul said to the centurion and to the soldiers, "Except these abide in the ship, ye cannot be saved." Then the soldiers cut away the ropes of the boat, and let it fall off. While the day was coming on, Paul besought them all to take some food, saying, "This day is the fourteenth day that ye wait and continue fasting, having taken nothing. Wherefore I beseech you to take some food; for this is for your safety: for there shall not a hair perish from the head of any of you."

When he had said this, and had taken bread, he gave thanks to God in presence of all; and he broke it, and began to eat. Then were they all of good cheer, and they also took some food. And we were in all in the ship two hundred threescore and sixteen souls. And when they had eaten enough, they lightened the ship, throwing out the wheat into the sea.

"They All Escaped Safe to Land"

When it was day, they knew not the land; but they perceived a certain bay with a beach, and they took counsel whether they could drive the ship upon it. And casting off the anchors, they left them in the sea, at the same time loosing the bands of the rudders; and hoisting up the foresail to the wind, they made for the beach. But lighting upon a place where two seas met, they ran the vessel aground; and the bow struck, and remained immovable, but the stern began to break up by the violence of the waves.

And the soldiers' counsel was to kill the prisoners, lest any of them should swim out, and escape. But the centurion, desiring to save Paul, kept them from their purpose; and commanded that those who could swim should cast themselves overboard, and get first to the land: and the rest, some on planks, and some on other things from the ship. And so it came to pass, that they all escaped safe to land.

A KNIGHT OF MALTA
From a painting by Giorgione

Paul Finds Hospitality at Malta

And when we had escaped, then we knew that the island was called Melita [Malta]. And the barbarians showed us no common kindness; for they kindled a fire, and received us all, because of the present rain, and because of the cold.

But when Paul had gathered a bundle of sticks, and laid them on the fire, a viper came out by reason of the heat, and fastened on his hand. And when the barbarians saw the venomous creature hanging from his hand, they said one to another, "No doubt this man is a murderer, whom, though he hath escaped from the sea, yet Justice hath not allowed to live." Howbeit he shook off the creature into the fire, and took no harm.

But they expected that he would have swollen, or fallen down dead suddenly; but after they had looked a great while, and saw no harm come to him, they changed their minds, and said that he was a god.

Now in the neighborhood of that place were lands belonging to the chief man of the island, whose name was Publius; who received us, and entertained us three days courteously.

And it came to pass, that the father of Publius lay sick of fever and dysentery: and to him Paul entered in, and prayed, and laid his hands on him, and healed him. And when this was done, others also who had diseases in the island came, and were cured; who also honored us with many honors; and when we sailed, they put on board such things as we needed.

THE END OF THE VOYAGE

"And so We Went Toward Rome"

And after three months we set sail in a ship of Alexandria, which had wintered in the island, whose sign was The Twin Brothers.[30] And touching at Syracuse, we tarried there three

HARBOR OF SYRACUSE WHERE PAUL LANDED

Syracuse was a famous Greek city, once the center of Hellenic influence in the West. The siege and capture of Syracuse by the Spartans forms the most tragic episode in the Peloponnesian War. Syracuse was the birthplace of Archimedes, the great mathematician. Its population has now shrunk to twenty-five thousand people.

days. And from thence we made a circuit, and arrived at Rhegium; and after one day a south wind sprang up, and on the second day we came to Puteoli; where we found brethren, and were entreated to tarry with them seven days: and so we came to Rome. And from thence, when the brethren heard of us, they came to meet us as far as Appii Forum [The Market of Appius] and The Three Taverns; whom when Paul saw, he thanked God, and took courage.

PUTEOLI, THE HARBOR IN ITALY WHERE PAUL LANDED
From a painting by Edoardo Forti

PAUL'S JOURNEY TO ROME

When we came to Rome,[31] Paul was allowed to abide by himself with a soldier that guarded him. And it came to pass, that after three days he called together those who were the chief of the Jews; and when they had come together, he said to them: "I, brethren, though I have done nothing against the people, or the customs of our fathers, yet was delivered prisoner from Jerusalem into the hands of the Romans: who, when they had examined me, would have let me go, because there was no cause of death in me. But when the Jews spoke against it, I was constrained to appeal to Cæsar; not that I had anything to accuse my nation of. For this cause therefore have I called for you, to see you, and to speak with you: for because of the hope of Israel I am bound with this chain."

And they said to him: "We neither received letters from Judea concerning thee, neither did any of the brethren come hither and report or speak any harm of thee. But we desire to hear of thee what thou thinkest: for as concerning this sect, we know that everywhere it is spoken against."

Paul Has Opportunity to Preach in Rome

And when they had appointed him a day, they came to him into his lodging in great number; to whom he expounded the matter, testifying the kingdom of God, and persuading

THE HARBOR IN ITALY WHERE PAUL LANDED
From a painting by Edoardo Forti

Puteoli (modern Pozzuoli), which was the terminus of Paul's voyage, was one of the most ancient Greek cities in Italy. It lies on the north shore of the Bay of Naples, famous for its scenery and its wonderful climate. Behind the town the hills rise boldly, their summits in Paul's day crowned with temples and villas. This whole shore was the most frequented watering place in the Roman Empire, for thither came the senators, the aristocracy, and the rich merchants of Rome, to spend their holidays in the most extravagant pleasures. The picture gives a hint of this life of luxury and sensuality. Side by side with this gayety was the intense commercial life of a city that was the chief port of entry for the world's capital and the terminus of all the eastern trade routes by which the grain essential to the life of Rome and the luxuries essential to its pleasure were brought from the eastern provinces. The town has met the fate of many others—destruction by earthquakes and wars, and in addition by submergence under the sea. The ancient remains of quays and other buildings may still be discerned beneath the blue waves of the bay.

THE CLAUDIAN AQUEDUCT NEAR THE APPIAN WAY

This aqueduct, newly built, to carry water from the Apennines to the city, was seen by Paul as he drew near to Rome. It is one of the conspicuous monuments on the Campagna, its lofty arches being visible for many a mile. Rome had many of these aqueducts; and in spite of wars and earthquakes, three of them are still in use!

them concerning Jesus, both from the law of Moses, and from the prophets, from morning till evening.

And some believed the things which were spoken, and some believed not.

When they agreed not among themselves, they departed, after Paul had spoken one word: "Well spoke the Holy Spirit by Isaiah the prophet to your fathers, saying:

"'Go unto this people, and say:
Hearing ye shall hear, and shall not understand;
And seeing ye shall see, and not perceive:
For the heart of this people hath become gross,
And their ears are dull of hearing,
And their eyes have they closed;
Lest they should see with their eyes,
And hear with their ears,
And understand with their heart,
And should turn again, and I should heal them.'

THE PYRAMID OF CAIUS CESTIUS, ROME

This monument stands on the western side of the Appian Way just before the traveler enters the city of Rome. It was built as the tomb of a Roman nobleman of the early empire. It would be seen by Paul as he entered the city by this gate. Years later he passed it on his last sad exit from the eternal city as he was being taken to the place of his execution. In fact, among the works of man, this pyramid, though of no important significance itself, is the only surviving witness of the martyrdom of Paul.

The inclosure to the left is the Protestant cemetery, in which the English poets Shelley and Keats are buried.

"Be it known therefore to you, that this salvation of God is sent to the Gentiles: they will also hear."

And Paul dwelt two whole years in his own hired house, and welcomed all that came in to him; preaching the kingdom of God, and teaching those things which concern the Lord Jesus Christ, with all boldness, no man forbidding him.[32]

THE APPIAN WAY

From a painting by Edoardo Forti

Along this ancient highway passed soldiers and generals marching to their wars, proconsuls and procurators going to take possession of their provinces, philosophers and rhetoricians going to study in Athens, and slaves on errands of business or villainy for their masters. Between the chariots of the great ones, might be seen, as in this picture, the gorgeous litter of some fashionable Roman beauty. One wonders what Paul saw and what he thought as he mingled with this throng on the way from The Three Taverns.

IMPRISONMENT AND LAST DAYS

PAUL IN PRISON

He Has Companions During His Imprisonment

Besides Timothy, other friends and associates of Paul are mentioned in various places in his writings as may be seen from the following:

EPAPHRAS, my fellow-prisoner in Christ Jesus, saluteth thee; and so do Mark, Aristarchus, Demas, Luke, my fellow-workers.

Aristarchus my fellow-prisoner saluteth you, and Mark, the cousin of Barnabas (touching whom ye received commandments, "If he come to you, receive him"), and Jesus that is called Justus, who are of the Jews: these only are my fellow-workers unto the kingdom of God, men that have been a comfort to me.

Epaphras, who is one of you, a servant of Christ Jesus, saluteth you, always striving for you in his prayers, that ye may stand perfect and fully assured in all the will of God. For I bear him witness, that he hath a great zeal for you, and for them in Laodicea, and for them in Hierapolis. Luke, the beloved physician, and Demas salute you.

I beseech thee for my child, who hath been born to me in my bonds, Onesimus, who once was unprofitable to thee, but now is profitable to thee and to me: whom I have sent back to thee in his own person, that is, my very heart: whom I would fain have kept with me, that in thy behalf he might minister to me in the bonds of the gospel.

TRADITIONAL HOUSE OF PAUL, ROME

"And Paul dwelt two whole years in his own hired house, and welcomed all that came in to him, preaching the kingdom of God, and teaching those things which concern the Lord Jesus Christ, with all boldness, no man forbidding him."

I have all things, and abound: I am filled, having received from Epaphroditus the things which were sent from you, an odor of a sweet smell, a sacrifice acceptable, well-pleasing to God.

Paul Writes to the Colossians

To us, the most interesting fruits of Paul's Roman imprisonment are the remarkable letters which he wrote during these years to different Christian churches. The arrangement below is selected in order to bring out the occasion for or the principal message of each letter. The great teachings are arranged in this volume in the section entitled "Christian Thought."

The Colossians had been beguiled to accept a curious mixture of teaching in which ritual, mystic fancy, and foolish asceticism had taken the place of the simplicity of the Gospel. Paul wrote to tell them that all they needed was to follow Christ. He cleared the fog of their thinking and living when he reminded them that they would find the light by living His life.

The Father made us worthy to be partakers of the inheritance of the saints in light; who delivered us out of the power of darkness, and translated us into the kingdom of his dear Son; in whom we have our redemption, the forgiveness of our sins. And you, being dead through your sins, did he make alive together with him, having forgiven us all our trespasses.

Let no man judge you in food, or in drink, or in respect of a feast day or a new moon or a sabbath day: which are a shadow of the things to come; but the body is Christ's. If ye died with Christ from the world's elements, why, as though living in the world, do ye subject yourselves to ordinances, "Handle not, nor taste, nor touch" (all which things are to perish with the using), after the precepts and doctrines of men?

If then ye were raised together with Christ, seek the things that are above, where Christ is, seated on the right hand of God. Set your mind on the things that are above, not on the things that are upon the earth. Put to death therefore your members which are upon the earth: vice, uncleanness,

RUINS OF THE PALACES OF THE CÆSARS, ROME

The structure in the foreground is a restoration made in order to show the modern visitor how this portion of Cæsar's palace used to look. The archæologists have cleared the ground to the foundations, and have built upon them a structure which reproduces the shape of the original and which bears, imbedded within it, all of the ancient architectural fragments that have been found on the site. The restored portions are easily detected by the fresh appearance of the bricks. It is quite possible that all of this brickwork was originally faced with marble and that there was a marble mosaic pavement. But in the Middle Ages much of this material was burned up in order to make lime, or was carried away to be used in the building of other structures. The general result of this vandalism is seen in the upper portion of the picture, where only the gaunt hulk of the stripped ruin rears its unlovely form against the sky.

These ruins comprise the remains of several imperial palaces, among them those of the sumptuous Golden House of Nero, which he built after the great fire at Rome. The influence of Christianity penetrated even to this stronghold of its enemies, for we know that some of "Cæsar's household" became followers of the new Way of life, and had no doubt heard Paul preach.

passion, evil desire, and covetousness, which is idolatry. Put on therefore, as God's elect, holy and beloved, a heart of compassion, kindness, lowliness, meekness, longsuffering; forbearing one another, and forgiving one another, if any man have a complaint against any; even as the Lord forgave you, so also do ye: and above all these things put on love, which is the bond of perfectness.

And let the peace of Christ rule in your hearts, to which also ye were called in one body; and be ye thankful. And whatsoever ye do, in word or in deed, do all in the name of the Lord Jesus.

A Circular Letter Is Sent to Asia Minor

This letter was probably written just after the letter to the Colossians. In some of the earliest manuscripts, the phrase "to the Ephesians" is missing. It is thought that the epistle was a sort of encyclical, sent to several of the churches in Asia Minor, of which the one in Ephesus was the chief.

In this letter, Paul carries further the thought in the earlier one. There he had laid emphasis on the supremacy of the Christ. Now, writing to a group of Christian churches representing two great races, he holds up the vital thought of the unity of the church in this supreme Christ. This essential unity, deeper than all races, diversities of thought and talent, difference of work and service, he extols in the following eloquent passage:

There is one body, and one Spirit, even as also ye were called in one hope of your calling; one Lord, one faith, one baptism, one God and Father of all, who is over all, and through all, and in all.

And he gave some to be apostles; and some, prophets; and some, evangelists; and some, pastors and teachers; for the perfecting of the saints, unto the work of ministering, unto the building up of the body of Christ: till we all attain to the unity of the faith, and of the knowledge of the Son of God, unto a full-grown man, unto the measure of the stature of the fulness of Christ: that we may grow up in all things into him, who is the head, even Christ; from whom all the body fitly framed and knit together through that which every joint supplieth, according to the working in due measure of each several part, maketh the increase of the body unto the building up of itself in love.

RESTORATION OF THE ROMAN FORUM
This picture gives an idea of the magnificence of Rome in the days of Paul, for nearly all the buildings here represented had been built previous to his coming there in the year 62 A.D. The low, broad structure in the center foreground is the famous Rostrum from which the orators of Rome addressed the citizens. Behind are temples to the gods, and the long Hall of Records where were kept the public archives of the Republic and the Empire; and on the very summit we see the Temple of Jupiter dominating the Capitoline hill.

Paul Writes to the Philippians

Although written in old age and from a Roman prison, this is the most joyous of Paul's letters. It was written to a church which he himself had founded, and which he had at least three times visited, a church which had been generous to him in gifts of love, and the character of whose members gave him many causes of satisfaction. Therefore, the keynote of this letter is the word "Rejoice!" The selections below bring out Paul's affection and courage, and his message of joy.

I thank my God upon all my remembrance of you, always in every prayer of mine for you all making request with joy, for your fellowship in furtherance of the gospel from the first day until now; being confident of this very thing, that he who began a good work in you will perfect it until the day of Jesus Christ.

TEMPLE OF VESTA

When Paul came into Rome over the Appian Way and found shelter in his own house in the Ghetto, he passed by this ancient temple. By reason of its grace and delicacy, it is one of the most beautiful in Rome, though sadly marred by the vicissitudes of fortune. The original temple, attributed to King Numa, perished in the first sack of Rome. Its successor, though damaged and restored, was still in use when Paul came hither, for within it the Vestals guarded the sacred fire which stood for the purity of the Roman home. It was the most nearly Christian thing in that pagan city.

I would have you know, brethren, that the things which happened to me have fallen out rather unto the furtherance of the gospel; so that my bonds became manifest in Christ throughout the whole prætorian guard, and to all the rest; and that most of the brethren in the Lord, being confident through my bonds, are much more bold to speak the word of God without fear. I know that this shall turn out to my salvation, through your prayer and the supply of the Spirit of Jesus Christ, according to my earnest expectation and my hope, that in nothing shall I be put to shame, but that with all boldness, as always, so now also Christ shall be magnified in my body, whether it be by life, or by death.

For to me to live is Christ, and to die is gain. But if to live in the flesh — if this shall bring fruit from my work, then what I shall choose I know not. But I am in a strait betwixt the two, having a desire to depart and be with Christ; for it is very far better: yet to abide in the flesh is more needful for your sake. And having this confidence, I know that I shall abide, yea, and abide with you all, for your progress and joy in the faith.

Hold forth the word of life, that I may rejoice in the day of Christ, that I have not run in vain, neither labored in vain. Yea, and if I am offered upon the sacrifice and service of your faith, I joy, and rejoice with you all.

Rejoice in the Lord always: again I will say, Rejoice![33] Let your forbearance be known to all men. The Lord is at hand. In nothing be anxious; but in everything by prayer and supplication with thanksgiving let your requests be made known to God. And the peace of God, which passeth all understanding, shall guard your hearts and your thoughts in Christ Jesus.

LATER ACTIVITIES AND LAST DAYS OF PAUL

Was Paul ever Released from Rome?

It was Paul's own expectation that he would be acquitted, and there is good ground for the belief that his expectation was fulfilled, and that he then entered upon another missionary enterprise, in the course of which he was again arrested and taken prisoner to Rome, later to suffer martyrdom there. There are a few passages in the letters of Paul which mention visits that cannot well be connected with any of the earlier journeys, and which probably occurred in the interval between his two Roman imprisonments. These passages are given in this section.

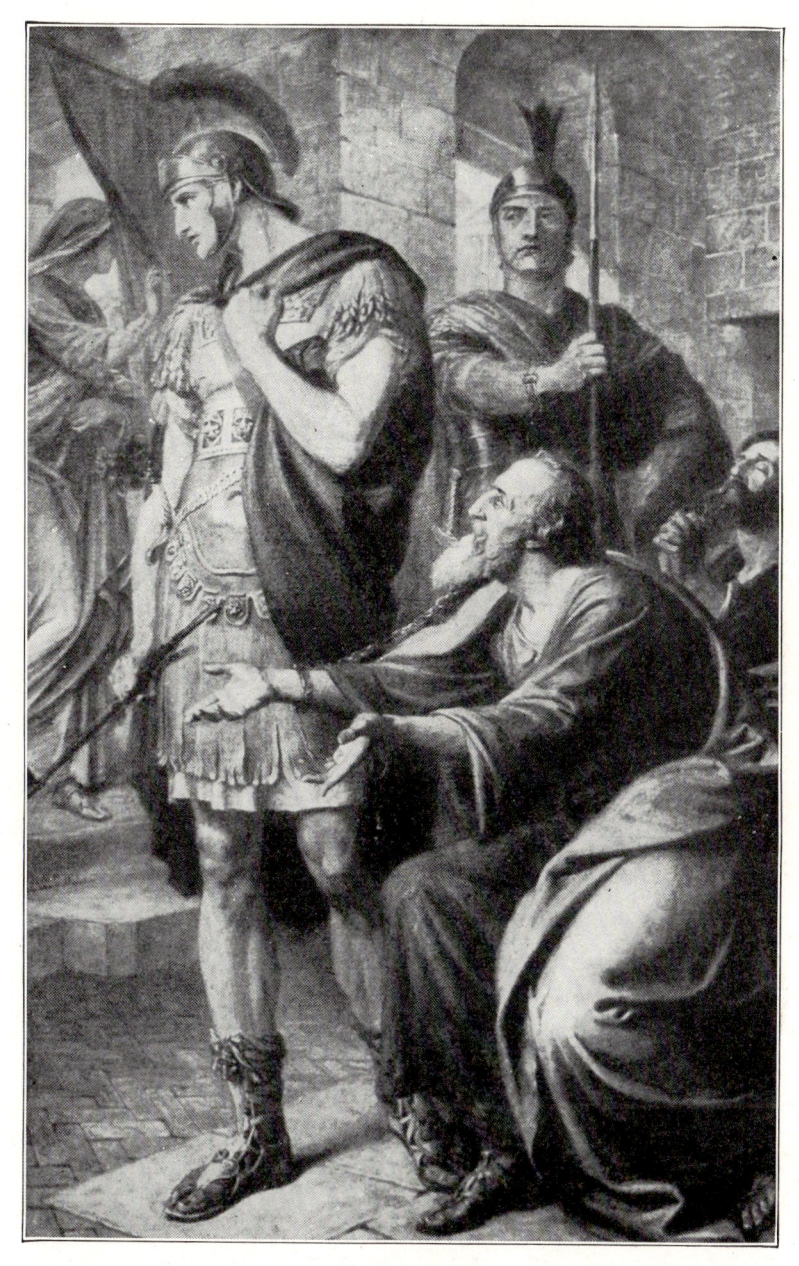

PAUL AT ROME
From a painting by Frederick Shields

The testimony of Clement, who lived only a generation later, is of great interest. He says: "Paul, having been a herald both in the East and in the West, received the high glory of his faith. When he had taught righteousness to the whole world, and had come to the limit of the West, and borne witness before the rulers, he so departed from the world and went to the holy place." The "limit of the West" was certainly farther west than Rome, and suggests at least Spain.

There is a tradition that he passed even the Pillars of Hercules, and reached Britain. It is very interesting to recall that there was a civilization in the land of our forefathers as early as the days of the apostolic church.

The insurrection in Britain under Queen Boadicea occurred in the year 61 A.D., while Paul was alive. If Paul ever went to Britain, as some suppose, he may have seen this queen.

I exhorted thee to tarry at Ephesus, when I was going into Macedonia, that thou mightest charge certain men not to teach a different doctrine.

Give diligence to come to me to Nicopolis; for I have determined to winter there.

The cloak that I left at Troas with Carpus, when thou comest, bring with thee, and the books, especially the parchments.

I left thee in Crete, that thou shouldst set in order the things that were wanting, and appoint elders in every city, as I gave thee charge.

Erastus remained at Corinth; but Trophimus have I left at Miletus sick.

Prepare me also a lodging; for I hope that through your prayers I shall be granted to you.

THE GHETTO, ROME

In Rome, the Ghetto, or section of a city set aside for the residence of Jews, has always been where it is now, along the left bank of the River Tiber, not far from the famous bridge which Horatio and his two companions held in the face of Tarquin's host. Fragments of ancient buildings may be seen on the right. The arches that span the narrow lane are old also, as is evidenced by the peculiar character of both the stone and the brick. It is more than probable that Paul passed under these arches during his sojourn in Rome.

The Loneliness and the Courage of Paul

This thou knowest, that all who are in Asia turned away from me; of whom are Phygelus and Hermogenes. The Lord grant mercy to the house of Onesiphorus: for he oft refreshed

THE VIA SACRA AND THE PALACES OF THE CÆSARS

The smooth, white, irregular blocks that form the roadway in the foreground are the ancient paving stones of the Sacred Way, down which wound the triumphal procession of all Rome's great conquerors. The broken stumps of masonry are the cores of resplendent piers and walls that in Paul's day made the Roman Forum a place of imperial glory. Farther up the hill are the remains of the Palaces of the Cæsars, notably those of Augustus and Tiberius.

me, and was not ashamed of my chain; but, when he was in Rome, he sought me out very diligently, and found me (the Lord grant to him that he may find mercy of the Lord in that day); and in how many things he ministered to me at Ephesus, thou knowest very well.

Give diligence to come shortly to me: for Demas hath forsaken me, having loved this present world, and hath departed to Thessalonica; Crescens to Galatia, Titus to Dalmatia. Only Luke is with me. Take Mark, and bring him with thee; for he is useful to me for ministering. And Tychicus have I sent to Ephesus.

Alexander the coppersmith did me much evil: the Lord will render to him according to his works. At my first defense no one took my part, but all men forsook me: I pray God that it may not be laid to their account. But the Lord stood by me, and strengthened me; that through me the message might be fully proclaimed, and that all the Gentiles might hear; and I was delivered out of the mouth of the lion.

The Lord will deliver me from every evil work, and will save me unto his heavenly kingdom: to whom be the glory forever and ever. Amen.

The Spirit in Which Paul Faced Death

It is the general tradition, accepted as early as the first century, that Paul suffered martyrdom under the Emperor Nero.

THE TRADITIONAL TOMB OF LUKE AT EPHESUS

Luke joined Paul at Troas on his second missionary journey. He was probably with Paul during his sojourn in Ephesus. Whether or not he died and was buried here, we have no sure indication, but tradition at least has decided that here is his tomb.

I suffer hardship, as an evildoer, even unto bonds; but the word of God is not bound. Therefore I endure all things for the elect's sake, that they also may obtain the salvation which is in Christ Jesus with eternal glory.

Our citizenship is in heaven; whence also we wait for a Saviour, the Lord Jesus Christ; who shall fashion anew the

UPPER CHAMBER, MAMERTINE PRISON

The grating in the floor of this room covers the opening to the lower dungeon which originally was to be entered only by this means. Now there is a stairway. In this lower dungeon, which was most repulsive and terrible, perished Jugurtha, the African king, and Vercingetorix whom Cæsar made captive in Gaul. The dungeon contains a tiny spring which, according to the legend, sprang miraculously at the bidding of Peter, in order that he might baptize his jailor. This tradition of Peter's imprisonment accounts for the fact that since the fifteenth century the place has been named San Pietro in Carcere (Saint Peter in Prison). The tablet on the wall commemorates the restoration of this prison in the year 1667 in the belief that both Peter and Paul were confined in it.

body of our humiliation, that it may be conformed to the body of his glory, according to the working whereby he is able even to subject all things to himself.

Though we walk in the flesh, we do not war according to the flesh (for the weapons of our warfare are not of the flesh, but mighty before God to the casting down of strongholds); casting down imaginations, and every high thing that is exalted against the knowledge of God, and bringing every thought into captivity to the obedience of Christ.

CHURCH OF SAINT PAUL WITHOUT THE WALLS

Paul is said to have been executed at a place called Three Fountains, and to have been buried where now stands this magnificent basilica that bears his name. The beautiful coffin in which his body is said to rest, the gift of a noble woman of Rome, is still in the crypt. Until the Reformation, the kings of England were the protectors of this church. It stands on the site of a church founded by Anacletus and enlarged by Constantine the Great. It has been plundered by Vandals and Saracens, and in 1823 was burned and reduced to ruins, after having been used as a place of Christian worship for nearly fifteen centuries.

Though several times destroyed and rebuilt, the church preserves wonderful mosaics that date from the fifth and the thirteenth centuries. The cloister pictured above is one of the most beautiful works of Romanesque architecture that have come down to us. Some of the twisted and fluted columns still carry the intricate mosaic patterns that were the glory of Rome in the Middle Ages. In the crypt beneath the church were found many wonderful sculptured marble sarcophagi—which indicates that the aristocracy of Rome in the fifth and sixth centuries wished to be buried as near as possible to the tomb of the great Apostle to the Gentiles.

I am now ready to be offered, and the time of my departure is at hand. I have fought a good fight, I have finished my course, I have kept the faith. Henceforth there is laid up for me a crown of righteousness, which the Lord, the righteous judge, will give me at that day; and not to me only, but to all them also that love his appearing.

WALKING WITH PAUL

Paul, with what strength you tread the Ostian Way,
Holding your aged head as calm and high
As some glad youth who goes to festival!
Has not the damp of dreary days and nights
'Midst nameless horrors of the Mamertine
Quenched the proud spirit that has striven with kings?

What think you, brother, was the road so long
That led without the walls to Golgotha?
How beats the sun! And with what cloudless glare
Fiercely bends o'er us this Italian sky!
Or do the eyes once blinded by the Light
Face without flinching all these lesser rays?

There is the place! We shall descend this hill,
Move but a little forward — mark the spot.
You will be given an hour to think of God
In that mean cell beyond yon little mound;
Then, to the left — you cannot see it now —
Stands the last milepost on the dolorous way.

See where Rome stands behind you, proud, secure
Temples that fell not when you spoke of Christ;
Homes of the Cæsars, whom you own as kings.
What serves your loyalty today, old man?
What was the merit of your vain appeal?
Jew, Roman, Christian, going forth to die!

Can nothing daunt you? Hear you not my voice?
Have you forgotten that you walk in chains,
Death-doomed by Cæsar? Tell me what you see?
Why is that rapture sweeping o'er your face?
Surely some voice proclaims within your soul,
"Cæsar has failed, and Paul has won his crown!"

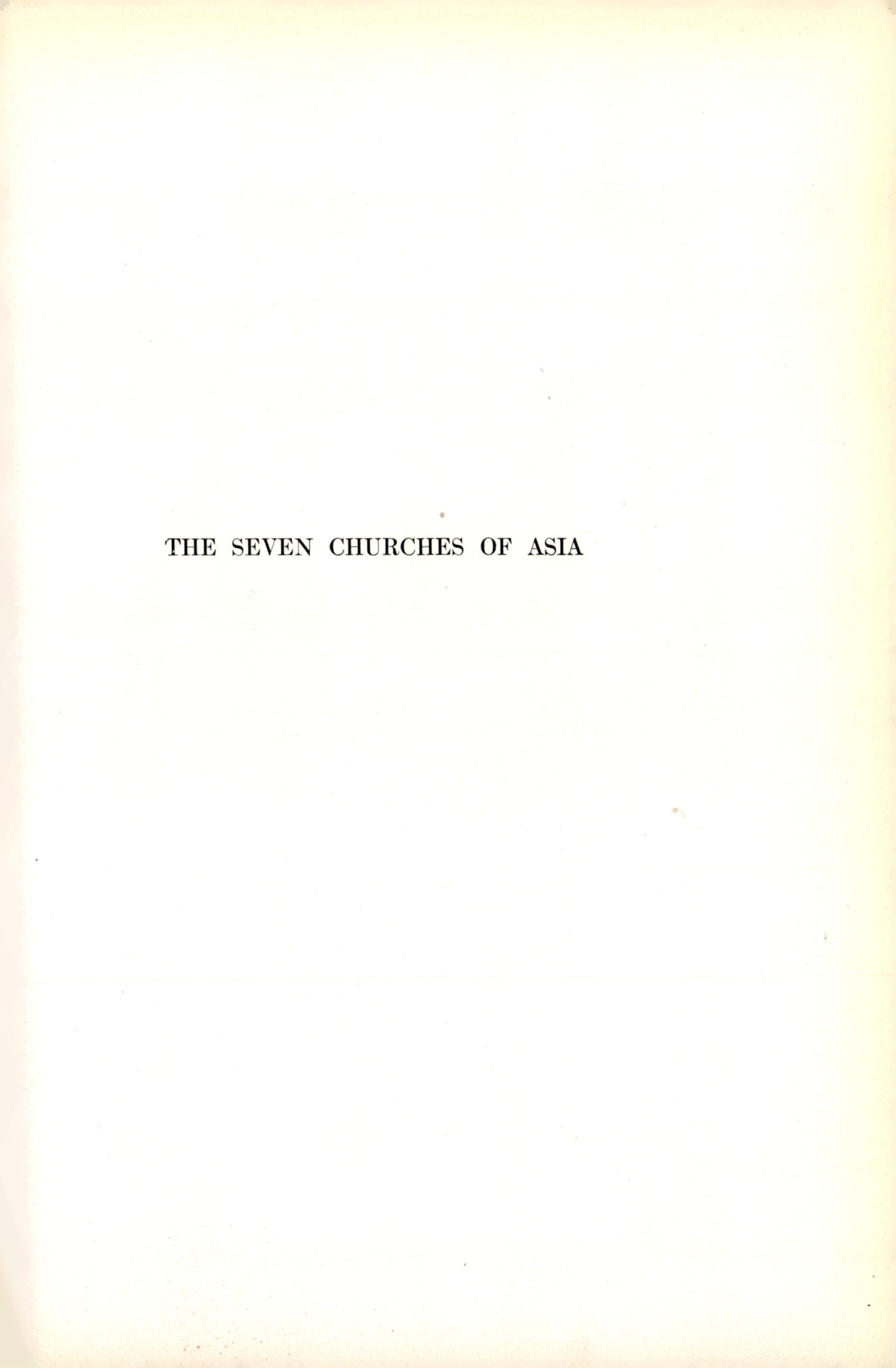

THE SEVEN CHURCHES OF ASIA

THE SEVEN CHURCHES OF ASIA

IN the seven short letters to the seven churches of Asia Minor, found in the Book of Revelation, we have a valuable collection of pictures of the early Christian communities that existed near the end of the first century. It was probably about 77 A.D., during the reign of Vespasian, that these letters were written. The "seven" are believed to be typical of a larger number—perhaps of all the churches in that part of the world at that time. We may recognize many characteristics of these early churches in churches that exist today.

The "angels" to whom the letters are directed may have been their leaders, their teachers, or pastors; but they have also been thought to be "a symbolical representation in which the active, as distinguished from the passive, life of the church finds expression"; that is, their spirit as it shows itself in conduct.

There seems to be a difference in the degree of fidelity of the first three and the last four. In none of the first three is the church perfect, but in none is she really faithless. In the second group, the churches as a whole seem to have been faithless; it is only a remnant which is acknowledged as faithful. In them, the struggle is fiercer, the issue more in doubt, and the promises are fuller and more eloquent of victory for those who endure to the end.

Canon Benham says: "Each message is prefaced by some feature of Christ as described in the first chapter of the Book of Revelation. To each church it is said, 'I know thy works,' and there is a promise in each 'to him that overcometh.' The first, Ephesus, is reproved for lapsing from its first love; Smyrna is not rebuked, but is warned that tribulation is coming upon her; Pergamum is faithful, but has some false teachers; Thyatira is suffering a foul spirit to devastate the church with its abominations; Sardis is formal and unreal, and so true religion is ready to die, though there are some who are leading holy lives; Philadelphia remains pure, but is weak; Laodicea is lukewarm and worldly. In all this, we are at no loss to see the types of the different forms of evil by which churches and individuals alike are infected in all ages."

"HOLD THAT FAST WHICH THOU HAST, THAT NO ONE TAKE THY CROWN"
From a painting by L. M. Roth

SEVEN CHRISTIAN CHURCHES

Some Years After the Death of Paul

TO EPHESUS

This was the city in which Paul ministered longer than in any other, a city of great importance and influence in his time, chiefly remembered now as the site of a famous temple of Diana. Many Jews had settled in this cosmopolitan center, and to them Paul preached first, turning later to the general populace when he lectured in the school of Tyrannus. His long ministry here laid a solid foundation for a thriving Christian church. Because it was the seaport of Asia Minor for Rome, Christians were often deported from Ephesus to die in the Colosseum. Ignatius, who was bishop of Ephesus, wrote touchingly to his city, "Ye are a highroad of them that are on their way to die unto God."

TO the angel of the church in Ephesus write: "These things saith he that holdeth the seven stars in his right hand, he that walketh in the midst of the seven golden candlesticks:

"'I know thy works, and thy toil and thy patience, and that thou canst not bear evil men: and didst try them who call themselves apostles, and they are not, and didst find them false; and thou hast patience, and didst bear for my name's sake, and hast not grown weary.

"'Nevertheless I have this against thee, that thou didst leave thy first love. Remember therefore from whence thou art fallen, and repent, and do the first works; or else I will come to thee quickly, and will move thy candlestick out of its place, except thou repent. But this thou hast, that thou hatest the works of the Nicolaitans, which I also hate.

"'He that hath an ear, let him hear what the Spirit saith to the churches. To him that overcometh, to him will I give to eat of the tree of life, which is in the midst of the Paradise of God.'"

SMYRNA

"Infidel Smyrna," the Turks call it, because it has been inhabited so largely by Greeks, who are of course Christians. The city is magnificently situated. It lies at the head of a long gulf of the Ægean Sea, surrounded by lofty mountains. The picture shows the city and the harbor from the top of Mount Pagus, which rises abruptly to the south. On the other side of this mountain is pointed out the site of the church of which the Apostle John was once a member. During the late war the Turks largely dismantled the ancient theater to find stones for their new war college. This city was utterly ruined in the great sack and massacre of September, 1922.

TO SMYRNA

Smyrna is the only one of the seven cities that has retained its identity. It was given to Greece as a result of the Great War, and has since fallen into the hands of the Turks. The church there was characterized by a poverty rich in good works, and to it was promised the victor's wreath.

And to the angel of the church in Smyrna write: "These things saith the first and the last, who was dead, and lived again:

"'I know thy tribulation, and thy poverty (but thou art rich), and the blasphemy of those who say they are Jews, and they are not, but are a synagogue of Satan.

"'Fear none of those things which thou art about to suffer: behold, the devil is about to cast some of you into prison, that ye may be tried; and ye shall have tribulation ten days. Be thou faithful unto death, and I will give thee the crown of life.

"'He that hath an ear, let him hear what the Spirit saith to the churches. He that overcometh shall not be hurt of the second death.'"

TO THYATIRA

In this city there was a woman or a party that encouraged a sensual philosophy destructive of Christian morality. To this church, if it could conquer this one influence, was promised authority and glory.

And to the angel of the church in Thyatira write: "These things saith the Son of God, who hath his eyes like a flame of fire, and his feet are like burnished brass:

"'I know thy works, and thy love and faith and ministry and patience, and that thy last works are more than the first.

"'But I have this against thee, that thou sufferest the woman Jezebel, who calleth herself a prophetess; and she teacheth and seduceth my servants to commit evil, and to eat things sacrificed to idols. And I gave her time that she should repent; and she repented not. Behold, I will cast her and them that sin with her into great tribulation, unless they repent of her deeds. And I will kill her children with death; and all the churches shall know that I am he who searcheth the inmost heart: and I will give to every one of you according to your works. But to you I say, to the rest that are in Thyatira, as many as have not this teaching, who know not the deep things of Satan, as they say; I cast upon you none other burden. But that which ye have, hold fast till I come.

THE GREAT ALTAR OF PERGAMUM

"'He that overcometh, and he that keepeth my works to the end, to him will I give authority over the nations: and he shall rule them with a rod of iron, as the vessels of the potter are broken to shivers; as I also have received of my Father: and I will give him the morning star. He that hath an ear, let him hear what the Spirit saith to the churches.'"

TO PERGAMUM

Pergamum was a center of the popular emperor-worship, which was so abhorrent to the Christians. This fact, no doubt, accounts for the allusion to "Satan's seat" being there. The church at Pergamum, though tempted, was faithful, and was promised a reward of secret spiritual strength.

And to the angel of the church in Pergamum write: "These things saith he that hath the sharp two-edged sword:

"'I know where thou dwellest, even where Satan's seat is: and thou holdest fast my name, and didst not deny my faith, even in the days of Antipas my witness, my faithful one, who was killed among you, where Satan dwelleth.

"'But I have a few things against thee, because thou hast there some that hold the doctrine of Balaam, who taught Balak to cast a stumbling block before the children of Israel, to eat things sacrificed to idols. So hast thou also some that hold the teaching of the Nicolaitans in like manner.

THE GREAT ALTAR OF PERGAMUM

In the third and second centuries before Christ, Pergamum was one of the great cities of Asia Minor. It was the seat of a school of Greek sculpture that made a specialty of heroic figures and dramatic action. Eumenes II, king of Pergamum (191–159 B.C.), has the honor of having built at Pergamum, in connection with a temple to Zeus, one of the largest and most splendid altars ever constructed. Much of this wonderful work has perished. In the early part of the twentieth century, excavators from Germany made extensive diggings on the site of the old city, and recovered many fragments of the altar and other architectural pieces. These are now in the Museum at Berlin. In the picture, one may easily detect these ancient fragments, set as they are in a modern restoration that represents the original form of the altar. Fragments may be seen, not only on the base of the altar, but also on the cornice above the columns. These sculptures speak eloquently of the wealth and the power that lay back of the classic religion with which Christianity had to contend, and they partly account for the long struggle of three centuries necessary to unseat the Olympians and enthrone the Christ. It is possible that this very altar was in the mind of the writer when he said of the church in Pergamum, "I know where thou dwellest, even where Satan's seat is."

SARDIS

Sardis lies inland from Smyrna on the great trunk line that connects Europe with the heart of Asia. It was once the brilliant capital of Crœsus, the richest man of his day, and was later the administrative center of Persia. Its importance was due to its military strength, its location on an important highway, and its command of the fertile plain of Hermus. It was the burning of Sardis by the Ionian Greeks with the aid of men of Athens that caused Darius to vow vengeance and to initiate the famous Persian Wars. In the days of the Apostle John, it was still a flourishing city, and the seat of one of the seven churches of Asia. An earthquake in the Middle Ages precipitated upon the city a huge section of the mountain. From that day until the twentieth century, Sardis disappeared from history.

An expedition sent out by Princeton University in 1909 has laid bare the ruins of the ancient town disclosing, among other interesting things, the remains of a little Christian church which had been built in a corner of the disused temple of Cybele. This little structure, dating from the fourth century of our era, is mute evidence of the conquest of the new religion which appropriated to itself the once splendid precincts of the heathen goddess.

"'Repent therefore; or else I will come to thee quickly, and I will make war against them with the sword of my mouth.

"'He that hath an ear, let him hear what the Spirit saith to the churches. To him that overcometh, to him will I give of the hidden manna, and I will give him a white stone, and upon the stone a new name written, which no one knoweth but he that receiveth it.'"

TO SARDIS

Sardis is today only a heap of ruins, but it was once the capital of Lydia and the home of the opulent King Crœsus. It was noted for its luxury and vice. Against these the church had struggled ineffectively, and its life had nearly died out. But there were a few even in Sardis who had not "defiled their garments," and who should walk eternally in white.

And to the angel of the church in Sardis[34] write: "These things saith he that hath the seven Spirits of God, and the seven stars:

"'I know thy works, that thou hast a name that thou livest, and thou art dead. Be watchful, and establish the things that remain, which were ready to die: for I have found no works of thine perfected before my God.

"'Remember therefore how thou hast received and didst hear; and keep it, and repent. If therefore thou shalt not watch, I will come on thee as a thief, and thou shalt not know what hour I will come upon thee.

"'Thou hast a few names even in Sardis who have not defiled their garments; and they shall walk with me in white; for they are worthy.

"'He that overcometh shall thus be arrayed in white garments; and I will not blot his name out of the book of life, but I will confess his name before my Father, and before his angels. He that hath an ear, let him hear what the Spirit saith to the churches.'"

TO LAODICEA

"Laodicean" has long been a synonym for a person of lukewarm temperament. This failing is attacked in this letter with evident disgust. Only those whose patience and fidelity last to the end of the day can sup with Christ and win the rewards that belong to perseverance.

And to the angel of the church in Laodicea write: "These things saith the Amen, the faithful and true witness, the beginning of the creation of God:

"'I know thy works, that thou art neither cold nor hot: I would thou wert cold or hot. So then because thou art lukewarm, and neither hot nor cold, I will spew thee out of my mouth. Because thou sayest, I am rich, and have gotten riches, and have need of nothing; and knowest not that thou art the wretched one, and miserable, and poor, and blind, and naked: I counsel thee to buy of me gold refined by fire, that thou mayest become rich; and white garments, that thou mayest clothe thyself, and that the shame of thy nakedness be not made manifest; and eye salve to anoint thine eyes, that thou mayest see.

"'As many as I love, I reprove and chasten: be zealous therefore, and repent. Behold, I stand at the door and knock: if any man hear my voice and open the door, I will come in to him, and will sup with him, and he with me.

"'To him that overcometh, will I grant to sit with me on my throne, even as I also overcame, and sat down with my Father on his throne.

"'He that hath an ear, let him hear what the Spirit saith to the churches.'"

TO PHILADELPHIA

The only church in which no fault is found. Philadelphia was an important center of trade, a city in which there was a great opportunity, to which the church had been found faithful.

And to the angel of the church in Philadelphia write: "These things saith he that is holy, he that is true, he that hath the key of David, he that openeth, and none shall shut, and shutteth, and none openeth:

"'I know thy works (behold, I have set before thee a door opened which none can shut), that thou hast a little power, and didst keep my word, and didst not deny my name. Behold, I give of the synagogue of Satan, of those who say they are Jews, and they are not, but do lie; behold, I will make

PHILADELPHIA

This flourishing Turkish city occupies the site of old Philadelphia, founded in the second century before Christ. It was called the City of Brotherly Love after its founder, King Attalus Philadelphus of Pergamum, whose second name was given him because of his devotion to his brother Eumenes II. The city was built for the purpose of spreading Hellenism in the Provinces of Lydia and Phrygia. When Christianity took root here, Philadelphia became the city of a new apostleship, and won immortality by being included among the seven chief churches of Asia.

them to come and worship before thy feet, and to know that I have loved thee.

"'Because thou didst keep the word of my patience, I also will keep thee from the hour of trial, that hour which is to come upon all the world, to try them that dwell upon the earth. Behold, I come quickly: hold fast that which thou hast, that no man take thy crown.

"'Him that overcometh will I make a pillar in the temple of my God, and he shall go out thence no more: and I will write upon him the name of my God, and the name of the city of my God, the new Jerusalem, which cometh down out of heaven from my God, and mine own new name. He that hath an ear, let him hear what the Spirit saith to the churches.'"

THE FELLOWSHIP OF ALL THE SAINTS

For all the saints who from their labors rest,
Who thee by faith before the world confessed,
Thy name, O Jesus, be forever blessed.
    Hallelujah, Hallelujah!

Thou wast their Rock, their Fortress, and their Might;
Thou, Lord, their Captain in the well-fought fight;
Thou, in the darkness drear, their one true Light.
    Hallelujah, Hallelujah!

Oh, may thy soldiers, faithful, true, and bold,
Fight as the saints who nobly fought of old,
And win with them the victor's crown of gold.
    Hallelujah, Hallelujah!

O blest communion, fellowship divine!
We feebly struggle, they in glory shine;
Yet all are one in thee, for all are thine.
    Hallelujah, Hallelujah!

And when the strife is fierce, the warfare long,
Steals on the ear the distant triumph song,
And hearts are brave again, and arms are strong.
    Hallelujah, Hallelujah!

The golden evening brightens in the west;
Soon, soon to faithful warriors comes their rest;
Sweet is the calm of Paradise the blest.
        Hallelujah, Hallelujah!

But lo, there breaks a yet more glorious day;
The saints triumphant rise in bright array;
The King of glory passes on his way.
        Hallelujah, Hallelujah!

From earth's wide bounds, from ocean's farthest coast,
Through gates of pearl streams in the countless host,
Singing to Father, Son, and Holy Ghost,
        Hallelujah, Hallelujah!

                  —William Walsham How

CHRIST KNOCKING AT THE DOOR
From a painting by Bernhard Plockhorst

CHRISTIAN THOUGHT

CHRISTIAN THOUGHT

THIS is an arrangement of the Epistles under the great themes of which they treat. The plan here followed is the same as the one used in arranging the Teachings of Jesus, and the topics are similar.

This treatment is particularly helpful in studying the letters of Paul, which constitute much the larger portion of this section. That great Christian thinker, dictating or writing under the pressure of his many activities, often turned abruptly from his main discourse to include some subsidiary thought or some fresh aspect of the truth. In such instances, it is difficult to follow his argument. By the present plan, as in the letter to the Romans, for example, all that bears upon the central truth is here included in one consecutive series, while the minor diverging thoughts are grouped together logically and are placed where they may be conveniently studied. The arrangement, of course, is not designed as a substitute for the usual order of reading any epistle, but as an additional opportunity to master the whole truth regarding any one theme, by a consecutive reading of all that these sacred writers said about it.

In the sections devoted to the shorter sayings, single sentences, separated from long passages, often acquire an unexpected significance. These striking sayings remind us that the New Testament writers frequently resemble in their literary method the sententious sages of the Old Testament, whose proverbs are gathered in Volume Four.

THE TWO NATURES
From a sculpture by George G. Barnard

These two figures are twins—similar in appearance and equally matched in strength It is impossible to distinguish which stands for the higher nature, and which for the lower. Are there not times when it is difficult for struggling man himself to determine whether the nature that triumphs for the moment is his higher or his lower one? The truth remains, however, that life is a continuous struggle between the greater and the lesser good, if not between good and evil; and, as in this statue, the struggle is keen, even intense. "I delight in the law of God after the inward man, but I see another law in my members, warring against the law of my mind."

THE MANIFESTATION OF GOD'S LOVE

A Summary of the New Testament

THE GRACE OF GOD THAT BRINGETH SALVATION HATH APPEARED TO ALL MEN, TEACHING US THAT, DENYING UNGODLINESS AND WORLDLY DESIRES, WE SHOULD LIVE SOBERLY, RIGHTEOUSLY AND GODLY, IN THIS PRESENT WORLD; LOOKING FOR THAT BLESSED HOPE AND THE GLORIOUS APPEARING OF THE GREAT GOD AND OUR SAVIOUR JESUS CHRIST; WHO GAVE HIMSELF FOR US, THAT HE MIGHT REDEEM US FROM ALL INIQUITY, AND PURIFY UNTO HIMSELF A PEOPLE FOR HIS OWN POSSESSION, ZEALOUS OF GOOD WORKS.

GOD'S RELATIONSHIP TO MAN

God Is Man's Light and Strength

This is the message which we have heard of him and declare to you, that God is light, and in him is no darkness at all.

Behold what manner of love the Father hath bestowed upon us, that we should be called children of God.

Love is of God; and every one that loveth is born of God, and knoweth God. He that loveth not knoweth not God; for God is love. Herein was the love of God manifested in us, that God sent his only Son into the world, that we might live through him. Herein is love, not that we loved God, but that he loved us, and sent his Son to be the propitiation for our sins.

God is love; and he that abideth in love abideth in God, and God abideth in him. We love, because he first loved us.

Every good gift and every perfect boon is from above, and cometh down from the Father of lights, with whom can be no variation, neither shadow that is cast by turning.

Now he that establisheth us, with you, in Christ, and anointed us, is God; who also sealed us, and gave the earnest of the Spirit in our hearts.

It is God who worketh in you, both to will and to work, for his good pleasure.

God Is Rich in Mercy and Forbearance

O the depth of the riches both of the wisdom and the knowledge of God!
> How unsearchable are his judgments!
> And his ways past tracing out!
> Who hath known the mind of the Lord?
> Or who hath been his counselor?
> Who hath first given to him,
> And it shall be recompensed to him again?

For of him, and through him, and unto him, are all things. To him be the glory forever and ever. Amen.

Thou art inexcusable, O man, whosoever thou art that judgest; for wherein thou judgest another, thou condemnest thyself; for thou that judgest dost practice the same things.

But we are sure that the judgment of God is according to truth against those who practice such things. And thinkest thou this, O man, who judgest them that practice such things, and doest the same, that thou shalt escape the judgment of God? Or despisest thou the riches of his goodness and forbearance and longsuffering, not knowing that the goodness of God leadeth thee to repentance? but after thy hardness and impenitent heart treasurest up for thyself wrath in the day of wrath and revelation of the righteous judgment of God.

The same Lord is Lord of all, and is rich unto all that call upon him.

Not as the trespass, so also is the free gift. For if through the trespass of the one the many died, much more did the grace of God, and the gift by the grace of the one man, Jesus Christ, abound to the many.

God is not unrighteous to forget your work and the love which ye showed toward his name, in that ye ministered to the saints, and still do minister.

Forget not this one thing, beloved, that one day is with the Lord as a thousand years, and a thousand years as one day. The Lord is not slack concerning his promise, as some count slackness; but is longsuffering toward you, not wishing that any should perish, but that all should come to repentance.

THE GOSPEL OF RIGHTEOUSNESS AND LOVE

From the Letter to the Romans

This, in brief, is Paul's great explanation of the Gospel in his letter to the Romans. God, he says, loves the world; but the world, since Adam's disobedience, has been entangled in sin. God's will is to save men from their sins and to help them, through faith in him, to live the life of righteousness.

"I Am not Ashamed of the Gospel"

I am not ashamed of the gospel: for it is the power of God unto salvation to every one that believeth; to the Jew first, and also to the Greek. For therein is revealed a righteousness of God from faith to faith: as it is written, "But the righteous shall live by faith."

God's Wrath Is Against Men's Wilful Sin

The just and righteous God cannot but be angry at the sin which has corrupted men, sin which they have committed against the light of their own knowledge of good.

For the wrath of God is revealed from heaven against all ungodliness and unrighteousness of men, who hinder the truth by unrighteousness; because that which is known of God is manifest in them; for God manifested it to them. For the invisible things of him since the creation of the world are clearly seen, being perceived through the things that are made, even his eternal power and divinity; that they may be without excuse; because that, knowing God, they glorified him not as God, neither gave thanks; but became vain in their reasonings, and their senseless heart was darkened. Professing themselves to be wise, they became fools, and changed the glory of the incorruptible God for the likeness of an image of corruptible man, and of birds, and four-footed beasts, and creeping things.

Wherefore God gave them up in the desires of their hearts to uncleanness, that their bodies should be dishonored among themselves: for that they exchanged the truth of God for a lie, and worshiped and served the creature rather than the Creator, who is blessed forever. Amen.

Both Jew and Gentile Have Fallen Short

The Jew had his Law to guide him, but he has not obeyed it; the Gentile had his conscience, but neither has he obeyed that.

THE COLOSSEUM SEEN FROM THE ARCH OF TITUS

The Arch of Titus in the foreground is a memorial of victory, erected after the destruction of Jerusalem by Titus. It marks Rome's domination over a rebellious subject nation. The Colosseum, erected by the same family, is associated with the Roman contempt for the rising sect of the Christians. It is eloquent of the worst elements in the Roman character —of brutality, indifference to suffering, and love of gross pleasure.

Despisest thou the riches of his goodness and forbearance and longsuffering, not knowing that the goodness of God leadeth thee to repentance? but after thy hardness and impenitent heart treasurest up for thyself wrath in the day of wrath and revelation of the righteous judgment of God; who will render to every man according to his works: to them that by patience in well-doing seek for glory and honor and incorruption, eternal life: but to them that are contentious, and do not obey the truth, but obey unrighteousness, shall be wrath and indignation, tribulation and anguish, upon every soul of man that worketh evil, of the Jew first, and also of the Greek; but glory, honor, and peace to every man that worketh good, to the Jew first, and also to the Greek: for there is no respect of persons with God.

For as many as have sinned without the law shall also perish without the law; and as many as have sinned under the law shall be judged by the law; for not the hearers of the law are just before God, but the doers of the law shall be justified (for when Gentiles who have not the law do by nature the things of the law, these, not having the law, are the law unto themselves; in that they show the work of the law written in their hearts, their conscience bearing witness therewith, and their thoughts one with another accusing or else excusing them).

What then? are we better than they? No, in no wise: for we before laid to the charge both of Jews and Greeks, that they are all under sin: as it is written:

> "There is none righteous, no, not one;
> There is none that understandeth,
> There is none that seeketh after God;
> They have all turned aside,
> They have together become unprofitable;
> There is none that doeth good, no, not one."

Therefore by the works of the law shall no flesh be justified in his sight: for through the law cometh the knowledge of sin.

The Old Law Prepared the Way for Christ

The Law had its place in showing men their sinfulness and preparing them for a higher life and for a Saviour yet to come. This Saviour, the Messiah, God's own Son, has appeared, and by his death has manifested the greatness of the saving and forgiving love of God for men. Because of their faithfulness, not their righteousness, those who are loyal to him are forgiven and accepted in the kingdom of God.

But now apart from the law a righteousness of God hath been manifested, being witnessed by the law and the prophets; even the righteousness of God through faith in Jesus Christ unto all them that believe; for there is no distinction. For all have sinned, and fall short of the glory of God; being justified freely by his grace through the redemption that is in Christ Jesus, whom God set forth to be a propitiation, through faith.

Christ Has Brought Us Peace with God

Therefore being justified by faith, we have peace with God through our Lord Jesus Christ; through whom also we have had our access by faith into this grace wherein we stand; and we rejoice in hope of the glory of God.

And not only so, but we also rejoice in our tribulations: knowing that tribulation worketh steadfastness; and steadfastness, approvedness; and approvedness, hope: and hope putteth not to shame; because the love of God hath been shed abroad in our hearts through the Holy Spirit which was given to us.

For while we were yet weak, in due season Christ died for the ungodly. For scarcely for a righteous man will one die: yet peradventure for a good man some would even dare to die. But God commendeth his own love toward us, in that, while we were yet sinners, Christ died for us. Much

A BAS-RELIEF FROM THE ARCH OF TITUS

This panel depicts a part of the triumphal procession in which the soldiers of Titus carried the spoils of Jerusalem which were brought to Rome. We see them bearing the table of showbread taken from Herod's temple, and the long trumpets of silver which the priests blew in times of festival, and the famous seven-branched candlestick. Were it not for this particular bit of sculpture, we should never have known how the seven branches were arranged to form this candelabrum. The sacred objects brought from Jerusalem after its destruction by Titus were deposited by the Emperor Vespasian in his magnificent Temple of Peace.

more then, being now justified by his blood, shall we be saved from the wrath of God through him. For if, while we were enemies, we were reconciled to God through the death of his Son, much more, being reconciled, we shall be saved by his life. And not only so, but we also rejoice in God through our Lord Jesus Christ, through whom we have now received the reconciliation.

We May Be Victorious in the Spirit

Freed now from the curse and condemnation of sin, we are empowered by the Spirit to live victorious lives that realize the righteousness demanded by the Law.

There is therefore now no condemnation to them that are in Christ Jesus. For the law of the Spirit of life in Christ Jesus made me free from the law of sin and of death. For what the law could not do, in that it was weak through the flesh, God, sending his own Son in the likeness of sinful flesh and for sin, condemned sin in the flesh: that the ordinance of the law might be fulfilled in us, who walk not after the flesh, but after the Spirit.

Ye are not in the flesh, but in the Spirit, if so be that the Spirit of God dwelleth in you.

We Are Debtors to Live That New Life Daily

So then, brethren, we are debtors, not to the flesh, to live after the flesh: for if ye live after the flesh, ye must die; but if by the Spirit ye put to death the deeds of the body, ye shall live. For as many as are led by the Spirit of God, these are sons of God. For ye received not the spirit of bondage again unto fear; but ye received the spirit of adoption, whereby we cry, "Abba" (Father). The Spirit himself beareth witness with our spirit, that we are children of God: and if children, then heirs; heirs of God, and joint-heirs with Christ; if so be that we suffer with him, that we may be also glorified together.

There Is Satisfaction for Those Who Trust in God's Love

The Spirit also helpeth our infirmity: for we know not how to pray as we ought; but the Spirit himself maketh intercession for us with groanings which cannot be uttered; and he that searcheth the hearts knoweth what is the mind of the Spirit, because he maketh intercession for the saints accord-

A CHARIOT ON THE APPIAN WAY
From a painting by Edoardo Forti

This is a picture of the Appian Way just outside of Rome—one of the fashionable drives where any day Paul might have seen chariots like this, or litters bearing the aristocratic ladies of the city to some rendezvous in the Campagna. The tombs that lined the old road might well have reminded them of the shortness of life and the need for some ideal other than that of worldly pleasure. It was to the Christians living in daily contact with these luxury-loving Romans that Paul wrote, "Be not conformed to this world."

ing to the will of God. And we know that all things work together for good to them that love God, even to them that are called according to his purpose. For whom he foreknew, he also foreordained to be conformed to the image of his Son, that he might be the first-born among many brethren: and whom he foreordained, them he also called: and whom he called, them he also justified: and whom he justified, them he also glorified.

What then shall we say to these things? If God is for us, who can be against us? He that spared not his own Son, but delivered him up for us all, how shall he not also with him freely give us all things? Who shall lay anything to the charge of God's elect? It is God that justifieth. Who is he that shall condemn? It is Christ that died, yea rather, that was raised from the dead, who is even at the right hand of God, who also maketh intercession for us. Who shall separate us from the love of Christ? shall tribulation, or distress, or persecution, or famine, or nakedness, or peril, or sword? Even as it is written:

> "For thy sake we are killed all the day long;
> We are accounted as sheep for the slaughter."

Nay, in all these things we are more than conquerors through him that loved us. For I am persuaded, that neither death, nor life, nor angels, nor principalities, nor powers, nor things present, nor things to come, nor height, nor depth, nor any other creature, shall be able to separate us from the love of God, which is in Christ Jesus our Lord.

"Present Your Bodies a Living Sacrifice"

Paul now describes the responsibility of those whose bodies and spirits have been redeemed for divine ends.

I beseech you therefore, brethren, by the mercies of God, that ye present your bodies a living sacrifice, holy, acceptable to God, which is your reasonable service. And be not conformed to this world: but be ye transformed by the renewing of your mind, that ye may prove what is that good and acceptable and perfect will of God.

For I say, through the grace that was given to me, to every man that is among you, not to think of himself more highly than he ought to think; but to think soberly, according as God hath dealt to each man a measure of faith. For even as we have many members in one body, and all the members have not the same office: so we, who are many, are one body in Christ, and severally members one of another.

And having gifts differing according to the grace that was given to us, whether prophecy, let us prophesy according to the proportion of our faith; or ministry, let us give ourselves

THE ARCH OF TITUS AND THE COLOSSEUM

to our ministry; or he that teacheth, to his teaching; or he that exhorteth, to his exhorting: he that giveth, let him do it with liberality; he that ruleth, with diligence; he that showeth mercy, with cheerfulness.

We that are strong ought to bear the infirmities of the weak, and not to please ourselves. Let each one of us please his neighbor for that which is good, unto edifying. For Christ also pleased not himself.
Now the God of patience and of consolation grant you to be of the same mind one with another according to Christ Jesus: that with one accord ye may with one mouth glorify the God and Father of our Lord Jesus Christ.

JESUS IN HUMAN LIFE

Jesus Is the Source of Spiritual Life

God so loved the world that he gave his only begotten Son, that whosoever believeth on him might not perish, but have everlasting life.

This is his commandment, that we should believe in the name of his Son Jesus Christ, and love one another.

We preach Christ crucified, to Jews a stumbling block, and to Gentiles foolishness; but to them that are called, both Jews and Greeks, Christ the power of God, and the wisdom of God.

That which was from the beginning, that which we have heard, that which we have seen with our eyes, that which we beheld, and our hands handled, concerning the Word of life (and the life was manifested, and we have seen, and bear witness, and declare to you the life, the eternal life, which was with the Father, and was manifested to us); that which we have seen and heard declare we to you.

If ye know that he is righteous, ye know that every one that doeth righteousness is begotten of him.

If any man sin, we have an Advocate with the Father, Jesus Christ the righteous. And he is the propitiation for our sins; and not for ours only, but also for the sins of the whole world.

Ye were redeemed, not with corruptible things, like silver and gold, from your vain manner of life handed down from your fathers; but with precious blood, as of a lamb without blemish and without spot, even the blood of Christ: who was foreknown indeed before the foundation of the world, but was manifested at the end of the times for your sake, who through him are believers in God, who raised him up from the dead, and gave him glory; so that your faith and hope might be in God.

The witness is this, that God gave to us eternal life, and this life is in his Son.
He that hath the Son hath the life; he that hath not the Son of God hath not the life.

Redemption Through Christ

The Father delivered us out of the power of darkness, and translated us into the kingdom of his dear Son; in whom we have our redemption, the forgiveness of our sins; who is the image of the invisible God, the first-born of all creation; for in him were all things created, that are in the heavens and that

CHRIST THE GUEST

From a painting by Albert W. Holden

Christ is frequently represented as the guest of the lowly: seldom indeed is he shown, as in this picture, as the guest of the rich. Possibly he would enter more frequently the homes of affluence if the owners were more conscious of their need of him.

are upon the earth, things visible and things invisible, whether thrones or dominions or principalities or powers; all things were created through him, and unto him; and he is before all things, and in him all things consist. He is the head of the body, the church: who is the beginning, the first-born from the dead; that in all things he might have the preëminence.

For it was the good pleasure of the Father that in him should all the fulness dwell; and through him to reconcile all things to himself, having made peace through the blood of his cross; through him, I say, whether things upon the earth, or things in the heavens.

And you, being in time past alienated and enemies in your mind in your evil works, yet now hath he reconciled in the body of his flesh through death, to present you holy and without blemish and unreprovable before him.

Christ also suffered for sins once, the righteous for the unrighteous, that he might bring us to God; being put to death in the flesh, but made alive in the spirit; who is on the right hand of God, having gone into heaven; angels and authorities and powers being made subject to him.

We did not follow cunningly devised fables, when we made known to you the power and coming of our Lord Jesus Christ, but were eyewitnesses of his majesty.

For he received from God the Father honor and glory, when there was borne such a voice to him by the Majestic Glory, "This is my beloved Son, in whom I am well pleased." And this voice we ourselves heard borne out of heaven, when we were with him in the holy mount.

Have this mind in you, which was also in Christ Jesus: who, existing in the form of God, counted not the being on an equality with God a thing to be grasped, but emptied himself, taking the form of a servant, being made in the likeness of men; and being found in fashion as a man, he humbled himself, becoming obedient even unto death, yea, the death of the cross. Wherefore also God highly exalted him, and gave to him the name which is above every name; that in the name of Jesus every knee should bow, of things in heaven and things on earth and things under the earth, and that every tongue should confess that Jesus Christ is Lord, to the glory of God the Father.

He Brings Us into Sonship with God

Before faith came, we were kept in ward under the law, shut up unto the faith which should afterwards be revealed. So that the law became our schoolmaster to bring us to Christ, that we might be justified by faith. But now that faith hath come, we are no longer under a schoolmaster. For ye are all sons of God, through faith, in Christ Jesus. For as many of you as were baptized into Christ, put on Christ. There can be neither Jew nor Greek, there can be neither bond nor free, there can be no male and female; for ye are all one man in Christ Jesus. And if ye are Christ's, then are ye Abraham's true descendants, heirs according to promise.

But I say, that the heir, as long as he is a child, differeth nothing from a bondservant, though he is lord of all; but is under guardians and stewards until the day appointed by the father.

Even so we, when we were children, were held in bondage under the elements of the world. But when the fulness of the time came, God sent forth his Son, born of a woman, born under the law, that he might redeem them that were under the law, that we might receive the adoption of sons. And because ye are sons, God sent forth the Spirit of his Son into our hearts, crying, "Abba" (Father). Wherefore thou art no longer a bondservant, but a son; and if a son, then an heir through God.

Christ redeemed us from the curse of the law, having become a curse for us: for it is written, "Cursed is every one that hangeth on a tree": that upon the Gentiles might come the blessing of Abraham in Christ Jesus; that we might receive the promise of the Spirit through faith.

The Gospel Has a World-wide Message

christ's missionary purpose

For this purpose the Son of God was manifested, that he might destroy the works of the devil.

> As by the offense of one judgment came upon all men to condemnation;
> Even so by the righteousness of one the free gift came upon all men to justification of life.
> As by one man's disobedience many were made sinners,
> So by the obedience of one shall many be made righteous.

christ's appeal, first to the jew

He chose us in him before the foundation of the world, that we should be holy and without blemish before him in love: having foreordained us unto adoption as sons through Jesus Christ unto himself, according to the good pleasure of his will, to the praise of the glory of his grace, which he freely bestowed on us in the Beloved.

In him we have our redemption through his blood, the forgiveness of our trespasses, according to the riches of his grace, which he made to abound toward us in all wisdom and prudence, having made known to us the mystery of his will, according to his good pleasure which he purposed in him unto a dispensation of the fulness of the times, to sum up all things in Christ, the things in the heavens, and the things upon the earth; in him, I say, to the end that we [Jews]

THADDEUS
From a painting by Ribera

should be to the praise of his glory, we who had before hoped in Christ.

He raised him from the dead, and made him to sit at his right hand in the heavenly places, far above all rule, and authority, and power, and dominion, and every name that is named, not only in this world, but also in that which is to come: and he put all things in subjection under his feet, and gave him to be head over all things to the church, which is his body, the fulness of him that filleth all in all.

THE GENTILES, FELLOW-HEIRS

God was pleased to make known what is the riches of the glory of this mystery among the Gentiles, which is Christ in you, the hope of glory.

For this cause I Paul, the prisoner of Christ Jesus in behalf of you Gentiles,— if so be that ye have heard of the dispensation of that grace of God which was given me toward you; how that by revelation was made known to me the mystery, as I wrote before in few words, whereby, when ye read, ye can perceive my understanding in the mystery of Christ; which in other generations was not made known to the sons of men, as it hath now been revealed unto his holy apostles and prophets in the Spirit; to wit, that the Gentiles are fellow-heirs, and fellow-members of the body, and fellow-partakers of the promise in Christ Jesus through the gospel, whereof I was made a minister, according to the gift of that grace of God which was given me according to the working of his power.

To me, who am less than the least of all saints, was this grace given, to preach among the Gentiles the unsearchable riches of Christ; and to make all men see what is the dispensation of the mystery which for ages hath been hid in God who created all things; to the intent that now to the principalities and the powers in the heavenly places might be made known through the church the manifold wisdom of God, according to the eternal purpose which he purposed in Christ Jesus our Lord: in whom we have boldness and access in confidence through our faith in him.

    You did he make alive, when ye were dead through your trespasses and sins, wherein in time past ye walked according to the course of this world, according to the prince of the powers of the air, of the spirit that now worketh in the sons of disobedience. Among whom we also all once lived in the desires of our flesh, doing the desires of the flesh and of the mind, and were by nature children of wrath, even as the rest.

    But God, being rich in mercy, for his great love wherewith he loved us, even when we were dead through our trespasses, made us alive together with Christ (by grace have ye been saved), and raised us up with him, and made us to sit with him in the heavenly places in Christ Jesus: that in the ages to come he might show the exceeding riches of his grace in kindness toward us in Christ Jesus: for by grace have ye been saved through faith; and that not of yourselves, it is the gift of God; not of works, that no man should glory. For we are his workmanship, created in Christ Jesus for good works, which God afore prepared that we should walk in them.

    Wherefore remember, that once ye, the Gentiles in the flesh, were separate from Christ, alienated from the commonwealth of Israel, and strangers from the covenants of the promise, having no hope and without God in the world. But now in Christ Jesus ye who once were far off are made nigh in the blood of Christ. For he is our peace, who made both one, and broke down the middle wall of partition between us; having abolished in his flesh the enmity, even the law of commandments contained in ordinances; that he might create in himself of the two one new man, so making peace; and might reconcile them both in one body unto God through the cross, having slain the enmity thereby. And he came and preached peace to you that were far off, and peace to them that were nigh: for through him we both have our access in one Spirit to the Father.

So then ye are no more strangers and sojourners, but ye are fellow citizens with the saints, and of the household of God, being built upon the foundation of the apostles and prophets, Christ Jesus himself being the chief corner stone[35]; in whom each several building, fitly framed together, groweth into a holy temple in the Lord. In him ye also are built together for a habitation of God in the Spirit.

Christ Gives to Us a New Nature

The love of Christ constraineth us; because we thus judge, that one died for all, therefore all died; and he died for all, that they that live should no longer live unto themselves, but unto him who for their sakes died and rose again. Wherefore we henceforth know no man after the flesh: even though we have known Christ after the flesh, yet now we know him so no more.

Wherefore if any man is in Christ, he is a new creature: the old things have passed away; behold, they have become new. But all things are of God, who reconciled us to himself through Christ, and gave to us the ministry of reconciliation; to wit, that God was in Christ reconciling the world to himself, not reckoning unto them their trespasses, and having committed to us the word of reconciliation.

Knowing that a man is not justified by the works of the law, but through faith in Jesus Christ, even we believed on Christ Jesus, that we might be justified by faith in Christ, and not by the works of the law: because by the works of the law shall no flesh be justified.

CHRIST THE CONSOLER
From a painting by Bernhard Plockhorst

The young pilgrim has at last found the object of his pilgrimage. He kneels in penitence, and receives not only the Saviour's forgiveness but his love. Above the head of Christ is the glorified cross, a symbol of the sacrificial love which embraces the whole world of sinners.

I have been crucified with Christ; and it is no longer I that live, but Christ liveth in me: and that life which I now live in the flesh I live in faith, the faith which is in the Son of God, who loved me, and gave himself up for me.

This I say, and testify in the Lord, that ye no longer walk as the Gentiles also walk, in the vanity of their mind, being darkened in their understanding, alienated from the life of God, because of the ignorance that is in them, because of the hardening of their heart; who being past feeling have given themselves up to lasciviousness, to work all uncleanness with greediness.

But ye did not so learn Christ; if so be that ye heard him, and were taught in him, even as truth is in Jesus: that ye put away, as concerning your former manner of life, the old self, that becometh corrupt after the desires of deceit; and that ye be renewed in the spirit of your mind, and put on the new self, that after God hath been created in righteousness and holiness of truth.

Wherefore putting away falsehood, speak ye truth each one with his neighbor: for we are members one of another.

Christ Is the Corner Stone

Ye have tasted that the Lord is gracious: to whom coming, a living stone, rejected indeed of men, but with God elect, precious, ye also, as living stones, are built up a spiritual house, to be a holy priesthood, to offer up spiritual sacrifices, acceptable to God through Jesus Christ. Because it is contained in scripture:

> "Behold, I lay in Zion a chief corner stone, elect, precious:
> And he that believeth on him shall not be put to shame."

For you therefore who believe is the preciousness: but for such as disbelieve:

"The stone which the builders rejected,
 The same was made the head of the corner";

and,

"A stone of stumbling, and a rock of offense";

for they stumble at the word, being disobedient: whereunto also they were appointed.

But ye are an elect race, a royal priesthood, a holy nation, a people for God's own possession, that ye may show forth the excellencies of him who called you out of darkness into his marvelous light: who in time past were no people, but are now the people of God: who had not obtained mercy, but now have obtained mercy.

All Things Are Ours in Christ

All things are yours; whether Paul, or Apollos, or Cephas, or the world, or life, or death, or things present, or things to come; all are yours; and ye are Christ's; and Christ is God's.

Already are ye filled, already have ye become rich, ye have come to reign without us; yea and I would that ye did reign, that we also might reign with you.

He was crucified through weakness, yet he liveth through the power of God. For we also are weak in him, but we shall live with him through the power of God toward you.

Christ, having been once offered to bear the sins of many, shall appear a second time, apart from sin, to them that wait for him, unto salvation.

©Braun, Clement & Co.   "YE ARE THE BODY OF CHRIST"
From a painting by Joseph Wencker

"And when he had given thanks, he broke it, and said, 'Take, eat: this is my body, which is broken for you: this do in remembrance of me.'"

CHRISTIAN UNITY AND COURAGE

PRIVILEGES AND RESPONSIBILITIES

Unity of Spirit, Diversity of Service
THE ONE BODY

THERE is one body, and one Spirit, even as also ye were called in one hope of your calling; one Lord, one faith, one baptism, one God and Father of all, who is over all, and through all, and in all. But to each one of us was the grace given according to the measure of the gift of Christ.

Wherefore he saith:

"When he ascended on high, he led captivity captive,
And gave gifts unto men."

(Now this, "He ascended," what is it but that he also descended into the lower parts of the earth? He that descended is the same also that ascended far above all the heavens, that he might fill all things.)

And he gave some to be apostles; and some, prophets; and some, evangelists; and some, pastors and teachers; for the perfecting of the saints, unto the work of ministering, unto the building up of the body of Christ: till we all attain to the unity of the faith, and of the knowledge of the Son of God, unto a full-grown man, unto the measure of the stature of the fulness of Christ.

From him all the body, fitly framed and knit together through that which every joint supplieth, according to the working in due measure of each several part, maketh the increase of the body unto the building up of itself in love.

CO-LABORERS WITH GOD

When one saith, "I am of Paul"; and another, "I am of Apollos"; are ye not men? What then is Apollos? and what is Paul? Ministers through whom ye believed; and each as the Lord gave to him. I planted, Apollos watered; but God gave the increase. So then neither is he that planteth anything, neither he that watereth; but God that giveth the increase. Now he that planteth and he that watereth are one: but each shall receive his own reward according to his own labor. For we are God's fellow-workers: ye are God's husbandry, God's building.

According to the grace of God which is given to me, as a wise master builder I laid a foundation; and another buildeth thereon. But let each man take heed how he buildeth thereon. For other foundation can no man lay than that which is laid, which is Jesus Christ. But if any man buildeth on the foundation gold, silver, precious stones, wood, hay, stubble; each man's work shall be made manifest: for the day shall declare it, because it is revealed in fire; and the fire itself shall prove each man's work of what sort it is. If any man's work shall abide which he built thereupon, he shall receive a reward. If any man's work shall be burned, he shall suffer loss: but he himself shall be saved; yet so as through fire.

Know ye not that ye are a temple of God, and that the Spirit of God dwelleth in you? If any man destroyeth the temple of God, him shall God destroy; for the temple of God is holy, which temple ye are.

ONE BODY, MANY MINISTRIES

I say, through the grace that was given to me, to every man that is among you, not to think of himself more highly than he ought to think; but to think soberly, according as God hath dealt to each man a measure of faith. For even as we have many members in one body, and all the members have not the same office: so we, who are many, are one body in Christ, and severally members one of another. And having gifts differing according to the grace that was given to us, whether prophecy, let us prophesy according to the proportion of our faith; or ministry, let us give ourselves to our ministry; or he that teacheth, to his teaching; or he that exhorteth, to his exhorting: he that giveth, let him do it with liberality; he that ruleth, with diligence; he that showeth mercy, with cheerfulness.

> Now there are diversities of gifts, but the same Spirit.
> And there are diversities of ministrations, but the same Lord.
> And there are diversities of workings, but the same God, who worketh all things in all.

But the manifestation of the Spirit is given to every man to profit withal.

For to one is given through the Spirit the word of wisdom; and to another the word of knowledge, according to the same Spirit: to another faith, in the same Spirit; and to another gifts of healings, in the one Spirit; and to another workings of miracles; and to another prophecy; and to another discernings of spirits: to another various kinds of tongues; and to another the interpretation of tongues. But all these the one and the same Spirit worketh, dividing to each one severally even as he will.

For as the body is one, and hath many members, and all the members of the body, being many, are one body; so also is Christ. For in one Spirit were we all baptized into one body, whether Jews or Greeks, whether bond or free; and were all made to drink of one Spirit. For the body is not one member, but many. If the foot shall say, "Because I am not the hand, I am not of the body"; it is not therefore not of the body. And if the ear shall say, "Because I am not the eye, I am not of the body"; it is not therefore not of the body.

If the whole body were an eye, where were the hearing? If the whole were hearing, where were the smelling? But now hath God set the members each one of them in the body, even as it pleased him. And if they were all one member, where were the body? But now they are many members, but one body. And the eye cannot say to the hand, "I have no need of thee": or again the head to the feet, "I have no need of you."

Nay, much rather, those members of the body which seem to be more feeble are necessary: and those parts of the body, which we think to be less honorable, upon these we bestow more abundant honor; and our uncomely parts have more abundant comeliness; whereas our comely parts have no need: but God tempered the body together, giving more abundant honor to that part which lacked; that there should be no schism in the body; but that the members should have the same care one for another.

> And whether one member suffereth, all the members suffer with it;
> Or one member is honored, all the members rejoice with it.

Now ye are the body of Christ, and severally members thereof. And God hath set some in the church, first apostles, secondly prophets, thirdly teachers, then miracles, then gifts of healings, helps, governments, various kinds of tongues. Are all apostles? are all prophets? are all teachers? are all workers of miracles? have all gifts of healings? do all speak with tongues? do all interpret? But desire earnestly the greater gifts.

THE HEAVENLY BRIDEGROOM

The woman who hath a husband is bound by law to the husband while he liveth; but if the husband die, she is discharged from the law of the husband. So then if, while the husband liveth, she be joined to another man, she shall be called an adulteress: but if the husband die, she is free from the law; so that she is no adulteress, though she be joined to another man.

Wherefore, my brethren, ye also were made dead to the law through the body of Christ; that ye should be joined to another, even to him who was raised from the dead, that we might bring forth fruit to God.

THE ABIDING WORD OF GOD

I write unto you, my little children, because your sins are forgiven you for his name's sake.
I write unto you, fathers, because ye know him who is from the beginning.
I write unto you, young men, because ye have overcome the evil one.
I have written unto you, little children, because ye know the Father.
I have written unto you, fathers, because ye know him who is from the beginning.
I have written unto you, young men, because ye are strong,
And the word of God abideth in you, and ye have overcome the evil one.

The Missionary Duty of Christians

"Whosoever shall call upon the name of the Lord shall be saved."

How then shall they call on him in whom they have not believed? and how shall they believe in him whom they have not heard? and how shall they hear without a preacher? and how shall they preach, unless they be sent? Even as it is written:

"How beautiful are the feet of them that preach the gospel of peace,
And bring glad tidings of good things!"

Ye were once darkness, but are now light in the Lord; walk as children of light (for the fruit of the light is in all goodness and righteousness and truth), proving what is well-pleasing to the Lord: and have no fellowship with the unfruitful works of darkness, but rather even reprove them.

Let a man so account of us, as of ministers of Christ, and stewards of the mysteries of God. Here, moreover, it is required in stewards, that a man be found faithful.

If I preach the gospel, I have nothing to glory of; for necessity is laid upon me; for woe is to me, if I preach not the gospel! For if I do this of mine own will, I have a reward; but if not of mine own will, I have a stewardship intrusted to me. What is my reward then? Verily that, when I preach the gospel, I may make the gospel without charge, so as not to use to the full my right in the gospel. For though I was free from all men, yet I brought myself under bondage to all, that I might gain the more.

Continue steadfastly in prayer, and watch therein with thanksgiving; withal praying for us also, that God may open to us a door for the word, to speak the mystery of Christ, for which I am also in bonds; that I may make it manifest, as I ought to speak.

The Glory That Excelleth

Are we beginning again to commend ourselves? or need we, as do some, epistles of commendation to you or from you?

Ye are our epistle, written in our hearts, known and read of all men; being made manifest that ye are an epistle of Christ, ministered by us, written not with ink, but with the Spirit of the living God; not in tables of stone, but in tables that are hearts of flesh.

And such confidence have we through Christ toward God: not that we are sufficient of ourselves, to account anything as from ourselves; but our sufficiency is from God; who also made us sufficient as ministers of a new covenant; not of the letter, but of the spirit: for the letter killeth, but the spirit giveth life.

But if the ministration of death, written, and engraven on stones, came with glory, so that the children of Israel could not look steadfastly on the face of Moses for the glory of his countenance; which glory was passing away: how shall not rather the ministration of the spirit be with glory? For if the ministration of condemnation hath glory, much rather doth the ministration of righteousness exceed in glory. For verily that which hath been made glorious hath not been made glorious in this respect, by reason of the glory that excelleth. For if that which passeth away was with glory, much more that which remaineth is in glory.

Where the Spirit of the Lord is, there is liberty.

The Christian Race

Know ye not that they that run in a race run all, but one receiveth the prize? Even so run, that ye may attain. And every man that striveth in the games is temperate in all things. Now they do it to receive a corruptible crown,[36] but we an incorruptible. I therefore so run, as not uncertainly; so fight I, not as one that beateth the air: but I keep my body under, and bring it into subjection: lest by any means, when I have preached to others, I myself should be a castaway.

Not that I have already obtained, or am already made perfect: but I press on, if so be that I may apprehend that for which also I was apprehended by Christ Jesus. Brethren, I count not myself yet to have apprehended: but one thing I

THE ROMAN GAMES
From a painting by Edoardo Forti
"Know ye not that they that run in a race run all, but one receiveth the prize? Even so run, that ye may attain."

do, forgetting the things which are behind, and stretching forward to the things which are before, I press on toward the goal unto the prize of the high calling of God in Christ Jesus.

THE GOOD FIGHT

The Weapons of the Christian Warrior

Finally, my brethren, be strong in the Lord, and in the power of his might. Put on the whole armor[37] of God, that ye may be able to stand against the wiles of the devil. For we wrestle not against flesh and blood, but against the principalities, against the powers, against the world rulers of this darkness, against the spiritual hosts of wickedness in the heavenly places.

Wherefore take unto you the whole armor of God, that ye may be able to withstand in the evil day, and, having done all, to stand. Stand therefore, having your loins girded about[38] with truth, and having put on the breastplate of righteousness; and your feet shod with the preparation of the gospel of peace; above all, taking the shield of faith, wherewith ye shall be able to quench all the fiery darts of the evil one. And take the helmet of salvation, and the sword of the Spirit, which is the word of God.

Ye, brethren, are not in darkness, that that day should overtake you as a thief. For ye are all sons of light and sons of the day: we are not of the night, nor of darkness.

Therefore let us not sleep, as do the rest, but let us watch and be sober.

For they that sleep sleep in the night;
And they that are drunken are drunken in the night.
But let us, since we are of the day, be sober, putting on the breastplate of faith and love; and for a helmet, the hope of salvation.

Though we walk in the flesh, we do not war according to the flesh (for the weapons of our warfare are not of the flesh, but mighty before God to the casting down of strongholds); casting down imaginations, and every high thing that is exalted against the knowledge of God, and bringing every thought into captivity to the obedience of Christ; and being in readiness to avenge all disobedience, when your obedience shall be made full.

The Spiritual Warfare

We know that the law is spiritual: but I am carnal, sold under sin. For that which I do, I know not: for what I would, that do I not; but what I hate, that do I. If then I do that which I would not, I consent to the law that it is good. So now it is no more I that do it, but sin which dwelleth in me. For I know that in me, that is, in my flesh, dwelleth no good thing: for to will is present with me, but to do that which is good is not. For the good which I would I do not: but the evil which I would not, that I do. Now if I do that which I would not, it is no more I that do it, but sin which dwelleth in me. I find then a law, that, when I would do good, evil is present with me. For I delight in the law of God after the inward man: but I see another law in my members, warring against the law of my mind, and bringing me into captivity to the law of sin which is in my members. O wretched man that I am! who shall deliver me from the body of this death?

I thank God through Jesus Christ our Lord.

The Rules of Christian Warfare

Be sober! be vigilant! because your adversary the devil, as a roaring lion, walketh about, seeking whom he may devour: whom resist, steadfast in the faith, knowing that the same afflictions are accomplished in your brethren who are in the world.

And the God of all grace, who called you to his eternal glory in Christ, after ye have suffered a little while, shall himself perfect, establish, strengthen you. To him be the dominion forever and ever. Amen.

Now it is high time for you to awake out of sleep: for now is salvation nearer to us than when we first believed.

The night is far spent, the day is at hand: let us therefore cast off the works of darkness, and let us put on the armor of light.

Let us walk honestly, as in the day: not in reveling and drunkenness, not in debauchery and wantonness, not in strife and jealousy. But put ye on the Lord Jesus Christ, and make not provision for the flesh, to fulfil the passions thereof.

Thou, O man of God, flee these things; and follow after righteousness, godliness, faith, love, patience, meekness. Fight the good fight of the faith, lay hold on the life eternal, whereunto thou wast called, and didst confess the good confession in the sight of many witnesses.

I charge thee in the sight of God, who giveth life to all things, and of Christ Jesus, who before Pontius Pilate witnessed the good confession; that thou keep the commandment, without spot, without reproach, until the appearing of our Lord Jesus Christ: which in its own times he shall show, who is the blessed and only Potentate, the King of kings, and Lord of lords; who only hath immortality, dwelling in light unapproachable; whom no man hath seen, nor can see: to whom be honor and power everlasting. Amen.

My brethren dearly beloved and longed for, my joy and crown, so stand fast in the Lord, my dearly beloved.

"THEY LOVED NOT THEIR LIVES UNTO THE DEATH"

Many loved Truth, and lavished life's best oil
    Amidst the dust of books to find her,
Content at last, for guerdon of their toil,
    With the cast mantle she hath left behind her.
        Many in sad faith sought for her,
        Many with crossed hands sighed for her;
        But these, our brothers, fought for her,
        At life's dear peril wrought for her,
        Tasting the raptured fleetness
        Of her divine completeness:
        Their higher instinct knew
Those love her best who to themselves are true,
And what they dare to dream of, dare to do;
        They followed her and found her
        Where all may hope to find,
Not in the ashes of the burnt out mind,
But beautiful, with danger's sweetness round her.
        Where faith made whole with deed
        Breathes its awakening breath
        Into the lifeless creed,
        They saw her, plumed and mailed,
        With sweet, stern face unveiled,
    And all-repaying eyes, look proud on them in death.
                —*James Russell Lowell*

THE CHALLENGE OF THE CHRISTIAN LIFE

TEMPTATIONS AND SUFFERINGS

Temptation Is Opportunity

COUNT it all joy, my brethren, when ye fall into manifold temptations; knowing that the proving of your faith worketh patience. And let patience have its perfect work, that ye may be perfect and entire, lacking in nothing.

Blessed is the man that endureth temptation: for when he hath been approved, he shall receive the crown of life, which the Lord promised to them that love him. Let no man say when he is tempted, "I am tempted of God": for God cannot be tempted with evil, neither tempteth he any man: but every man is tempted, when he is drawn away by his own desire, and enticed. Then when the desire hath conceived, it beareth sin: and the sin, when it is full-grown, bringeth forth death.

There hath no temptation taken you but such as man can bear: but God is faithful, who will not suffer you to be tempted above that ye are able; but will with the temptation make also the way of escape, that ye may be able to bear it.

Greatly rejoice, though now for a little while, if need be, ye have been put to grief in manifold trials; that the proof of your faith, being more precious than gold that perisheth, though it is proved by fire, may be found unto praise and honor and glory at the revelation of Jesus Christ: whom

THE TWO SORROWS
From a sculpture by Louis Rivière

Here are presented two aspects of sorrow. In the younger woman, a sense of bitter loss is uppermost, unrelieved by any comprehension of the larger life in which sorrow is but an incident. The older figure represents that comprehension of the meaning of suffering which Christ had when, with the hour of death imminent, he could say, "My peace I give unto you." The crushing sorrows of earth are seen to be a part of the ordered plan of heaven, when looked at, in the phrase of one of the ancient fathers, "from the viewpoint of eternity."

having not seen, ye love; on whom, though now ye see him not, yet believing, ye rejoice greatly with joy unspeakable and full of glory: receiving the end [object] of your faith, even the salvation of your souls.

Faith Overcomes Suffering

I reckon that the sufferings of this present time are not worthy to be compared with the glory which shall be revealed toward us. For the earnest expectation of the creation waiteth for the revealing of the sons of God. For the creation was subjected to vanity, not of its own will, but by reason of him who subjected it, in hope that the creation itself also shall be delivered from the bondage of corruption into the liberty of the glory of the children of God. For we know that the whole creation groaneth and travaileth in pain together until now. And not only so, but ourselves also, who have the firstfruits of the Spirit, even we ourselves groan within ourselves, waiting for our adoption, to wit, the redemption of our body. For by hope were we saved.

Working together with him, we entreat also that ye receive not the grace of God in vain: giving no occasion of stumbling in anything, that our ministration be not blamed; but in all things commending ourselves, as ministers of God, in much patience, in afflictions, in necessities, in distresses, in stripes, in imprisonments, in tumults, in labors, in watchings, in fastings; in pureness, in knowledge, in longsuffering, in kindness, in the Holy Spirit, in love unfeigned, in the word of truth, in the power of God; by the armor of righteousness on the right hand and on the left, by glory and dishonor, by evil report and good report; as deceivers, and yet true; as unknown, and yet well known; as dying, and behold, we live; as chastened, and not killed; as sorrowful, yet always rejoicing; as poor, yet making many rich; as having nothing, and yet possessing all things.

234 THE MASTER LIBRARY

THE LAST PRAYER
From a painting by Jean L. Gérôme

Persecution and Martyrdom Are Ways to Life

Beloved, think it not strange concerning the fiery trial among you, which cometh upon you to prove you, as though a strange thing happened to you; but rejoice, insomuch as ye are partakers of Christ's sufferings; that, when his glory shall be revealed, ye may be glad also with exceeding joy. If ye are reproached for the name of Christ, happy are ye; for the Spirit of glory and the Spirit of God resteth upon you. For let none of you suffer as a murderer, or a thief, or an evildoer, or as a meddler in other men's affairs: but if a man suffer as a Christian, let him not be ashamed; but let him glorify God in this name.

For the time hath come for judgment to begin at the house of God: and if it begin first at us, what shall be the end of them that obey not the gospel of God? And if the righteous is scarcely saved, where shall the ungodly and sinner appear?

Wherefore let them also that suffer according to the will of God commit their souls in well-doing to a faithful Creator.

A great door and effectual is opened to me, and there are many adversaries.

We who live are always delivered to death for Jesus' sake, that the life also of Jesus may be manifested in our mortal flesh. So then death worketh in us, but life in you.

We having the same spirit of faith, according to that which is written, "I believed, and therefore did I speak"; we also believe, and therefore also we speak; knowing that he who raised up the Lord Jesus shall raise up us also with Jesus, and shall present us with you. For all things are for your sakes, that the grace, being multiplied through the many, may cause the thanksgiving to abound unto the glory of God.

CHRISTIAN CHARACTER

On Love

AN ODE TO HEAVENLY LOVE

If I speak with the tongues of men and of angels,
But have not love,[39]
I am become sounding brass, or a clanging cymbal.
And if I have the gift of prophecy,
And know all mysteries and all knowledge;
And if I have all faith, so as to remove mountains,
But have not love,
I am nothing.
And if I bestow all my goods to feed the poor,
And if I give my body to be burned,
But have not love,
It profiteth me nothing.
Love suffereth long, and is kind;
Love envieth not;
Love vaunteth not itself,
Is not puffed up,
Doth not behave itself unseemly,
Seeketh not its own,
Is not provoked,
Taketh not account of evil,
Rejoiceth not in unrighteousness, but rejoiceth with the truth;
Beareth all things,
Believeth all things,
Hopeth all things,
Endureth all things.
Love never faileth:
But whether there be prophecies, they shall be done away;
Whether there be tongues, they shall cease;
Whether there be knowledge, it shall be done away.

AMOR–CARITAS
From a sculpture by Augustus Saint Gaudens

For we know in part,
And we prophesy in part:
But when that which is perfect is come,
That which is in part shall be done away.
When I was a child, I spoke as a child,
I felt as a child,
I thought as a child:
Now that I have become a man, I have put away childish
    things.
For now we see in a mirror, darkly;
But then face to face!
Now I know in part;
But then shall I know fully even as also I was fully known.
But now abideth faith, hope, love — these three:
And the greatest of these is love.

LOVE TOWARD ONE ANOTHER

Hereby know we love, because he laid down his life for us; and we ought to lay down our lives for the brethren. But whoso hath the world's goods, and beholdeth his brother in need, and shutteth up his compassion from him, how doth the love of God abide in him? My little children, let us not love in word, neither with the tongue; but in deed and truth.

Beloved, let us love one another: for love is of God; and every one that loveth is born of God, and knoweth God. He that loveth not knoweth not God; for God is love. Herein was the love of God manifested in us, that God sent his only Son into the world, that we might live through him. Herein is love, not that we loved God, but that he loved us, and sent his Son to be the propitiation for our sins. Beloved, if God so loved us, we also ought to love one another. No man hath seen God at any time. If we love one another, God dwelleth in us, and his love is perfected in us.

THE CHALLENGE OF THE CHRISTIAN LIFE

Brethren, ye were called for freedom; only use not your freedom for an occasion to the flesh, but through love be servants one to another. For the whole law is fulfilled in one word, even in this, "Thou shalt love thy neighbor as thyself." But if ye bite and devour one another, take heed that ye be not consumed one of another.

Owe no man anything, save to love one another; for he that loveth his neighbor hath fulfilled the law. For this:
> "Thou shalt not commit adultery,
> Thou shalt not kill,
> Thou shalt not steal,
> Thou shalt not bear false witness,
> Thou shalt not covet,"

and if there be any other commandment, it is summed up in this saying, namely,
> "Thou shalt love thy neighbor as thyself."

Love worketh no ill to his neighbor; love therefore is the fulfilment of the law.

Be ye of sound mind, and be sober unto prayer: above all things being fervent in your love among yourselves; for love covereth a multitude of sins: using hospitality one to another without murmuring: according as each hath received a gift, ministering it among yourselves, as good stewards of the manifold grace of God.

If there is therefore any exhortation in Christ, if any consolation of love, if any fellowship of the Spirit, if any tender mercies and compassions, make full my joy, that ye be of the same mind, having the same love, being of one accord, of one mind; doing nothing through faction or through vainglory, but in lowliness of mind each counting other better than himself; not looking each of you to his own things, but each of you also to the things of others.

On Magnanimity and Forgiveness

Bless them that persecute you:
Bless, and curse not.
Rejoice with them that do rejoice;
And weep with them that weep.
Be of the same mind one toward another.
Mind not high things,
But condescend to men of low estate.
Be not wise in your own conceits.
Recompense to no man evil for evil.
Provide things honest in the sight of all men.
If it be possible, as much as in you lieth,
Live peaceably with all men.
Dearly beloved, avenge not yourselves,
But rather give place unto wrath.
For it is written: "Vengeance is mine;
I will repay," saith the Lord.
Therefore if thine enemy hunger, feed him;
If he thirst, give him drink:
For in so doing thou shalt heap coals of fire on his head.
Be not overcome of evil,
But overcome evil with good.

I therefore, the prisoner in the Lord, beseech you to walk worthily of the calling wherewith you were called, with all lowliness and meekness, with longsuffering, forbearing one another in love; giving diligence to keep the unity of the Spirit in the bond of peace.

Let all bitterness, and wrath, and anger, and clamor, and railing, be put away from you, with all malice; and be ye kind to one another, tender-hearted, forgiving one another, even as God also in Christ forgave you.

LIGHT OF THE WORLD
From a painting by Holman Hunt

LIGHT OF THE WORLD

From a painting by Holman Hunt

HUNT painted two pictures of this type. One is found in the Chapel of Keble College, Oxford, the other hangs against one of the huge piers in Saint Paul's Cathedral, London. They are both wonderfully beautiful in color. Here are mingled the golden light of the lantern and the clear gray light of dawn—lights that sparkle in the dewy grass, flash from the rosy fruit, scintillate from the embroidered pearls and rubies and emeralds of the royal robe, and illuminate the seamless dress with a wonderful richness and color that constitute the emotional surcharge of the painting.

In his "Arrows of the Chase," Ruskin says: "The legend beneath the picture is the beautiful verse, 'Behold, I stand at the door and knock. If any man hear my voice, and open the door, I will come in to him, and will sup with him, and he with me.' On the left-hand side of the picture is seen this door of the human soul. It is fast barred; its bars and nails are rusty; it is knitted and bound to its stanchions by creeping tendrils of ivy, showing that it has never been opened. A bat hovers about it: its threshold is overgrown with brambles, nettles, and fruitless corn—the wild grass, 'whereof the mower filleth not his hand nor he that bindeth the sheaves his bosom.' Christ approaches it in the night time, Christ in his everlasting offices of Prophet, Priest, and King. He wears the white robe, representing the power of the Spirit upon him; the jeweled robe and breastplate, representing the sacerdotal investiture; the rayed crown of gold, inwoven with the crown of thorns—not dead thorns, but now bearing soft leaves, for the healing of the nations.

"Now, when Christ enters any human heart, he bears with him a twofold light: first, the light of conscience, which displays past sin, and afterwards the light of peace, the hope of salvation. The lantern, carried in Christ's left hand, is this light of conscience. Its fire is red and fierce; it falls only on the closed door, on the weeds which encumber it, and on an apple shaken from one of the trees of the orchard, thus marking that the entire awakening of the conscience is not merely to committed, but to hereditary guilt.

"The light is suspended by a chain wrapped about the wrist of the figure, showing that the light which reveals sin appears to the sinner also to chain the hand of Christ. The light which proceeds from the head of the figure, on the contrary, is that of the hope of salvation; it springs from the crown of thorns, and, though itself sad, subdued, and full of softness, is yet so powerful that it entirely melts into the glow of it the forms of the leaves and boughs, which it crosses, showing that every earthly object must be hidden by this light, where its sphere extends."

Be ye therefore imitators of God, as beloved children; and walk in love, even as Christ also loved you, and gave himself up for us, an offering and a sacrifice to God for a sweet-smelling odor.

Christ also suffered for you, leaving you an example, that ye should follow in his steps: who did no sin, neither was guile found in his mouth: who, when he was reviled, reviled not again; when he suffered, threatened not; but committed himself to him that judgeth righteously.

My brethren, if any among you do err from the truth, and one convert him; let him know, that he who converteth a sinner from the error of his way shall save a soul from death, and shall cover a multitude of sins.

> Whatsoever things are true,
> Whatsoever things are honest,
> Whatsoever things are just,
> Whatsoever things are pure,
> Whatsoever things are lovely,
> Whatsoever things are of good report,
> If there be any virtue, and if there be any praise —
> Think on these things.

Brethren, even if a man be overtaken in any trespass, ye who are spiritual, restore such a one in a spirit of meekness; looking to thyself, lest thou also be tempted.

On Confessing Our Faith

The righteousness which is of faith saith thus: "Say not in thy heart, 'Who shall ascend into heaven?' (that is, to bring Christ down from above): or, 'Who shall descend into the abyss?' (that is, to bring Christ up from the dead). But what saith it? 'The word is nigh thee, in thy mouth, and in thy heart: that is, the word of faith, which we preach: because if thou shalt confess with thy mouth Jesus as Lord, and shalt believe in thy heart that God raised him from the dead, thou shalt be saved. For with the heart man believeth unto righteousness; and with the mouth confession is made unto salvation.

For the scripture saith, "Whosoever believeth on him shall not be put to shame."

Every spirit that confesseth that Jesus Christ hath come in the flesh is of God: and every spirit that confesseth not Jesus is not of God: and this is the spirit of the antichrist, whereof ye have heard that it cometh; and now it is in the world already.

Whosoever shall confess that Jesus is the Son of God, God dwelleth in him, and he in God.

On Humility

HUMILITY IN THE SIGHT OF GOD

Putting away all filthiness and overflowing of wickedness, receive with meekness the implanted word, which is able to save your souls.

>Cleanse your hands, ye sinners;
>And purify your hearts, ye double-minded.
>Be afflicted, and mourn, and weep:
>Let your laughter be turned to mourning,
>And your joy to heaviness.
>Humble yourselves in the sight of the Lord,
>And he shall exalt you.

AN OLD SAINT
From a painting by Elihu Vedder

If a man thinketh himself to be something, when he is nothing, he deceiveth himself. But let each man prove his own work, and then shall he have his glorying in regard of himself alone, and not of his neighbor. For each man shall bear his own burden.

Ye younger, be subject to the elder. Yea, all of you gird yourselves with humility, to serve one another: for God resisteth the proud, but giveth grace to the humble. Humble yourselves therefore under the mighty hand of God, that he may exalt you in due time; casting all your anxiety upon him, because he careth for you.

If we say that we have no sin, we deceive ourselves, and the truth is not in us. If we confess our sins, he is faithful and just to forgive us our sins, and to cleanse us from all unrighteousness. If we say we have not sinned, we make him a liar, and his word is not in us.

THE BOLD HUMILITY OF PAUL

We are not bold to number or compare ourselves with certain of them that commend themselves: but they themselves, measuring themselves by themselves, and comparing themselves with themselves, are without understanding. But we will not glory beyond our measure, but according to the measure of the province which God apportioned to us as a measure, to reach even to you. For we stretch not ourselves overmuch, as though we reached not to you: for we came even as far as to you in the gospel of Christ: not glorying beyond our measure, that is, in other men's labors; but having hope that, as your faith groweth, we shall be magnified in you according to our province unto further abundance, so as to preach the gospel even unto the parts beyond you, and not to glory in another's man's province in regard of things ready to our hand.

But he that glorieth, let him glory in the Lord. For not he that commendeth himself is approved, but whom the Lord commendeth.

Would that ye could bear with me in a little foolishness: but indeed ye do bear with me. For I am jealous over you with a godly jealousy: for I espoused you to one husband, that I might present you as a pure virgin to Christ. But I fear, lest by any means, as the serpent beguiled Eve in his craftiness, your minds should be corrupted from the simplicity and the purity that is toward Christ. For if he that cometh preacheth another Jesus, whom we did not preach, or if ye receive a different spirit, which ye did not receive, or a different gospel, which ye did not accept, ye do well to bear with him.

For I reckon that I am not a whit behind the very chiefest apostles. But though I be rude in speech, yet am I not in knowledge; nay, in every way have we made this manifest to you in all things.

Or did I commit a sin in abasing myself that ye might be exalted, because I have preached to you the gospel of God for nought? I robbed other churches, taking wages of them that I might minister to you; and when I was present with you and was in want, I was not a burden on any man; for the brethren, when they came from Macedonia, supplied the measure of my want; and in all things I kept myself from being burdensome to you, and so will I keep myself.

As the truth of Christ is in me, no man shall stop me of this glorying in the regions of Achaia. Wherefore? because I love you not? God knoweth.

On Patience

Be patient, therefore, brethren, until the coming of the Lord. Behold, the husbandman waiteth for the precious fruit of the earth, being patient over it, until it receive the early and latter rain. Be ye also patient; establish your hearts: for the coming of the Lord is at hand. Murmur not against one another, brethren, lest ye be judged: behold, the judge standeth before the doors!

Take, brethren, the prophets who spoke in the name of the Lord, as an example of suffering and patience. Behold, we call them blessed who endured: ye have heard of the patience of Job, and have seen the end of the Lord, how that the Lord is full of pity, and merciful.

The proving of your faith worketh patience. And let patience have its perfect work, that ye may be perfect and entire, lacking nothing.

On Moral Impurity

OUR BODIES ARE GOD'S TEMPLE

Know ye not that your bodies are members of Christ? He that is joined to the Lord is one spirit. Or know ye not that your body is a temple of the Holy Spirit which is in you, which ye have from God? and ye are not your own; for ye were bought with a price: glorify God therefore in your body.

Know ye not that ye are a temple of God, and that the Spirit of God dwelleth in you? If any man destroyeth the temple of God, him shall God destroy; for the temple of God is holy, which temple ye are.

HOLINESS OF LIFE

This is the will of God, even your sanctification, that ye abstain from unclean living; and that each one of you should learn mastery over his own bodily desires in sanctification and honor; that no man transgress, and wrong his brother in the matter: because the Lord is an avenger in all these things, as also we forewarned you and testified. For God called us not for uncleanness, but in sanctification. Therefore he that rejecteth, rejecteth not man, but God, who giveth his Holy Spirit to you.

Know ye not that a little leaven leaveneth the whole lump? Purge out the old leaven, that ye may be a new lump, even as ye are unleavened. For our passover also hath been sacrificed, even Christ; therefore let us keep the feast, not with old leaven, neither with the leaven of malice and wickedness, but with the unleavened bread of sincerity and truth.

THE KNIGHT'S DREAM
From a painting by Raphael

Raphael has here given his own expression to a very ancient theme. He places before the sleeping knight the choice of service or pleasure which here appear in the guise of two young women — on the left, Virtue, who holds out the book of knowledge and the sword of action; on the right, Pleasure, whose gayer dress, jewels, and spray of flowers all suggest the path of ease and dalliance. To Raphael the choice seemed like a dream; to Saint Paul it was a stern reality, for "the mind of the flesh is death, but the mind of the Spirit is life and peace."

They that are after the flesh mind the things of the flesh;
But they that are after the Spirit the things of the Spirit.
For the mind of the flesh is death;
But the mind of the Spirit is life and peace.

On Matters of Conscience

FOOD OFFERED TO IDOLS

Now concerning things sacrificed to idols, we know that we all have knowledge.

Knowledge puffeth up, but love edifieth. If any man thinketh that he knoweth anything, he knoweth not yet as he ought to know; but if any man loveth God, the same is known by him. Concerning therefore the eating of things sacrificed to idols, we know that no idol is anything in the world, and that there is no God but one.

For though there be that are called gods, whether in heaven or on earth; as there are gods many, and lords many; yet to us there is one God, the Father, of whom are all things, and we unto him; and one Lord, Jesus Christ, through whom are all things, and we through him.

Howbeit there is not in all men that knowledge: but some, being used until now to the idol, eat as of a thing sacrificed to an idol; and their conscience being weak is defiled. But food will not commend us to God: neither, if we eat not, are we the worse; nor, if we eat, are we the better.

But take heed lest by any means this liberty of yours become a stumbling block to the weak. For if a man see thee who hast knowledge sitting at meat in an idol's temple, will not his conscience, if he is weak, be emboldened to eat things sacrificed to idols? For through thy knowledge he that is weak perisheth, the brother for whose sake Christ died. And thus, sinning against the brethren, and wounding their conscience when it is weak, ye sin against Christ.

Wherefore, if food causeth my brother to stumble, I will eat no flesh forevermore, lest I cause my brother to stumble.

"GIVE NO OCCASION OF STUMBLING"

What say I then? that an idol is anything, or that which is offered in sacrifice to idols is anything?

250 THE MASTER LIBRARY

DIANA OR CHRIST
From a painting by Edwin Long

But I say, that the things which the Gentiles sacrifice, they sacrifice to demons, and not to God: and I would not that ye should have communion with demons.

> Ye cannot drink the cup of the Lord, and the cup of demons;
> Ye cannot partake of the table of the Lord, and of the table of demons.
> Do we provoke the Lord to jealousy?
> Are we stronger than he?
> "All things are lawful"; but not all things are expedient.
> "All things are lawful"; but not all things edify.
> Let no man seek his own,
> But every man his neighbor's good.

Whatsoever is sold in the shambles, eat, asking no question for conscience' sake; for the earth is the Lord's, and the fulness thereof.

If one of them that believe not biddeth you to a feast, and ye are disposed to go; whatsoever is set before you, eat, asking no question for conscience' sake. But if any man say to you, "This hath been offered in sacrifice to idols," eat not, for his sake that showed it, and for conscience' sake: conscience, I say, not thine own, but the other's; for why is my liberty judged by another conscience? If I partake with thankfulness, why am I evil spoken of for that for which I give thanks?

> Whether therefore ye eat, or drink,
> Or whatsoever ye do,
> Do all to the glory of God.

Give no occasion of stumbling, either to Jews, or to Greeks, or to the church of God: even as I also please all men in all things, not seeking mine own profit, but the profit of the many, that they may be saved.

Be ye imitators of me, even as I also am of Christ.

WHATEVER MAY BE A STUMBLING BLOCK

One man hath faith to eat all things; but he that is weak eateth herbs [vegetables].

Let not him that eateth set at nought him that eateth not;
And let not him that eateth not judge him that eateth:
For God hath received him.

Who art thou that judgest the servant of another? to his own lord he standeth or falleth. Yea, he shall be made to stand; for the Lord hath power to make him stand.

One man esteemeth one day above another: another esteemeth every day alike. Let every man be fully assured in his own mind.

He that regardeth the day, regardeth it unto the Lord:
And he that eateth, eateth to the Lord, for he giveth God thanks;
And he that eateth not, to the Lord he eateth not, and giveth God thanks.
For none of us liveth to himself,
And none dieth to himself.
For whether we live, we live unto the Lord;
Or whether we die, we die unto the Lord:
Whether we live therefore, or die, we are the Lord's.
For to this end Christ died, and lived again,
That he might be Lord of both the dead and the living.
But thou, why dost thou judge thy brother?
Or thou again, why dost thou set at nought thy brother?

For we shall all stand before the judgment seat of God. For it is written:

"As I live, saith the Lord,
To me every knee shall bow,
And every tongue shall confess to God."

CHRIST AND THE WORLD
From a painting by Louise Max-Ehrler

That stern choice between duty and pleasure is here again represented. On one side is the suggestion of great wealth, not merely dreamt about as possible of attainment, but actually present to be grasped with a single act. On the other hand is the crown of thorns, symbolic of the path of duty which is ofttimes also a path of suffering. The young woman has laid her hand upon the crown, as if to verify its sharpness even in the act of acceptance. We can divine by the position of the other hand and the look on her face that the choice has been made. One must not overlook the fact that it is a slave who presents the wealth, but an angel who holds the crown of thorns.

So then each one of us shall give account of himself to God. Let us not therefore judge one another any more; but judge ye this rather, that no man put a stumbling block in his brother's way, or an occasion of falling.

I know, and am persuaded in the Lord Jesus, that nothing is unclean of itself: save that to him who accounteth anything to be unclean, to him it is unclean. For if because of thy food thy brother is grieved, thou walkest no longer in love. Destroy not with thy food him for whom Christ died. Let not then your good be evil spoken of: for the kingdom of God is not eating and drinking, but righteousness and peace and joy in the Holy Spirit. For he that herein serveth

Christ is well-pleasing to God, and approved of men. So then let us follow after things which make for peace, and things whereby we may edify one another. Overthrow not for food's sake the work of God. All things indeed are clean; howbeit it is evil for that man who eateth with offense.

It is good not to eat flesh, nor to drink wine, nor to do anything whereby thy brother stumbleth.

"THE LIBERTY WHEREWITH CHRIST HATH MADE US FREE"

We take thought for things honorable, not only in the sight of the Lord, but also in the sight of men.

Look carefully how ye walk, not as unwise, but as wise; redeeming the time, because the days are evil. Wherefore be ye not foolish, but understand what the will of the Lord is.

Walk in wisdom toward them that are without, redeeming the time.

Not knowing God, ye were in bondage to them that by nature are no gods: but now that ye have come to know God, or rather to be known by God, how turn ye back again to the weak and beggarly elements, whereunto ye desire to be in bondage over again? Ye observe days, and months, and seasons, and years. I am afraid of you, lest by any means I have bestowed upon you labor in vain.

For freedom did Christ set us free[40]: stand fast therefore, and be not entangled again in a yoke of bondage.

Ye were running well; who hindered you that ye should not obey the truth? This persuasion came not of him that calleth you.

All things are lawful for me; but not all things are expedient;
All things are lawful for me; but I will not be brought under
    the power of any.
Foods for the stomach, and the stomach for foods;
But God shall bring to nought both it and them.

Let no man therefore judge you in food, or in drink, or in respect of a feast day or a new moon or a sabbath day: which are a shadow of the things to come; but the body is Christ's.

Let no man rob you of your prize by a voluntary humility and worshiping of the angels, dwelling in the things which he hath seen, vainly puffed up by his fleshly mind, and not holding fast the Head, from whom all the body, being supplied and knit together through the joints and bands, increaseth with the increase of God.

On Benevolence

As ye abound in everything, in faith, and utterance, and knowledge, and in all earnestness, and in your love to us, see that ye abound in this grace also. I speak not by way of commandment, but as proving through the earnestness of others the sincerity also of your love. For ye know the grace of our Lord Jesus Christ, that, though he was rich, yet for your sakes he became poor, that ye through his poverty might become rich.

And herein I give my judgment: for this is expedient for you, who were the first to make a beginning a year ago, not only to do, but also to will.

But now complete the doing also; that as there was the readiness to will, so there may be the completion also out of your ability.

For if the readiness is there, it is acceptable according as a man hath, not according as he hath not.

This I say:

He that soweth sparingly shall reap also sparingly;
And he that soweth bountifully shall reap also bountifully.

Let each man do according as he hath purposed in his heart; not grudgingly, or of necessity: for God loveth a cheerful giver. And God is able to make all grace abound to you; that ye, having always all sufficiency in all things, may abound unto every good work: as it is written:

"He hath scattered abroad, he hath given to the poor;
His righteousness abideth forever."

Now he that supplieth seed to the sower and bread for food, shall supply and multiply your seed for sowing, and increase the fruits of your righteousness: ye being enriched in everything to all liberality, which worketh through us thanksgiving to God. For the ministration of this service not only filleth up the measure of the wants of the saints, but aboundeth also through many thanksgivings to God; seeing that through the proving of you by this ministration they glorify God for the obedience of your confession to the gospel of Christ and for the liberality of your contribution to them and to all; while they themselves also, with supplication on your behalf, long after you by reason of the exceeding grace of God in you.

Thanks be to God for his unspeakable gift.

Let him that is taught in the word communicate to him that teacheth in all good things. Be not deceived; God is not mocked:

For whatsoever a man soweth, that shall he also reap.
He that soweth unto his own flesh shall of the flesh reap corruption;
But he that soweth unto the Spirit shall of the Spirit reap life everlasting.

And let us not be weary in well-doing; for in due season we shall reap, if we faint not. So then as we have opportunity, let us work that which is good toward all men, and especially toward them that are of the household of the faith.

I will most gladly spend and be spent for your souls. If I love you more abundantly, am I loved the less?

LIGHT

"He was the true light."

How beautiful is light!
Light, as it dawns and deepens into day;
Light, tender, wistful as it dies away;
Light of the moon appearing through the trees,
Peacefully resting on the restless seas;
Light in the clouds of grandeur and of dread;
After long voyages, home-shore lights ahead;
Lamplight that streams through open cottage door,
Telling of joy and rest when toil is o'er;
Firelight within (while storms without we hear),
Shining on books beloved and friends long dear;
When dark the night descends across the plain,
Lights of a village twinkling through the rain;
Starlight that, silent, whispers of God's throne;
Light of the love in eyes that meet our own;
Glow of church windows in a scene snow-white,
While songs of worship ring out in the night;
Sunlight that softly seeks the hallowed place
Where sinners pray for God's forgiving grace.
O Thou, the true and everlasting Light,
Who art the source of all things pure and bright,
These lesser rays on earthly paths that shine
Speak of the cloudless sunlight, Love Divine!
Father of lights, by Spirit and by word,
Lighten our darkness, we beseech thee, Lord!

—From *"The Living Church,"* by *Maud Frazer Jackson*

JAMES THE LESS
From a painting by Frederick Shields

CHRISTIAN CONDUCT AND BELIEF

FOOLISH THOUGHT AND SINFUL ACT

Shallow Philosophies

TAKE heed lest there shall be any one that maketh spoil of you through his philosophy and vain deceit, after the tradition of men, after the elements of the world, and not after Christ: for in him dwelleth all the fulness of the Godhead bodily, and in him ye are made full, who is the head of all principality and power.

Neither give heed to fables and endless genealogies, which minister questionings, rather than a dispensation of God which is in faith.

Now the end of the charge is love out of a pure heart and a good conscience and faith unfeigned: from which things some having swerved have turned aside to vain talking; desiring to be teachers of the law, though they understand neither what they say, nor whereof they confidently affirm.

You, being in time past alienated and enemies in your mind in your evil works, yet now hath he reconciled in the body of his flesh through death, to present you holy and without blemish and unreprovable before him: if so be that ye continue in the faith, grounded and steadfast, and not moved away from the hope of the gospel which ye heard, which was preached in all creation under heaven; whereof I Paul was made a minister. Now I rejoice in my sufferings for your sake, and fill up on my part that which is lacking of the afflictions of Christ in my flesh for his body's sake, which is the church; whereof I was made a minister, according to the dispensation of God which was given me toward you, to fulfil the word of God.

Restless Unbelief

Let us fear therefore, lest haply, a promise being left of entering into his rest, any one of you should seem to have come short of it. For indeed we have had good tidings preached to us, even as also they: but the word of hearing did not profit them, because it was not united by faith with them that heard.

For we who have believed enter into that rest: even as he hath said:

"As I swore in my wrath,
They shall not enter into my rest":

although the works were finished from the foundation of the world.

For he hath said somewhere of the seventh day on this wise, "And God rested on the seventh day from all his works"; and in this place again, "They shall not enter into my rest."

Seeing therefore it remaineth that some should enter thereinto, and they to whom the good tidings were before preached failed to enter in because of disobedience, he again defineth a certain day, "Today," saying in David so long a time afterward (even as hath been said before):

"Today if ye shall hear his voice,
Harden not your hearts."

For if Joshua had given them rest, he would not have spoken afterwards of another day. There remaineth therefore a rest for the people of God.

For he that hath entered into his rest, hath himself also rested from his works, as God did from his. Let us therefore give diligence to enter into that rest, lest any man fall after the same example of obedience.

For the word of God is living, and active, and sharper than any two-edged sword, and piercing even to the dividing of soul and spirit, of both joints and marrow, and quick to discern the thoughts and intents of the heart. Neither is there any creature that is not manifest in his sight: but all things are naked and laid open before the eyes of him with whom we have to do.

Take heed, brethren, lest haply there shall be in any one of you an evil heart of unbelief, in falling away from the living God: but exhort one another day by day, so long as it is called today; lest any one of you be hardened by the deceitfulness of sin.

Therefore we ought to give the more earnest heed to the things that were heard, lest haply we drift away from them. For if the word spoken through angels proved steadfast, and every transgression and disobedience received a just recompense of reward; how shall we escape, if we neglect so great a salvation? which having at first been spoken through the Lord, was confirmed to us by them that heard; God also bearing witness with them, both by signs and wonders, and by manifold powers, and by gifts of the Holy Spirit, according to his own will.

Wilful Sin

If we sin wilfully after that we have received the knowledge of the truth, there remaineth no more a sacrifice for sins, but a certain fearful expectation of judgment, and a fierceness of fire which shall devour the adversaries.

A man that hath set at nought Moses' law dieth without compassion on the word of two or three witnesses: of how much sorer punishment, think ye, shall he be judged worthy, who hath trodden under foot the Son of God, and hath counted the blood of the covenant wherewith he was sanctified an unholy thing, and hath done despite to the Spirit of grace? For we know him that said, "Vengeance belongeth to me, I will recompense." And again, "The Lord shall judge his people."

It is a fearful thing to fall into the hands of the living God.

Many walk, of whom I told you often, and now tell you even weeping, that they are the enemies of the cross of Christ: whose end is perdition, whose god is the belly, and whose glory is in their shame, who mind earthly things.

WANTONNESS

These, as creatures without reason, born mere animals to be taken and destroyed, railing in matters whereof they are ignorant, shall in their destroying surely be destroyed, suffering wrong as the hire of wrongdoing; men that count it pleasure to revel in the daytime, spots and blemishes, reveling in their deceivings while they feast with you; having eyes full of adultery, and that cannot cease from sin; enticing unsteadfast souls; having a heart exercised in covetousness; children of cursing; forsaking the right way, they went astray, having followed the way of Balaam the son of Beor, who loved the hire of wrongdoing; but he was rebuked for his own transgression: a dumb ass spoke with man's voice and stayed the madness of the prophet.

These are springs without water, and mists driven by a storm, for whom the blackness of darkness hath been reserved. For, uttering great swelling words of vanity, they entice in the passions of the flesh, by much wantonness, those who are just escaping from them that live in error; promising them liberty, while they themselves are bondservants of corruption; for of whom a man is overcome, of the same is he also brought into bondage.

For if, after they have escaped the defilements of the world through the knowledge of the Lord and Saviour Jesus Christ, they are again entangled therein and overcome, the last state hath become worse with them than the first. For it were better for them not to have known the way of righteousness, than, after knowing it, to turn back from the holy commandment delivered to them. It hath happened to them according to the true proverb:

"The dog turning to his own vomit again,
And the sow that had washed, to wallowing in the mire."

Beloved, while I was giving all diligence to write to you of our common salvation, it was needful for me to write to you exhorting you to contend earnestly for the faith which was once for all delivered to the saints.

For there are certain men crept in privily, even they who were of old written of beforehand to this condemnation, ungodly men, turning the grace of our God into lasciviousness, and denying our only Master and Lord, Jesus Christ.

Woe to them! for they went in the way of Cain, and ran riotously in the error of Balaam for hire, and perished in the gainsaying of Korah.

These are they who are hidden rocks in your love feasts, when they feast with you, shepherds that without fear feed themselves; clouds without water, carried along by winds; autumn trees without fruit, twice dead, plucked up by the roots; wild waves of the sea, foaming out their own shame; wandering stars, for whom the blackness of darkness hath been reserved forever. These are murmurers, complainers, walking after their own desires (and their mouth speaketh great swelling words), showing respect of persons for the sake of advantage.

But ye, beloved, remember ye the words which have been spoken before by the apostles of our Lord Jesus Christ;

©*Braun, Clement & Co.*

"LOVE NOT THE WORLD"
From a drawing by Eugène Burnand

The young people of this picture have caught a vision of the beauty of the spiritual life, in comparison with which the world and its pleasures shrink to nothingness. "The world passeth away, and the desire thereof, but he that doeth the will of God abideth forever."

that they said to you, "In the last time there shall be mockers, walking after their own ungodly desires." These are they who make separations, sensual, having not the Spirit.

But ye, beloved, building up yourselves on your most holy faith, praying in the Holy Spirit, keep yourselves in the love of God, looking for the mercy of our Lord Jesus Christ unto eternal life.

O MASTER, LET ME WALK WITH THEE
"He that is greatest among you shall be your servant."

O Master, let me walk with thee
In lowly paths of service free;
Tell me thy secret; help me bear
The strain of toil, the fret of care;

Help me the slow of heart to move
By some clear, winning word of love;
Teach me the wayward feet to stay,
And guide them in the homeward way.

O Master, let me walk with thee
Before the taunting Pharisee;
Help me to bear the sting of spite,
The hate of men who hide thy light,

The sore distrust of souls sincere
Who cannot read thy judgments clear
The dulness of the multitude
Who dimly guess that thou art good.

Teach me thy patience; still with thee
In closer, dearer company,
In work that keeps faith sweet and strong,
In trust that triumphs over wrong,

In hope that sends a shining ray
Far down the future's broadening way,
In peace that only thou canst give,
With thee, O Master, let me live!
— *Washington Gladden*

HOLY AND HAPPY LIVING

The Things of the Spirit

They that are after the flesh mind the things of the flesh;
But they that are after the Spirit the things of the Spirit.
For the mind of the flesh is death;
But the mind of the Spirit is life and peace.

Ye are of God, my little children, and have overcome them [the false prophets]: because greater is he that is in you than he that is in the world.

Know ye not, that to whom ye present yourselves as servants unto obedience, his servants ye are whom ye obey; whether of sin unto death, or of obedience unto righteousness?

But God be thanked, that, whereas ye were servants of sin, ye became obedient from the heart to that form of teaching whereunto ye were delivered; and being made free from sin, ye became servants of righteousness.

I speak after the manner of men because of the infirmity of your flesh. For as ye presented your members as servants to uncleanness and to iniquity unto iniquity, even so now present your members as servants to righteousness unto sanctification.

For when ye were servants of sin, ye were free in regard of righteousness. What fruit then had ye at that time in the things whereof ye are now ashamed? for the end of those things is death.

But now being made free from sin and become servants to God, ye have your fruit unto sanctification, and the end everlasting life. For the wages of sin is death; but the free gift of God is eternal life in Christ Jesus our Lord.

What shall we say then? Shall we continue in sin, that grace may abound? God forbid. How shall we, that died to sin, live any longer therein?

Know ye not that all we who were baptized into Christ Jesus were baptized into his death? Therefore we were buried with him through baptism into death; that like as Christ was raised from the dead through the glory of the Father, so we also might walk in newness of life. For if we have become united with him in the likeness of his death, we shall be also in the likeness of his resurrection; knowing this, that our old self is crucified with him, that the body of sin might be done away, that so we should no longer be in bondage to sin; for he that hath died is justified from sin.

Now if we died with Christ, we believe that we shall also live with him; knowing that Christ being raised from the dead dieth no more; death no more hath dominion over him. For the death that he died, he died unto sin once: but the life that he liveth, he liveth unto God. Likewise reckon ye also yourselves to be dead to sin, but alive to God in Christ Jesus.

Walk by the Spirit, and ye shall not fulfil the desires of the flesh. For the desire of the flesh is against the Spirit, and the desire of the Spirit is against the flesh; for these are contrary the one to the other; that ye may not do the things that ye would. But if ye are led by the Spirit, ye are not under the law.

Now the works of the flesh are manifest, which are these: vice, uncleanness, lasciviousness, idolatry, sorcery, enmities, strife, jealousies, wraths, factions, divisions, parties, envyings, drunkenness, revelings, and such like; of which I forewarn you, even as I forewarned you in times past, that they who practice such things shall not inherit the kingdom of God.

But the fruit of the Spirit is love, joy, peace, longsuffering, kindness, goodness, faithfulness, meekness, temperance; against such there is no law. And they that are of Christ Jesus have crucified the flesh with the passions and the desires thereof. If we live by the Spirit, by the Spirit let us also walk.

God forbid that I should glory, save in the cross of our Lord Jesus Christ, through which the world hath been crucified to me, and I to the world. For neither is circumcision anything, nor uncircumcision, but a new creature.

And as many as shall walk according to this rule, peace be upon them, and mercy, and upon the Israel of God.

The Marks of a True Christian

Seeing we have this ministry, even as we obtain mercy, we faint not: but we have renounced the hidden things of shame, not walking in craftiness, not handling the word of God deceitfully; but by the manifestation of the truth commending ourselves to every man's conscience in the sight of God.

Let a man so account of us, as of ministers of Christ, and stewards of the mysteries of God. Here, moreover, it is required in stewards, that a man be found faithful.

Only let your manner of life be worthy of the gospel of Christ: that, whether I come and see you or be absent, I may hear of your state, that ye stand fast in one spirit, with one soul striving for the faith of the gospel; and in nothing affrighted by the adversaries: which is for them an evident token of perdition, but of your salvation, and that from God.

For to you it hath been granted in the behalf of Christ, not only to believe on him, but also to suffer in his behalf: having the same conflict which ye saw in me, and now hear to be in me.

My beloved, even as ye have always obeyed, not as in my presence only, but now much more in my absence, work out your own salvation with fear and trembling; for it is God who worketh in you, both to will and to work, for his good pleasure.

Do all things without murmurings and questionings; that ye may become blameless and harmless, children of God without blemish, in the midst of a crooked and perverse generation, among whom ye are seen as lights in the world.

Walk worthily of God, who calleth you into his own kingdom and glory.

Let us consider one another to provoke to love and good works; not forsaking our own assembling together, as the custom of some is, but exhorting one another; and so much the more, as ye see the day approaching.

Every one that doeth sin doeth also lawlessness: and sin is lawlessness: and ye know that he was manifested to take away sins; and in him is no sin. Whosoever abideth in him sinneth not: whosoever sinneth hath not seen him, neither knoweth him.

In your faith supply virtue; and in your virtue knowledge; and in your knowledge temperance; and in your temperance patience; and in your patience godliness; and in your godliness brotherly kindness; and in your brotherly kindness love. For if these things are yours and abound, they make you to be not idle nor unfruitful unto the knowledge of our Lord Jesus Christ. For he that lacketh these things is blind, and cannot see afar off, and hath forgotten that he was cleansed from his old sins.

Wherefore, brethren, give the more diligence to make your calling and election sure: for if ye do these things, ye shall never stumble: for thus the entrance shall be richly supplied to you into the everlasting kingdom of our Lord and Saviour Jesus Christ.

Gird up your mind, be sober and set your hope perfectly on the grace that is to be brought to you at the revelation of Jesus Christ; as obedient children, not fashioning yourselves according to your former passions in the time of your ignorance: but like as he who called you is holy, be ye yourselves also holy in all manner of living; because it is written, "Ye shall be holy; for I am holy."

And if ye call on him as Father, who without respect of persons judgeth according to each man's work, pass the time of your sojourning in fear.

Sanctify in your hearts Christ as Lord: and be ready always to give answer to every man that asketh you a reason concerning the hope that is in you, yet with meekness and fear: having a good conscience; that, wherein ye are spoken against, they may be put to shame who revile your good manner of life in Christ. For it is better, if the will of God should so will, that ye suffer for well-doing than for evildoing.

Be ye of sound mind, and be sober unto prayer: above all things being fervent in your love among yourselves; for love covereth a multitude of sins: using hospitality one to another without murmuring: according as each hath received a gift, ministering it among yourselves, as good stewards of the manifold grace of God; if any man speaketh, speaking as it were oracles of God; if any man ministereth, ministering as

THE APOSTLE ANDREW
From a painting by Ribera

of the strength which God supplieth: that in all things God may be glorified through Jesus Christ, whose is the glory and the dominion forever and ever. Amen.

The Garments of Holiness

If then ye were raised together with Christ, seek the things that are above, where Christ is, seated on the right hand of God. Set your mind on the things that are above, not on the things that are upon the earth. For ye died, and your life is hid with Christ in God. When Christ, who is our life, shall be manifested, then shall ye also with him be manifested in glory.

Put to death therefore your members which are upon the earth: vice, uncleanness, passion, evil desire, and covetousness, which is idolatry. For these things' sake the wrath of God cometh upon the sons of disobedience: wherein ye also once walked, when ye lived in these things; but now do ye also put them all away: anger, wrath, malice, railing, shameful speaking out of your mouth: lie not to one another; seeing that ye have put off the old self with his doings, and have put on the new self, that is being renewed unto knowledge after the image of him that created him: where there is neither Greek nor Jew, barbarian, Scythian, bond, nor free; but Christ is all, and in all.

Put on therefore, as God's elect, holy and beloved, a heart of compassion, kindness, lowliness, meekness, longsuffering; forbearing one another, and forgiving one another, if any man have a complaint against any; even as the Lord forgave you, so also do ye: and above all these things put on love, which is the bond of perfectness. Let the peace of Christ rule in your hearts, to which also ye were called in one body; and be ye thankful.

Let the word of Christ dwell in you richly; in all wisdom teaching and admonishing one another with psalms and hymns and spiritual songs, singing with grace in your hearts to God. And whatsoever ye do, in word or in deed, do all in the name of the Lord Jesus, giving thanks to God the Father through him.

The Happiness of Christians

Finally, my brethren, rejoice in the Lord. To write the same things to you, to me indeed is not irksome, but for you it is safe.

Is any among you suffering? let him pray. Is any cheerful? let him sing praise. Is any among you sick? let him call for the elders of the church, and let them pray over him, anointing him with oil in the name of the Lord: and the prayer of faith shall save him that is sick, and the Lord shall raise him up; and if he have committed sins, it shall be forgiven him. Confess therefore your sins one to another, and pray one for another, that ye may be healed. The supplication of a righteous man availeth much in its working. Elijah was a man of like passions with us, and he prayed fervently that it might not rain; and it rained not on the earth for three years and six months. And he prayed again; and the heaven gave rain, and the earth brought forth her fruit.

Be not drunken with wine, wherein is riot, but be filled with the Spirit; speaking one to another in psalms and hymns and spiritual songs, singing and making melody with your heart to the Lord; giving thanks always for all things to God, even the Father, in the name of our Lord Jesus Christ.

Our glorying is this, the testimony of our conscience, that in holiness and sincerity of God, not in fleshly wisdom but in the grace of God, we behaved ourselves in the world, and more abundantly toward you.

THE APOSTLE THOMAS
From a painting by Ribera

God the Source of Holiness and Happiness

His divine power hath granted to us all things that pertain to life and godliness, through the knowledge of him that called us by his own glory and virtue; whereby he hath granted to us his exceeding great and precious promises; that through these ye may become partakers of the divine nature, having escaped from the corruption that is in the world by evil passion.

This is the boldness which we have toward him, that, if we ask anything according to his will, he heareth us: and if we know that he heareth us whatsoever we ask, we know that we have the petitions which we have asked of him.

Moses put a veil upon his face, that the children of Israel should not look steadfastly on the end of that which was passing away. But we all, with unveiled face, beholding as in a mirror the glory of the Lord, are transformed into the same image from glory to glory.

God, being minded to show more abundantly to the heirs of the promise the immutability of his counsel, interposed with an oath; that by two immutable things, in which it is impossible for God to lie, we may have a strong encouragement, who have fled for refuge to lay hold of the hope set before us: which we have as an anchor of the soul, a hope both sure and steadfast and entering into that which is within the veil; whither as a forerunner Jesus entered for us, having become a high priest forever after the order of Melchizedek.

We know that whosoever is begotten of God sinneth not;
But he that was begotten of God keepeth himself,
And that wicked one toucheth him not.

THE LIFE IMMORTAL

"The Glory of the Celestial"

If in this life only we have hope in Christ, we are of all men most miserable.

But now is Christ risen from the dead, and become the firstfruits of them that slept.

> For since by man came death,
> By man came also the resurrection of the dead.
> For as in Adam all die,
> Even so in Christ shall all be made alive.

But each in his own order: Christ the firstfruits; afterwards they that are Christ's at his coming. Then cometh the end, when he shall have delivered up the kingdom to God, even the Father; when he shall have put down all rule, and all authority and power. For he must reign, till he hath put all enemies under his feet. The last enemy that shall be destroyed is death. For he hath put all things under his feet.

But when he saith, "All things are put under him," it is manifest that he is excepted who did put all things under him. And when all things shall be subdued unto him, then shall the Son also himself be subject to him that put all things under him, that God may be all in all.

But some man will say, "How are the dead raised up? and with what body do they come?"[41]

Thou fool, that which thou sowest is not quickened, except it die: and that which thou sowest, thou sowest not that body that shall be, but bare grain, it may chance of wheat, or of some other grain: but God giveth it a body as it hath pleased him, and to each seed its own body. All flesh is not the same flesh: but there is one kind of flesh of men, another flesh of beasts, another of fishes, and another of birds.

> There are also celestial bodies,
> And bodies terrestrial:
> But the glory of the celestial is one,
> And the glory of the terrestrial is another.
> There is one glory of the sun,
> And another glory of the moon,
> And another glory of the stars;
> For one star differeth from another star in glory.

So also is the resurrection of the dead.

> It is sown in corruption,
> It is raised in incorruption:
> It is sown in dishonor,
> It is raised in glory:
> It is sown in weakness,
> It is raised in power:
> It is sown a natural body,
> It is raised a spiritual body.

There is a natural body, and there is a spiritual body. And so it is written:

> "The first man Adam was made a living soul":
> The last Adam was made a quickening spirit.
> Howbeit that was not first which is spiritual, but that which is natural;
> And afterwards that which is spiritual.
> The first man is of the earth, earthy:
> The second man is the Lord from heaven.
> As is the earthy, such are they also that are earthy:
> And as is the heavenly, such are they also that are heavenly.
> And as we have borne the image of the earthy,
> We shall also bear the image of the heavenly.

> Now this I say, brethren:
> Flesh and blood cannot inherit the kingdom of God;

CHRISTIAN MARTYRS
From a drawing by Gustave Doré

The Roman show is over; the applause has died away; the crowd has gone. The sun has set; dense shadows gather on the vacant seats of the great amphitheater and on the bloodstained sand of the arena. The hungry lions have sated themselves. But with the rising moon, a new and heavenly light shines down on this scene of suffering, and the angels of God wing hither in silent procession to sanctify and glorify even so fearful a place as this. We may almost hear them say, "These are they who come out of great tribulation."

Neither doth corruption inherit incorruption.
Behold, I show you a mystery:
We shall not all sleep,
But we shall all be changed,
In a moment,
In the twinkling of an eye,
At the last trump
For the trumpet shall sound,
And the dead shall be raised incorruptible,
And we shall be changed.
For this corruptible must put on incorruption,
And this mortal must put on immortality.

So when this corruptible shall have put on incorruption,
And this mortal shall have put on immortality,
Then shall be brought to pass the saying that is written:
"Death[42] is swallowed up in victory!
O death, where is thy sting!
O grave, where is thy victory!"
The sting of death is sin;
And the strength of sin is the law.

But thanks be to God, who giveth us the victory through our Lord Jesus Christ. Therefore, my beloved brethren, be ye steadfast, unmovable, always abounding in the work of the Lord, forasmuch as ye know that your labor is not in vain in the Lord.

The Temporal and the Eternal

If after the manner of men I fought with beasts at Ephesus, what doth it profit me? If the dead are not raised, let us eat and drink; for tomorrow we die.

We preach not ourselves, but Christ Jesus as Lord, and ourselves as your servants for Jesus' sake. Seeing it is God, who said, "Light shall shine out of darkness," who shined in our hearts, to give the light of the knowledge of the glory of God in the face of Jesus Christ.

But we have this treasure in earthen vessels, that the exceeding greatness of the power may be of God, and not from ourselves; we are pressed on every side, yet not straitened; perplexed, yet not unto despair; pursued, yet not forsaken; smitten down, yet not destroyed: always bearing about in the body the dying of Jesus, that the life also of Jesus may be manifested in our body.

For we who live are always delivered unto death for Jesus' sake, that the life also of Jesus may be manifested in our mortal flesh.

Wherefore we faint not; but though our outward man is decaying, yet our inward man is renewed day by day. For our light affliction, which is for the moment, worketh for us more and more exceedingly an eternal weight of glory:

> While we look not at the things that are seen,
> But at the things that are not seen:
> For the things that are seen are temporal;
> But the things that are not seen are eternal.

For we know that if the earthly house of our tabernacle be dissolved, we have a building from God, a house not made with hands, eternal, in the heavens. For verily in this we groan, longing to be clothed upon with our habitation which is from heaven: if so be that being clothed we shall not be found naked. For indeed we that are in this tabernacle groan, being burdened; not that we would be unclothed, but that we would be clothed upon, that what is mortal may be swallowed up of life. Now he that wrought us for this very thing is God, who gave to us the earnest of the Spirit.

Being therefore always of good courage, and knowing that, whilst we are at home in the body, we are absent from the Lord (for we walk by faith, not by sight); we are of good courage, I say, and are willing rather to be absent from the body, and to be at home with the Lord. Wherefore also we make it our aim, whether at home or absent, to be well-pleasing to him. For we must all appear before the judgment seat of Christ; that each one may receive the things done in his body, according to that he hath done, whether it be good or bad.

Our citizenship is in heaven; whence also we wait for a Saviour, the Lord Jesus Christ; who shall fashion anew the body of our humiliation, that it may be conformed to the body of his glory, according to the working whereby he is able even to subject all things to himself.

The Immortal Hope in Christ

Blessed be the God and Father of our Lord Jesus Christ, who according to his great mercy hath caused us to be born again to a living hope by the resurrection of Jesus Christ from the dead, to an inheritance incorruptible, and undefiled, and that fadeth not away, reserved in heaven for you, who by the power of God are guarded through faith to a salvation ready to be revealed in the last time.

God appointed us not unto wrath, but unto the obtaining of salvation through our Lord Jesus Christ, who died for us, that, whether we wake or sleep, we should live together with him. Wherefore exhort one another, and build up one another, even as also ye do.

God will render to every man according to his works: to them that by patience in well-doing seek for glory and honor and incorruption, eternal life.

To me to live is Christ, and to die is gain. I am in a strait betwixt the two, having a desire to depart, and to be with Christ; which is far better.

If any man have not the Spirit of Christ, he is none of his. And if Christ is in you, the body is dead because of sin; but the spirit is life because of righteousness.

We would not have you ignorant, brethren, concerning them that fall asleep; that ye sorrow not, even as the rest, who have no hope. For if we believe that Jesus died and rose again, even so them also that have fallen asleep in Jesus will

God bring with him. For this we say to you by the word of the Lord, that we that are alive, that are left unto the coming of the Lord, shall in no wise precede them that have fallen asleep. For the Lord himself shall descend from heaven, with a shout, with the voice of the archangel, and with the trump of God: and the dead in Christ shall rise first; then we that are alive, that are left, shall together with them be caught up in the clouds, to meet the Lord in the air: and so shall we ever be with the Lord.

Wherefore comfort one another with these words.

Our Duties in View of the Immortal Hope

If the Spirit of him that raised up Jesus from the dead dwelleth in you, he that raised up Christ Jesus from the dead shall give life also to your mortal bodies through his Spirit that dwelleth in you. So then, brethren, we are debtors, not to the flesh, to live after the flesh: for if ye live after the flesh, ye must die; but if by the Spirit ye put to death the deeds of the body, ye shall live.

The day of the Lord will come as a thief in the night; in which the heavens shall pass away with a great noise, and the elements shall melt with fervent heat; the earth also and the works that are therein shall be burned up.

Seeing that these things are thus all to be dissolved, what manner of persons ought ye to be in all holy living and godliness, looking for and earnestly desiring the coming of the day of God, by reason of which the heavens being on fire shall be dissolved, and the elements shall melt with fervent heat? Nevertheless we, according to his promise, look for new heavens and a new earth, wherein dwelleth righteousness.

Wherefore, beloved, seeing that ye look for these things, give diligence that ye may be found in peace, without spot and blameless in his sight.

Love not the world,
Neither the things that are in the world.
If any man love the world,
The love of the Father is not in him.
For all that is in the world,
The desire of the flesh,
And the desire of the eyes,
And the pride of life,
Is not of the Father,
But is of the world.
And the world passeth away, and the desire thereof:
But he that doeth the will of God abideth forever.

Beloved, now are we the sons of God, and it doth not yet appear what we shall be; but we know that, when he shall appear, we shall be like him; for we shall see him as he is.

And every man that hath this hope in him purifieth himself, even as he is pure.

VICTOR

"The last enemy that shall be destroyed is Death."

    Poor soul, the center of my sinful earth,
    Press'd by these rebel powers that thee array,
    Why dost thou pine within and suffer dearth,
    Painting thy outward walls so costly gay?
    Why so large cost, having so short a lease,
    Dost thou upon thy fading mansion spend?
    Shall worms, inheritors of this excess,
    Fat up thy charge? is this thy body's end?
    Then, soul, live thou upon thy servant's loss,
    And let that pine to aggravate thy store:
    Buy terms divine in selling hours of dross;
    Within be fed, without be rich no more:
      So shalt thou feed on Death, that feeds on men,
      And Death once dead, there's no more dying then.
                            — *Shakespeare*

SIMON THE ZEALOT
From a painting by Rubens

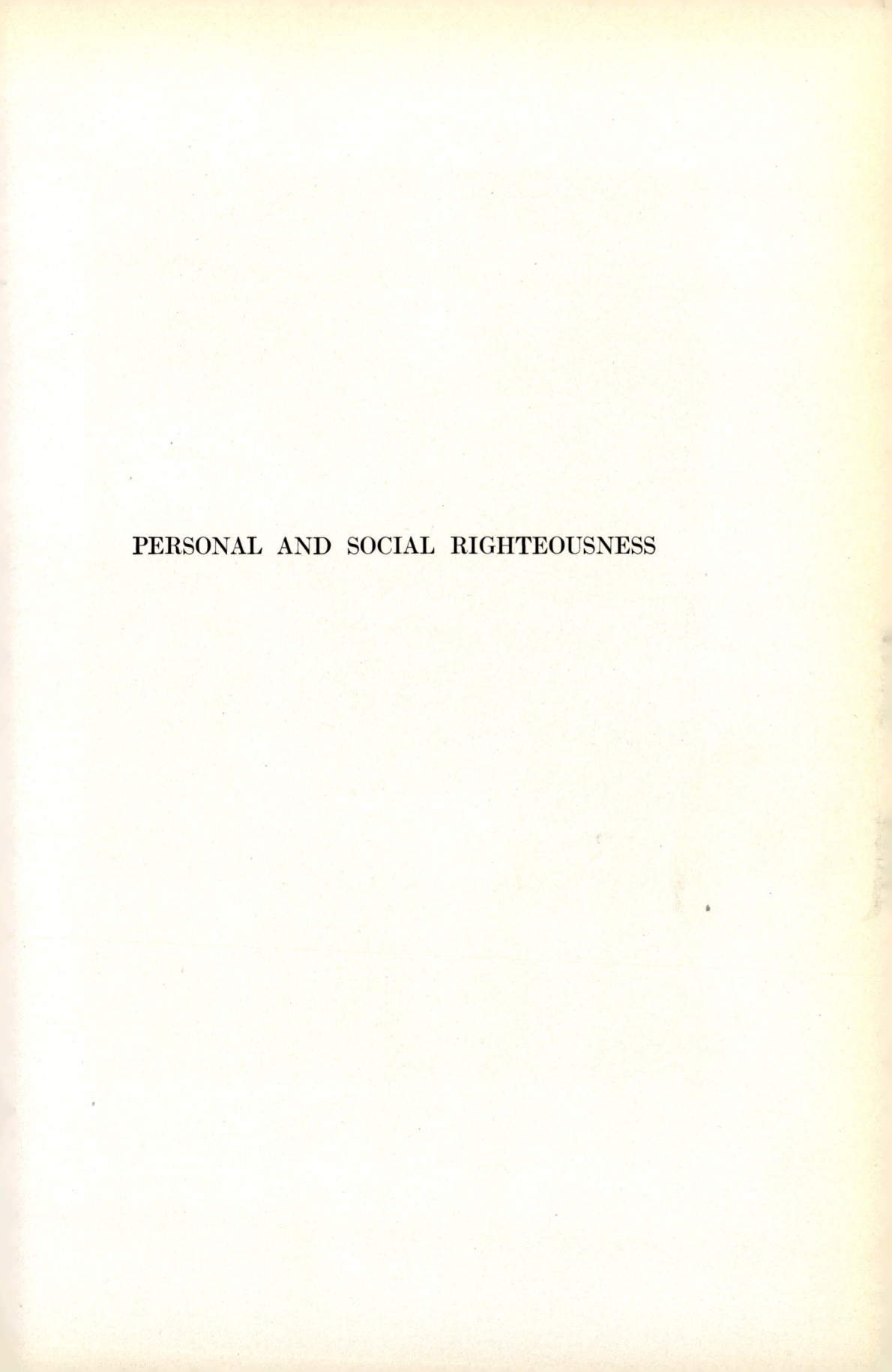

PERSONAL AND SOCIAL RIGHTEOUSNESS

PERSONAL AND SOCIAL RIGHTEOUSNESS

Words of Wisdom

WHILE reading the Hebrew Scriptures, we became familiar with the sages who wrote those sensible and prudent sayings of which so many have been left us in Proverbs and the Book of Ecclesiastes.

Similar sayings are found in the New Testament. Jesus, as we have already seen, not only used, but originated many proverbs. There are others scattered through the Christian writings, particularly in the Epistle of James. They cover much the same subjects as those in the Old Testament — wisdom, industry, the use of the tongue, humility, companionship, and religion in practice. These New Testament sayings are illumined by a higher light than the earlier ones, being conceived in the spirit of Jesus and made urgent as expressions of his life and example in the world.

The technical word "wisdom," which is used in the Old Testament as indicating the spirit of moral prudence, is employed in the New Testament to indicate rather that unselfish righteousness of the Christian, which sometimes does not seem to be prudent at all, but which nevertheless deserves and wins the favor of the Eternal.

THE OMNIPRESENCE OF CHRIST
From a painting by Heinrich Hofmann

PRINCIPLES OF RIGHTEOUS LIVING

RELIGION IN PRACTICE

"Faith Without Works Is Dead"

BE ye doers of the word, and not hearers only, deluding your own selves.

For if any one is a hearer of the word, and not a doer, he is like a man beholding his natural face in a mirror: for he beholdeth himself, and goeth away, and straightway forgetteth what manner of man he was.

But he that looketh into the perfect law, the law of liberty, and so continueth, being not a hearer that forgetteth, but a doer that worketh, this man shall be blessed in his doing.

If any man thinketh himself to be religious, while he bridleth not his tongue, but deceiveth his heart, this man's religion is vain.

Pure religion and undefiled before our God and Father is this, to visit the fatherless and widows in their affliction, and to keep oneself unspotted from the world.

What doth it profit, my brethren, if a man say he hath faith, but have not works? can that faith save him? If a brother or a sister be unclad, and in lack of daily food, and one of you say to them, "Go in peace, be ye warmed and filled"; and yet ye give them not the things which are needful to the body: what doth it profit? Even so faith, if it have not works, is dead in itself.

Yea, a man will say, "Thou hast faith, and I have works." Show me thy faith apart from thy works, and I by my works will show thee my faith.

Thou believest that God is one; thou doest well: the demons also believe, and tremble. But wilt thou know, O vain man, that faith without works is dead?

Was not Abraham our father justified by works, in that he offered Isaac his son upon the altar? Thou seest how faith wrought with his works, and by works was faith made perfect; and the scripture was fulfilled which saith, "Abraham believed God, and it was reckoned unto him for righteousness; and he was called the friend of God." Ye see that by works a man is justified, and not only by faith.

Likewise also was not Rahab justified by works, in that she received the messengers, and sent them out another way?

For as the body without the spirit is dead, even so faith without works is dead.

To him that knoweth to do good, and doeth it not, to him it is sin.

If a man saith, "I love God," and hateth his brother, he is a liar: for he that loveth not his brother whom he hath seen, how can he love God whom he hath not seen? And this commandment have we from him, that he who loveth God love his brother also.

Hereby we know that we know him, if we keep his commandments.

He that saith, "I know him," and keepeth not his commandments, is a liar, and the truth is not in him. But whoso keepeth his word, in him verily hath the love of God been perfected.

Hereby we know that we are in him: he that saith he abideth in him ought himself also to walk even as he walked.

He that saith he is in the light, and hateth his brother, is in the darkness even until now.

He that loveth his brother abideth in the light, and there is no occasion of stumbling in him.

But he that hateth his brother is in the darkness, and walketh in the darkness, and knoweth not whither he goeth, because the darkness hath blinded his eyes.

Hereby know we love, because he laid down his life for us; and we ought to lay down our lives for the brethren.

But whoso hath the world's goods, and beholdeth his brother in need, and shutteth up his compassion from him, how doth the love of God abide in him?

My little children, let us not love in word, neither with the tongue; but in deed and truth.

We know that we have passed from death to life because we love the brethren.

He that loveth not abideth in death. Whosoever hateth his brother is a murderer, and ye know that no murderer hath eternal life abiding in him.

In this the children of God are manifest, and the children of the devil: whosoever doeth not righteousness is not of God, neither he who loveth not his brother. For this is the message that ye heard from the beginning, that we should love one another.

If we say that we have fellowship with him, and walk in the darkness, we lie, and do not the truth; but if we walk in the light, as he is in the light, we have fellowship one with another, and the blood of Jesus his Son cleanseth us from all sin.

Dearly beloved, I beseech you as strangers and pilgrims,[43] abstain from fleshly passions, which war against the soul; having your behavior honest among the Gentiles, that, whereas they speak against you as evildoers, they may, by your good works, which they behold, glorify God in the day of visitation.

Building up yourselves on your most holy faith, praying in the Holy Spirit, keep yourselves in the love of God, looking for the mercy of our Lord Jesus Christ unto eternal life. And on some have mercy, who are in doubt; and some save, snatching them out of the fire; and on some have mercy with fear, hating even the garment spotted by the flesh.

Whosoever shall keep the whole law, and yet stumble in one point, he hath become guilty of all. For he that said, "Do not commit adultery," said also, "Do not kill." Now if thou dost not commit adultery, but killest, thou hast become a transgressor of the law. So speak ye, and so do, as men that are to be judged by a law of liberty; for judgment is without mercy to him that hath showed no mercy; mercy glorieth against judgment.

If we live by the Spirit, by the Spirit let us also walk.

Be not deceived; God is not mocked:
For whatsoever a man soweth, that shall he also reap.
He that soweth unto his own flesh shall of the flesh reap corruption;
But he that soweth unto the Spirit shall of the Spirit reap life everlasting.
And let us not be weary in well-doing; for in due season we shall reap, if we faint not.

Walk by the Spirit, and ye shall not fulfil the desires of the flesh. For the desire of the flesh is against the Spirit, and the desire of the Spirit is against the flesh; for these are contrary the one to the other; that ye may not do the things that ye would.

Ye cannot drink the cup of the Lord, and the cup of demons;
Ye cannot partake of the table of the Lord, and of the table of demons.

Rejoice always; pray without ceasing; in everything give thanks; for this is the will of God in Christ Jesus concerning you.

Quench not the Spirit; despise not prophesyings; prove all things; hold fast that which is good; abstain from every form of evil.

Resist the devil, and he will flee from you;
Draw nigh to God, and he will draw nigh to you.
Cleanse your hands, ye sinners;
And purify your hearts, ye double-minded.
Be afflicted, and mourn, and weep:
Let your laughter be turned to mourning,
And your joy to heaviness.
Humble yourselves in the sight of the Lord,
And he shall exalt you.

SELF–CONTROL IN SPEECH

"Let Your Speech Be Always with Grace"

Let every man be swift to hear, slow to speak, slow to wrath; for the wrath of man worketh not the righteousness of God.

If any man thinketh himself to be religious, while he bridleth not his tongue, but deceiveth his heart, this man's religion is vain.

In many things we all stumble. If any stumbleth not in word, the same is a perfect man, able to bridle the whole body also. Now if we put the horses' bridles into their mouths, that they may obey us, we turn about their whole body also. Behold, the ships also, though they are so great, and are driven by rough winds, are yet turned about by a very small rudder, whither the steersman willeth.

So the tongue also is a little member, and boasteth great things. Behold, how great a matter a little fire kindleth! And the tongue is a fire: the world of iniquity among our members is the tongue, which defileth the whole body, and setteth on fire the course of nature, and is set on fire by hell.

For every kind of beasts, and birds, of creeping things and things in the sea, is tamed, and hath been tamed by mankind; but the tongue can no man tame; it is an unruly evil, full of deadly poison.

Therewith bless we the Lord and Father;
And therewith curse we men, who are made after the likeness of God:
Out of the same mouth proceedeth blessing and cursing.

My brethren, these things ought not so to be.

Doth the fountain send forth from the same opening sweet water and bitter?
Can a fig tree, my brethren, yield olives,
Or a vine, figs?
Neither can salt water yield sweet.

Let your speech be always with grace, seasoned with salt, that ye may know how ye ought to answer every man.

SAINT MATTHEW
From a painting by Il Guercino

Lie not to one another; seeing that ye have put off the old self with his doings, and have put on the new self, that is being renewed unto knowledge after the image of him that created him.

Let no corrupt speech proceed out of your mouth, but such as is good for edifying as the need may be, that it may give grace to them that hear. And grieve not the Holy Spirit of God, in whom ye were sealed unto the day of redemption.

Let all bitterness, and wrath, and anger, and clamor, and railing, be put away from you, with all malice; and be ye kind to one another, tender-hearted, forgiving one another, even as God also in Christ forgave you.

Above all things, my brethren, swear not, neither by the heaven, nor by the earth, nor by any other oath. Let your yea be yea, and your nay, nay; that ye fall not under judgment.

Even things without life, giving a voice, whether pipe or harp, if they give not a distinction in the sounds, how shall it be known what is piped or harped? For if the trumpet give an uncertain voice, who shall prepare himself for war? So also ye, unless ye utter by the tongue speech easy to be understood, how shall it be known what is spoken? for ye will be speaking into the air.

Speak not one against another, brethren. He that speaketh against a brother, or judgeth his brother, speaketh against the law, and judgeth the law: but if thou judgest the law, thou art not a doer of the law, but a judge.

One only is the lawgiver and judge, even he who is able to save and to destroy: who art thou that judgest thy neighbor?

Be ye all like-minded, compassionate, loving as brethren, tender-hearted, humble-minded, not rendering evil for evil, or reviling for reviling; but on the contrary blessing; for hereunto were ye called, that ye should inherit a blessing.

> For he that would love life,
> And see good days,
> Let him refrain his tongue from evil,
> And his lips that they speak no guile;
> Let him turn away from evil, and do good;
> Let him seek peace, and pursue it.

And be ready always to give answer to every man that asketh you a reason concerning the hope that is in you, yet with meekness and fear.

COMPANIONSHIP AND SOCIAL INTERCOURSE

"Be of the Same Mind One Toward Another"

Know ye not that the friendship of the world is enmity with God?

Whosoever therefore would be a friend of the world maketh himself an enemy of God.

> Be not unequally yoked with unbelievers:
> For what fellowship hath righteousness with unrighteousness?
> Or what communion hath light with darkness?
> And what concord hath Christ with Belial?
> Or what portion hath a believer with an unbeliever?
> And what agreement hath a temple of God with idols?

For we are a temple of the living God; even as God said:

> "I will dwell in them, and walk in them;
> I will be their God, and they shall be my people."

Wherefore

> "Come ye out from among them,
> And be ye separate," saith the Lord,
> "And touch no unclean thing;

And I will receive you,
And I will be to you a Father,
And ye shall be to me sons and daughters."

Be ye angry, and sin not:
Let not the sun go down upon your wrath;
Neither give place to the devil.

Let love be without dissimulation.
Abhor that which is evil;
Cleave to that which is good.
Be kindly affected one to another with brotherly love,
In honor preferring one another;
Not slothful in business;
Fervent in spirit; serving the Lord;
Rejoicing in hope;
Patient in tribulation;
Continuing instant in prayer;
Distributing to the necessity of saints;
Given to hospitality.
Bless them that persecute you:
Bless, and curse not.
Rejoice with them that do rejoice,
And weep with them that weep.
Be of the same mind one toward another.
Mind not high things,
But condescend to men of low estate.
Be not wise in your own conceits.
Recompense to no man evil for evil.
Provide things honest in the sight of all men.
If it be possible, as much as lieth in you,
Live peaceably with all men.
Dearly beloved, avenge not yourselves,
But rather give place unto wrath:

For it is written,
"Vengeance is mine;
I will repay," saith the Lord.
Therefore if thine enemy hunger, feed him;
If he thirst, give him drink:
For in so doing thou shalt heap coals of fire on his head.
Be not overcome of evil,
But overcome evil with good.

Be at peace among yourselves.
Now we exhort you, brethren, admonish the disorderly, encourage the faint-hearted, support the weak, be longsuffering toward all. See that none render to any one evil for evil; but ever follow that which is good, one toward another, and toward all.

Know ye not that a little leaven leaveneth the whole lump? Purge out the old leaven, that ye may be a new lump, even as ye are unleavened.

THE PRIVILEGES OF THE JEW

"Having in the Law the Form of Knowledge and of the Truth"

What advantage then hath the Jew?
Much every way: first of all, that they were intrusted with the oracles of God.

I could wish that I myself were anathema from Christ for my brethren's sake, my kinsmen according to the flesh, Israelites, whose is the adoption, and the glory, and the covenants, and the giving of the law, and the service of God, and the promises; whose are the fathers, and of whom is Christ as concerning the flesh, who is over all, God blessed forever.

Behold, thou art called a Jew, and restest upon the law, and gloriest in God, and knowest his will, and approvest the things that are more excellent, being instructed out of the law; and art confident that thou thyself art a guide of the blind, a light of them that are in darkness, a corrector of the foolish, a teacher of babes, having in the law the form of knowledge and of the truth.

Thou therefore that teachest another, teachest thou not thyself?

Thou that preachest a man should not steal, dost thou steal?

Thou that sayest a man should not commit adultery, dost thou commit adultery?

Thou that abhorrest idols, dost thou rob temples?

Thou that gloriest in the law, through breaking the law dishonorest thou God?

WISDOM

"Who Is Wise and Understanding Among You?"

If any of you lack wisdom, let him ask of God, that giveth to all liberally and upbraideth not; and it shall be given him. But let him ask in faith, nothing doubting; for he that doubteth is like the surge of the sea driven by the wind and tossed. For let not that man think that he shall receive anything from the Lord, a double-minded man unstable in all his ways.

Who is wise and understanding among you? let him show by his good life his works in meekness of wisdom. But if ye have bitter jealousy and faction in your heart, glory not and lie not against the truth. This wisdom is not a wisdom that cometh down from above, but is earthly, sensual, devilish. For where jealousy and faction are, there is confusion and every vile deed.

But the wisdom that is from above is first pure, then peaceable, gentle, easy to be persuaded, full of mercy and good fruits, without variance, without hypocrisy. And the fruit of righteousness is sown in peace for them that make peace.

The word of the cross is to them that perish foolishness; but to us who are saved it is the power of God. For it is written:

"I will destroy the wisdom of the wise,
And the discernment of the discerning will I bring to nought."

Where is the wise? where is the scribe? where is the disputer of this world? hath not God made foolish the wisdom of the world? For seeing that in the wisdom of God the world through its wisdom knew not God, it was God's good pleasure through the foolishness of the preaching to save them that believe. Seeing that Jews ask for signs, and Greeks seek after wisdom: but we preach Christ crucified, to Jews a stumbling block, and to Gentiles foolishness; but to them that are called, both Jews and Greeks, Christ the power of God, and the wisdom of God.

Because the foolishness of God is wiser than men;
And the weakness of God is stronger than men.

For behold your calling, brethren, that not many wise after the flesh, not many mighty, not many noble, are called:

But God chose the foolish things of the world, that he might put to shame them that are wise;
And God chose the weak things of the world, that he might put to shame the things that are strong;
And the base things of the world, and the things that are despised, did God choose,

> Yea and the things that are not, that he might bring to nought the things that are;
> That no flesh should glory before God.

> We speak the wisdom of God in a mystery, even the wisdom that hath been hidden, which God foreordained before the worlds unto our glory: which none of the rulers of this world hath known: for had they known it, they would not have crucified the Lord of glory: but as it is written:
> "Eye hath not seen,
> Nor ear heard,
> Neither have entered into the heart of man,
> The things which God hath prepared for them that love him."
> But God hath revealed them to us through the Spirit; for the Spirit searcheth all things, yea, the deep things of God.
> What man knoweth the things of a man, save the spirit of the man, which is in him?
> Even so the things of God knoweth no man, save the Spirit of God.
> Now we have received, not the spirit of the world, but the spirit which is from God; that we might know the things that are freely given us of God. These things also we speak, not in the words which man's wisdom teacheth, but which the Spirit teacheth; combining spiritual things with spiritual words.

HE THAT DOETH THE WILL

What, then! doth Charity fail?
Is Faith of no avail?
Is Hope blown out like a light
By a gust of wind in the night?
The clashing of creeds, and the strife
Of the many beliefs, that in vain
Perplex man's heart and brain,
Are naught but the rustle of leaves,
When the breath of God upheaves

The boughs of the Tree of Life,
And they subside again!
And I remember still
The words, and from whom they came —
Not he that repeateth the name,
But he that doeth the will!

And Him evermore I behold
Walking in Galilee,
Through the cornfield's waving gold,
In hamlet, in wood, and in wold,
By the shores of the Beautiful Sea.
He toucheth the sightless eyes;
Before him the demons flee;
To the dead he sayeth, Arise!
To the living, Follow me!
And that voice still soundeth on
From the centuries that are gone
To the centuries that shall be!

From all vain pomps and shows,
From the pride that overflows,
And the false conceits of men;
From all the narrow rules
And subtleties of Schools,
And the craft of tongue and pen;
Bewildered in its search,
Bewildered with the cry,
Lo, here! lo, there, the Church!
Poor, sad Humanity
Through all the dust and heat
Turns back with bleeding feet,
By the weary road it came,
Unto the simple thought
By the Great Master taught,
And that remaineth still—
Not he that repeateth the name,
But he that doeth the will!

— *Henry Wadsworth Longfellow*

SAINT PETER
From a sculpture by Bernini

SOCIAL IDEALS

FAMILY RELATIONSHIPS

The Mutual Duties of Husbands and Wives

YE wives, be in subjection to your own husbands; that, even if any obey not the word, they may without the word be gained by the behavior of their wives; beholding your chaste behavior coupled with fear.

Whose adorning, let it not be the outward adorning of braiding the hair, and of wearing jewels of gold, or of putting on of apparel; but let it be the hidden man of the heart, in the incorruptible apparel of a meek and quiet spirit, which is in the sight of God of great price.

For after this manner in the old time the holy women also, who hoped in God, adorned themselves, being in subjection to their own husbands: as Sarah obeyed Abraham, calling him lord; whose children ye now are, if ye do well, and are not put in fear by any terror.

Likewise, ye husbands, dwell with your wives according to knowledge, giving honor to the woman, as to the weaker vessel, and as being also joint-heirs of the grace of life; to the end that your prayers be not hindered.

Subject yourselves one to another in the fear of Christ.

Wives, be in subjection to your own husbands, as to the Lord. For the husband is the head of the wife, even as Christ is the head of the church, being himself the Saviour of the body. Therefore as the church is subject to Christ, so let the wives be to their husbands in everything.

Husbands, love your wives, even as Christ also loved the church, and gave himself for it; that he might sanctify it, having cleansed it by the washing of water by the word, that he might present the church to himself a glorious church, not having spot or wrinkle or any such thing; but that it should be holy and without blemish. Even so ought husbands to love their wives as their own bodies. He that loveth his wife loveth himself: for no man ever hated his own flesh; but nourisheth and cherisheth it, even as Christ also the church; because we are members of his body. For this cause shall a man leave his father and mother, and shall be joined unto his wife, and they two shall be one flesh. This is a great mystery: but I speak concerning Christ and the church. Nevertheless, let every one of you in particular so love his wife even as himself; and the wife see that she reverence her husband.

Wives, be in subjection to your husbands, as is fitting in the Lord.

Husbands, love your wives, and be not bitter against them.

I would have you know, that the head of every man is Christ; and the head of the woman is the man; and the head of Christ is God.

Every man praying or prophesying, having his head covered, dishonoreth his head. But every woman praying or prophesying with her head unveiled dishonoreth her head; for that it is one and the same thing as if she were shaven. For if a woman is not veiled, let her also be shorn: but if it is a shame to a woman to be shorn or shaven, let her be veiled. For a man indeed ought not to have his head veiled, forasmuch as he is the image and glory of God: but the woman is the glory of the man. For the man is not of the woman; but the woman of the man: for neither was the man created for the woman; but the woman for the man: for this cause ought the woman to have a sign of authority on her head, because of the angels. Nevertheless, neither is the woman without the man, nor the man without the woman, in the Lord. For as the woman is of the man, so is the man also by the woman; but all things are of God.

Judge ye in yourselves: is it seemly that a woman pray to God unveiled? Doth not even nature itself teach you, that, if a man have long hair, it is a dishonor to him? But if a woman have long hair, it is a glory to her; for her hair is given her for a covering. But if any man seemeth to be contentious, we have no such custom, neither the churches of God.

Marriage, Divorce, and Remarriage

Shouldst thou marry, thou hast not sinned; and if a virgin marry, she hath not sinned. Yet such shall have tribulation in the flesh; and I would spare you.

The wife is bound by the law as long as her husband liveth; but if her husband be dead, she is at liberty to be married to whom she will; only in the Lord.

To the married I give charge, yea not I, but the Lord: "Let not the wife depart from her husband (but if she depart, let her remain unmarried, or else be reconciled to her husband); and let not the husband leave his wife."

But to the rest say I, not the Lord: If any brother hath a wife that believeth not, and she is content to dwell with him, let him not leave her. And the woman who hath a husband that believeth not, and he is content to dwell with her, let her not leave her husband. For the unbelieving husband is sanctified in the wife, and the unbelieving wife is sanctified in the husband: else were your children unclean; but now are they holy.

Yet if the unbelieving departeth, let him depart: the brother or the sister is not under bondage in such cases: but God hath called us in peace. For how knowest thou, O wife, whether thou shalt save thy husband? or how knowest thou,

O husband, whether thou shalt save thy wife? Only, as the Lord hath distributed to each man, as God hath called each, so let him walk.

Purity of Life

This is the will of God, even your sanctification, that ye abstain from unclean living; and that each one of you should learn mastery over his own bodily desires in sanctification and honor; that no man transgress, and wrong his brother in the matter: because the Lord is an avenger in all these things, as also we forewarned you and testified. For God called us not for uncleanness, but in sanctification.

Flee impure living. Every other sin that a man doeth is outside the body; but he that liveth impurely sinneth against his own body.
Or know ye not that your body is a temple of the Holy Spirit which is in you, which ye have from God? and ye are not your own; for ye were bought with a price: glorify God therefore in your body.

Duties of Parents and Children

Children, obey your parents in the Lord; for this is right. "Honor thy father and thy mother" (which is the first commandment with promise), "that it may be well with thee, and thou mayest live long upon the earth."
And, ye fathers, provoke not your children to wrath; but nurture them in the chastening and admonition of the Lord.

Children, obey your parents in all things, for this is well-pleasing in the Lord.
Fathers, provoke not your children, that they be not discouraged.

SERVANTS AND MASTERS

Servants, be in subjection to your masters with all fear; not only to the good and gentle, but also to the froward.

For this is acceptable, if for conscience toward God a man endureth griefs, suffering wrongfully.

For what glory is it, if, when ye sin, and are buffeted for it, ye shall take it patiently? but if, when ye do well, and suffer for it, ye shall take it patiently, this is acceptable with God. For hereunto were ye called: because Christ also suffered for you, leaving you an example, that ye should follow in his steps:

> Who did no sin,
> Neither was guile found in his mouth:
> Who, when he was reviled, reviled not again;
> When he suffered, threatened not;

but committed himself to him that judgeth righteously: who his own self bore our sins in his body upon the tree, that we, having died unto sins, might live unto righteousness; by whose stripes ye were healed. For ye were going astray like sheep; but have now returned to the Shepherd and Bishop of your souls.

Servants, be obedient to them that are your masters according to the flesh, with fear and trembling, in singleness of your heart, as to Christ; not in the way of eyeservice, as menpleasers; but as the servants of Christ, doing the will of God from the heart; with good will doing service, as to the Lord, and not to men: knowing that whatsoever good thing any man doeth, the same shall he receive again from the Lord, whether he be bond or free.

And, ye masters, do the same things to them, and forbear threatening; knowing that he who is both their Master and yours is in heaven, and there is no respect of persons with him.

THE HOUSE OF THE VETTII AT POMPEII
From a painting by Edoardo Forti

Whatsoever ye do, do it heartily, as unto the Lord, and not unto men; knowing that from the Lord ye shall receive the recompense of the inheritance: ye serve the Lord Christ. For he that doeth wrong shall receive again for the wrong that he hath done: and there is no respect of persons.

Masters, render to your servants that which is just and equal; knowing that ye also have a Master in heaven.

[In that new creation] there is neither Greek nor Jew, barbarian, Scythian, bond nor free; but Christ is all, and in all.

RICH AND POOR

The Transience of Riches

Let the brother of low degree glory in his high estate: and the rich, in that he is made low: because as the flower of the grass he shall pass away. For the sun ariseth with a scorching wind, and withereth the grass; and the flower thereof falleth, and the grace of the fashion of it perisheth: so also shall the rich man fade away in his goings.

Come now, ye that say, "Today or tomorrow we will go into this city, and spend a year there, and trade, and get gain": whereas ye know not what shall be on the morrow. What is your life? For ye are a vapor, that appeareth for a little

THE HOUSE OF THE VETTII AT POMPEII
From a painting by Edoardo Forti

This is a faithful restoration of a Roman home in the time of Paul. One sees the beautiful colonnade that surrounds the open court; one can almost smell the odor of flowers and hear the plash of falling water. In the cool shadow of this loggia are abundant suggestions of luxury, and of the pride of life that demands ever more and more. It is a fact that in the early centuries the Gospel appealed powerfully to women such as those pictured here—women weary of the eternal round of pleasure and the ennui of a useless life. By the fourth Christian century, there were scores of wealthy women who were members of the Christian church at Rome.

time, and then vanisheth away. Ye ought to say, "If the Lord will, we shall both live, and do this or that." But now ye glory in your vauntings: all such glorying is evil.

Therefore to him that knoweth to do good, and doeth it not, to him it is sin.

The Iniquity of Unjust Gain

Come now, ye rich, weep and howl for your miseries that are coming upon you.

Your riches are corrupted,
And your garments are moth-eaten;
Your gold and your silver are rusted;
And their rust shall be a testimony against you,
And shall eat your flesh, as if it were fire.
Ye have laid up your treasure in the last days.
Behold, the hire of the laborers who mowed your fields,
    which is by you kept back by fraud, crieth out:
And the cries of them that reaped have entered into the
    ears of the Lord of Sabaoth [hosts].
Ye have lived delicately on the earth, and taken your
    pleasure;
Ye have nourished your hearts in a day of slaughter.
Ye have condemned, ye have killed the righteous one; he
    doth not resist you.

They that buy [may be] as though they possessed not;
And they that use the world, as not using it to the full:
For the fashion of this world passeth away.

The Error of Subservience to the Rich

My brethren, do ye, in accepting persons, hold the faith of our Lord Jesus Christ, the Lord of glory? For if there come into your synagogue a man with a gold ring, in fine clothing, and there come in also a poor man in vile clothing;

and ye have regard to him that weareth the fine clothing, and say, "Sit thou here in a good place"; and ye say to the poor man, "Stand thou there, or sit under my footstool"; are ye not divided in your own mind and become judges with evil thoughts [wrong standards]?

Hearken, my beloved brethren; did not God choose them that are poor as to the world to be rich in faith, and heirs of the kingdom which he promised to them that love him? But ye have dishonored the poor man. Do not the rich oppress you, and themselves drag you before the judgment seats? Do not they blaspheme the honorable name by which ye are called? Howbeit if ye fulfil the royal law, according to the scripture, "Thou shalt love thy neighbor as thyself," ye do well; but if ye have respect of persons, ye commit sin, being convicted by the law as transgressors.

The Duty of Contented Industry

We exhort you, brethren, that ye abound more and more; and that ye study to be quiet, and to do your own business, and to work with your hands, even as we charged you, that ye may walk becomingly toward them that are outside, and may have need of nothing.

Let him that stole steal no more; but rather let him labor, working with his hands the thing that is good, that he may have whereof to give to him that hath need.

Now we command you, brethren, in the name of our Lord Jesus Christ, that ye withdraw yourselves from every brother that walketh disorderly, and not after the tradition which they received of us. For yourselves know how ye ought to imitate us: for we behaved not ourselves disorderly among you; neither did we eat bread for nought at any man's hand; but in labor and travail, working night and day, that we might not burden any of you: not because we have not the right, but to make ourselves an example to you, that ye should imitate us.

For even when we were with you, this we commanded you, If any will not work, neither let him eat. For we hear of some that walk among you disorderly, that work not at all, but are busybodies. Now them that are such we command and exhort in the Lord Jesus Christ, that with quietness they work, and eat their own bread.

The Duty of Taking Care of the Poor

To do good and to communicate forget not; for with such sacrifices God is well pleased.

Neither was there among them any that lacked; for as many as were possessors of lands or houses sold them, and brought the prices of the things that were sold, and laid them at the apostles' feet: and distribution was made to each, according as any one had need.

In all things I gave you an example, that so laboring ye ought to help the weak, and to remember the words of the Lord Jesus, that he said, "It is more blessed to give than to receive."

THE CITIZEN AND THE STATE

The Duty of Patriotic Loyalty

Let every soul be in subjection to the higher powers: for there is no power but of God; and the powers that be are ordained of God. Whosoever therefore resisteth the power, withstandeth the ordinance of God: and they that withstand shall receive to themselves judgment. For rulers are not a terror to the good work, but to the evil.

HAIL, CÆSAR
From a painting by Edoardo Forti

This is a scene from the Stadium in Rome. On the hill to the left is the palace of Cæsar. Two hundred thousand spectators look down from the lofty seats upon the race course where the drivers of the quadrigas, or four-horse chariots, contend with such skill and daring. The victor is just passing the royal box in which, under the canopy, in splendid isolation, sits the ruler of the world.

Paul and the early Christians must have been very familiar with such contests, so that the allusion of the Apostle was instantly comprehended by all when he said, "They do it to obtain a corruptible crown, but we an incorruptible."

And wouldst thou have no fear of the power? do that which is good, and thou shalt have praise from the same; for he is a servant of God to thee for good. But if thou do that which is evil, be afraid; for he beareth not the sword in vain: for he is a servant of God, an avenger for wrath to him that doeth evil.

Wherefore ye must needs be in subjection, not only because of the wrath, but also for conscience' sake. For for this cause ye pay tribute also; for they are ministers of God's service, attending continually upon this very thing.

Render to all their dues: tribute to whom tribute is due; custom to whom custom; fear to whom fear; honor to whom honor.

Be subject to every ordinance of man for the Lord's sake: whether to the king, as supreme; or to governors, as sent by him for vengeance on evildoers, and for praise to them that do well. For so is the will of God, that by well-doing ye should put to silence the ignorance of foolish men: as free, and not using your freedom for a cloak of wickedness, but as bondservants of God. Honor all men. Love the brotherhood. Fear God. Honor the king.

Caution Against Hasty Litigation

Dare any of you, having a matter against his neighbor, go to law before the unrighteous, and not before the saints? Or know ye not that the saints shall judge the world? and if the world is judged by you, are ye unworthy to judge the smallest matters? Know ye not that we shall judge angels? how much more things that pertain to this life? If then ye have to judge things pertaining to this life, do ye set them to judge who are of no account in the church? I say this to move you to shame. What, cannot there be found among you one wise man who shall be able to decide between his brethren, but brother goeth to law with brother, and that before unbelievers? Nay, already it is altogether a defect in you, that ye have lawsuits one with another. Why not rather take wrong? Why not rather be defrauded? Nay, but ye yourselves do wrong, and defraud, and that your brethren.

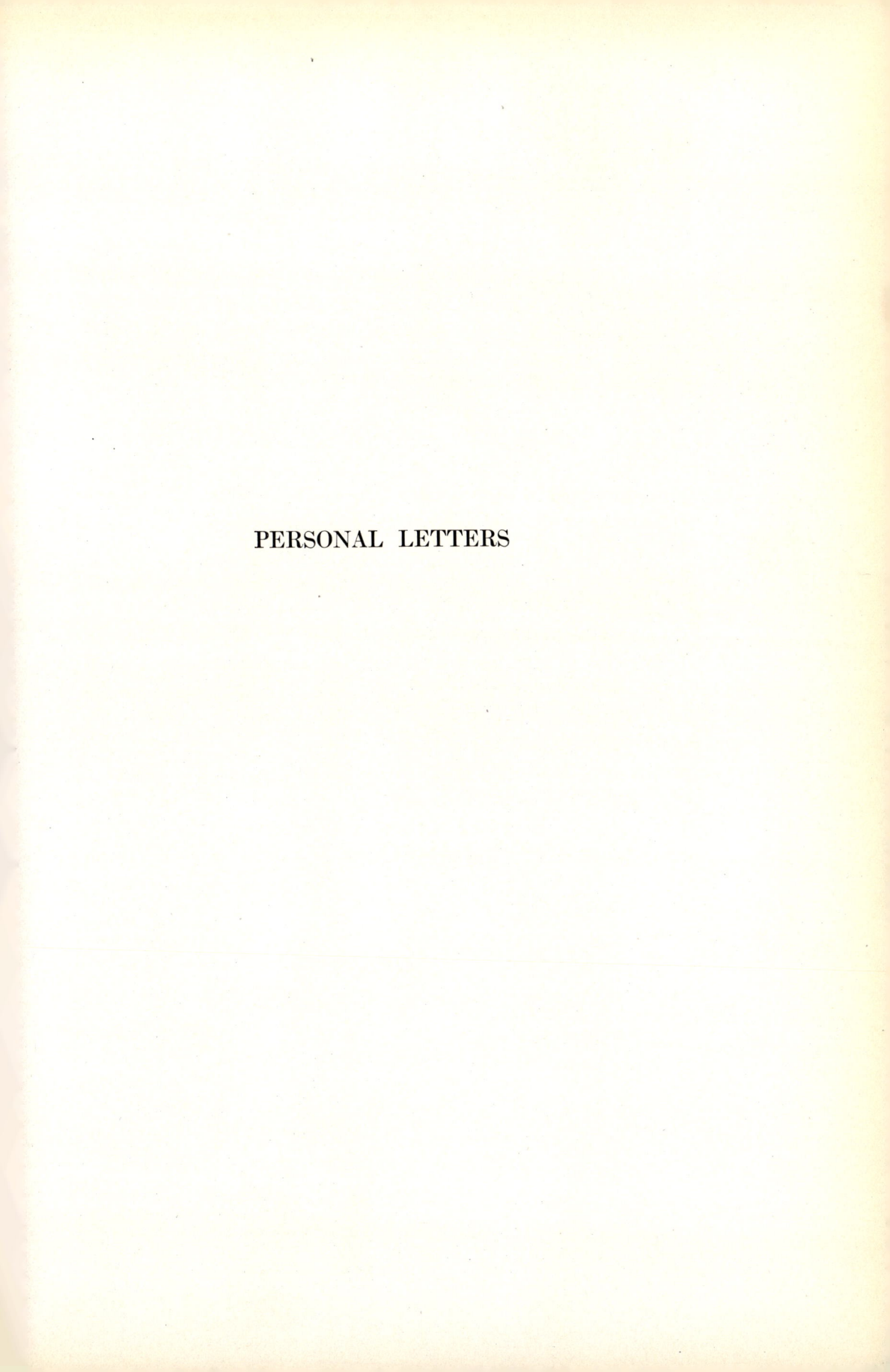

PERSONAL LETTERS

PERSONAL LETTERS

THE letters included in this section are for the most part of Paul's writing; but to these have been added two described in the Bible as the Second and Third Epistles of John.

The personal letters of Paul shed a flood of light upon a different side of his character from that which is revealed in his official letters to the churches. They show him highly appreciative of the kindness and coöperation of individual Christians, some leaders, some humble members of the churches. They reveal his loving heart and loyal nature.

The letters to Timothy and Titus, his young assistants, are products of Paul's old age. They come from a veteran whose battles are fought, whose race is run, and who is desirous of guiding to wise leadership of the churches those who are to take his place. "They show the administrative wisdom, the love of order, and the eye for practical detail, of the great church founder and pastor."

As Paul's dying testimony, these letters have a special pathos; they convey a practical message still useful to our churches, and present the strong and inspiring view of one who goes forward in faith and in fearlessness knowing that, after suffering a violent death, he will pass from this earth to receive the crown of life.

THE APOSTLE PAUL
From a sculpture by Bernini

PERSONAL LETTERS

MESSAGES OF GREETING AND FRIENDSHIP

From the Letters of Paul

A Letter of Introduction and of Greeting

Since Paul himself had never been in Rome when these words were written, it has been thought that they constituted originally a separate letter of introduction for Phœbe to the members of some church in Asia Minor. The letter is most interesting because of its affectionate tone and because it expresses Paul's appreciation of the services and sacrifices of many helpers, some of whom he mentions by name.

I COMMEND to you Phœbe our sister, who is a servant of the church that is at Cenchreæ; that ye receive her in the Lord, worthily of the saints, and that ye assist her in whatsoever matter she may have need of you: for she herself also hath been a helper of many, and of mine own self.

Salute Prisca and Aquila my fellow-workers in Christ Jesus, who for my life laid down their own necks; to whom not only I give thanks, but also all the churches of the Gentiles: and salute the church that is in their house.

Salute Epænetus my beloved, who is the firstfruits of Asia to Christ.

Salute Mary, who bestowed much labor on you.

Salute Andronicus and Junias, my kinsmen, and my fellow-prisoners, who are of note among the apostles, who also have been in Christ before me.

Salute Ampliatus my beloved in the Lord.

Salute Urbanus our fellow-worker in Christ, and Stachys my beloved.

Salute Apelles the approved in Christ.

Salute them that are of the household of Aristobulus.

Salute Herodion my kinsman.

"PAUL, AN APOSTLE OF JESUS CHRIST BY THE GRACE OF GOD"
From a drawing by Isings

The soldier guard has laid aside his helmet and his sword, and is probably stretching himself for a good nap, while the Apostle takes his pen and his sheet of papyrus and calls up before his mind's eye the friends to whom he is about to write.

Salute them of the household of Narcissus, that are in the Lord.

Salute Tryphæna and Tryphosa, who labor in the Lord.

Salute Persis the beloved, who labored much in the Lord.

Salute Rufus the chosen in the Lord, and his mother and mine.

Salute Asyncritus, Phlegon, Hermes, Patrobas, Hermas, and the brethren that are with them.

Salute Philologus, and Julia, Nereus and his sister, and Olympas, and all the saints who are with them.

Salute one another with a holy kiss. All the churches of Christ salute you.

Now I beseech you, brethren, mark them that are causing the divisions and occasions of stumbling, contrary to the doctrine which ye learned; and turn away from them. For they that are such serve not our Lord Christ, but their own belly; and by their smooth and fair speech they beguile the hearts of the innocent. For your obedience hath come abroad to all men.

I rejoice therefore over you; but I would have you wise unto that which is good, and simple unto that which is evil. And the God of peace shall bruise Satan under your feet shortly.

Timothy my fellow-worker saluteth you; and Lucius and Jason and Sosipater, my kinsmen.

I Tertius, who write the epistle, salute you in the Lord.

Gaius my host, and of the whole church, saluteth you.

Erastus the treasurer of the city saluteth you, and Quartus the brother.

Now to him that is able to establish you according to my gospel and the preaching of Jesus Christ, according to the revelation of the mystery which hath been kept in silence through times eternal, but now is manifested, and by the scriptures of the prophets, according to the commandment of the everlasting God, is made known to all the nations unto obedience of faith: to the only wise God, through Jesus Christ, to whom be the glory forever. Amen.

Greetings to the Colossians

At the close of the letter to the Colossians, the principal thoughts of which have been quoted earlier, come these tender personal remembrances, characteristic of the letters of Paul.

All my affairs shall Tychicus make known to you, the beloved brother and faithful minister and fellow-servant in the Lord: whom I have sent to you for this very purpose, that ye may know our estate, and that he may comfort your hearts; together with Onesimus, the faithful and beloved brother, who is one of you. They shall make known to you all things that are done here.

Aristarchus my fellow-prisoner saluteth you, and Mark, the cousin of Barnabas (touching whom ye received commandments, "If he come to you, receive him"), and Jesus that is called Justus, who are of the Jews: these only are my fellow-workers unto the kingdom of God, men that have been a comfort to me.

Epaphras, who is one of you, a servant of Christ Jesus, saluteth you, always striving for you in his prayers, that ye may stand perfect and fully assured in all the will of God. For I bear him witness, that he hath a great zeal for you, and for them in Laodicea, and for them in Hierapolis.

Luke, the beloved physician, and Demas salute you.

Salute the brethren that are in Laodicea, and Nymphas, and the church that is in their house. And when this epistle hath been read among you, cause that it be read also in the church of the Laodiceans; and that ye also read the epistle from Laodicea.

And say to Archippus, "Take heed to the ministry which thou hast received in the Lord, that thou fulfil it."

The salutation of me Paul with mine own hand. Remember my bonds. Grace be with you. Amen.

Affectionate Greetings to Other Christians

We, brethren, being taken from you for a short time, in presence, not in heart, endeavored the more exceedingly to see your face with great desire: because we would fain have come to you, even I Paul, once and again; but Satan hindered us.

For what is our hope, or joy, or crown of glorying? Are not even ye, before our Lord Jesus at his coming? For ye are our glory and joy.

Now when Timothy came even now from you to us, and brought us glad tidings of your faith and love, and that ye have good remembrance of us always, longing to see us, even

THE MAMERTINE PRISON, ROME

This prison is an excavation in the northern foot of the Palatine Hill. It is exceedingly ancient, possibly pre-Roman, though it was enlarged in Roman times, and was used during the republican period as one of the regular state prisons. Some of Catiline's fellow-conspirators were confined here. The lower story of the prison is frequently flooded with water, so that one can well imagine that Paul was willing to hire his own house rather than languish in such a place.

as we also to see you; for this cause, brethren, we were comforted over you in all our affliction and distress through your faith: for now we live, if ye stand fast in the Lord.

For what thanksgiving can we render to God again for you, for all the joy wherewith we joy for your sakes before our God; night and day praying exceedingly that we may see your face, and may perfect that which is lacking in your faith?

Finally, brethren, pray for us, that the word of the Lord may have free course, and be glorified, even as also it is with you; and that we may be delivered from unreasonable and evil men; for all have not faith. But the Lord is faithful, who shall establish you, and guard you from the evil one. And we have confidence in the Lord touching you, that ye both do and will do the things which we command. And the Lord direct your hearts into the love of God, and into the patience of Christ.

The things which ye both learned and received and heard and saw in me, these things do: and the God of peace shall be with you.

Though ye have ten thousand instructors in Christ, yet have ye not many fathers; for in Christ Jesus I have begotten you through the gospel.

Wherefore I beseech you, be ye imitators of me.

A Letter Asking Forgiveness for an Undeserving Servant

Paul, a prisoner of Christ Jesus, and Timothy our brother, to Philemon our beloved and fellow-worker, and to Apphia our sister, and to Archippus our fellow-soldier, and to the church in thy house: Grace to you and peace from God our Father and the Lord Jesus Christ.

I thank my God always, making mention of thee in my prayers, hearing of thy love, and of the faith which thou hast toward the Lord Jesus, and toward all the saints; [while I pray] that the fellowship of thy faith may become effectual, in the knowledge of every good thing which is in you, unto Christ. For we have great joy and consolation in thy love, because the hearts of the saints have been refreshed through thee, brother.

Wherefore, though I have all boldness in Christ to enjoin thee that which is befitting, yet for love's sake I rather beseech, being such a one as Paul the aged, and now a prisoner

SAINT BARTHOLOMEW
From a painting by Ribera

also of Jesus Christ: I beseech thee for my child, who hath been born to me in my bonds, Onesimus, who once was unprofitable to thee, but now is profitable to thee and to me: whom I have sent back to thee in his own person, that is, my very heart: whom I would fain have kept with me, that in thy behalf he might minister to me in the bonds of the gospel: but without thy mind I would do nothing; that thy kindness should not be as of necessity, but of free will. For perhaps he was therefore parted from thee for a season, that thou shouldst have him forever; no longer as a servant, but more than a servant, a brother beloved, especially to me, but how much rather to thee, both in the flesh and in the Lord? If thou countest me therefore a partner, receive him as myself. If he hath wronged thee at all, or oweth thee aught, put that to mine account; I Paul write it with mine own hand, I will repay it: that I say not to thee that thou owest to me even thine own self besides. Yea, brother, let me have joy of thee in the Lord; refresh my heart in Christ.

Having confidence in thine obedience, I write to thee, knowing that thou wilt do even beyond what I say. But withal prepare me also a lodging; for I hope that through your prayers I shall be granted to you.

Epaphras, my fellow-prisoner in Christ Jesus, saluteth thee; and so do Mark, Aristarchus, Demas, Luke, my fellow-workers.

The grace of our Lord Jesus Christ be with your spirit. Amen.

LETTERS OF CHRISTIAN COUNSEL

From the Epistles of John

A Letter to Gaius the Beloved

THE ELDER TO GAIUS THE BELOVED, WHOM I LOVE IN TRUTH. BELOVED, I PRAY THAT IN ALL THINGS THOU MAYEST PROSPER AND BE IN HEALTH, EVEN AS THY SOUL PROSPERETH.

I rejoiced greatly, when brethren came and bore witness to thy truth, even as thou walkest in truth. I have no greater joy than to hear that my children walk in truth.

Beloved, thou doest a faithful work in whatsoever thou doest toward them that are brethren and strangers withal; who bore witness to thy love before the church: whom thou wilt do well to set forward on their journey worthily of God: because for the sake of the Name they went forth, taking nothing of the Gentiles. We therefore ought to welcome such, that we may be fellow-workers for the truth.

I wrote somewhat to the church: but Diotrephes, who loveth to have the preëminence among them, receiveth us not. Therefore, if I come, I will bring to remembrance his works which he doeth, prating against us with wicked words: and not content therewith, neither doth he himself receive the brethren, and them that would he forbiddeth, and casteth them out of the church. Beloved, imitate not that which is evil, but that which is good. He that doeth good is of God: he that doeth evil hath not seen God. Demetrius hath the witness of all men, and of the truth itself: yea, we also bear witness; and thou knowest that our witness is true.

I had many things to write to thee, but I am unwilling to write them to thee with ink and pen; but I hope shortly to see thee, and we shall speak face to face. Peace be unto thee. The friends salute thee. Salute the friends by name.

A Letter to a Chosen Lady and Her Children

The Greek word "kuria" means lady, and is also a proper name; therefore this address may read, "to the elect lady," or "to the chosen Kuria." This note accordingly may be considered as addressed to a Christian woman and her children, or possibly to a Christian church.

THE ELDER TO THE ELECT LADY AND HER CHILDREN, WHOM I LOVE IN TRUTH; AND NOT I ONLY, BUT ALSO ALL THEY THAT KNOW THE TRUTH; FOR THE TRUTH'S SAKE WHICH DWELLETH IN US, AND IT SHALL BE WITH US FOREVER: GRACE, MERCY, PEACE SHALL BE WITH US, FROM GOD THE FATHER, AND FROM JESUS CHRIST, THE SON OF THE FATHER, IN TRUTH AND LOVE.

I rejoice greatly that I have found certain of thy children walking in truth, even as we received commandment from the Father.

And now I beseech thee, lady, not as though I wrote a new commandment to thee, but that which we had from the beginning, that we love one another. And this is love, that we should walk after his commandments.

THE BOY TIMOTHY READING THE SCRIPTURES
From a painting by James Sant
"Knowing that from a child thou hast known the holy Scriptures, which are able to make thee wise unto salvation."

This is the commandment, even as ye have heard from the beginning, that ye should walk in it.

For many deceivers have gone forth into the world, even they who confess not that Jesus Christ cometh in the flesh. This is the deceiver and the antichrist. Look to yourselves, that ye lose dot those things which we have wrought, but that ye receive a full reward. Whosoever goeth onward and abideth not in the doctrine of Christ, hath not Christ: he that abideth in the doctrine, he hath both the Father and the Son. If there come any to you, and bring not this doctrine, receive him not into your house, neither bid him Godspeed: for he that biddeth him Godspeed partaketh in his evil works.

Having many things to write to you, I would not write them with paper and ink: but I trust to come to you, and speak face to face, that your joy may be made full.

The children of thine elect sister greet thee. Amen.

THREE LETTERS ABOUT CHRISTIAN CHURCH LIFE

From the Letters of Paul

These letters, originally personal, to individual leaders in the early Christian church, were cherished and shared with many other church leaders. Eventually they attained their present form as manuals for the ideals and conduct of ministers of the Gospel.

THE FIRST LETTER TO TIMOTHY

PERSONAL GREETINGS

PAUL, AN APOSTLE OF CHRIST JESUS ACCORDING TO THE COMMANDMENT OF GOD OUR SAVIOUR, AND CHRIST JESUS OUR HOPE; TO TIMOTHY, MY TRUE CHILD IN FAITH: GRACE, MERCY, PEACE, FROM GOD THE FATHER AND CHRIST JESUS OUR LORD.

I thank him that enabled me, even Christ Jesus our Lord, because he counted me faithful, appointing me to his service; though I was before a blasphemer, and a persecutor, and injurious; but I obtained mercy, because I did it ignorantly in unbelief; and the grace of our Lord abounded exceedingly with faith and love which is in Christ Jesus. This is a faithful

THE APPIAN WAY

This famous road was built in 312 B.C. by Appius Claudius. It was the main thoroughfare from Rome to the East, and for many centuries the most important road in the empire. It was strongly built in the Roman fashion, and paved with huge blocks of stone fitted close together. Special chariots and relays of horses made it possible to travel on this road more than two hundred miles a day. Paul coming from Puteoli entered this road at Capua.

saying, and worthy of all acceptation, that Christ Jesus came into the world to save sinners; of whom I am chief: howbeit for this cause I obtained mercy, that in me as chief might Christ Jesus show forth all his longsuffering, for an example of them that should thereafter believe on him to life everlasting.

Now to the King eternal, immortal, invisible, the only God, be honor and glory forever and ever. Amen.

This charge I commit to thee, son Timothy, according to the prophecies which led the way to thee, that thou by them mayest war a good warfare; holding faith, and a good conscience; which some having thrust from them made shipwreck concerning the faith.

PRAYERS TO BE OFFERED FOR ALL MEN

I exhort therefore, first of all, that supplications, prayers, intercessions, thanksgivings, be made for all men; for kings, and for all that are in high place; that we may lead a tranquil and quiet life in all godliness and gravity.

This is good and acceptable in the sight of God our Saviour; who would have all men to be saved, and come to the knowledge of the truth. For there is one God, one mediator also between God and men, himself man, Christ Jesus, who gave himself a ransom for all; the testimony to be borne in its own times; whereunto I was appointed a preacher and an apostle (I speak the truth, I lie not), a teacher of the Gentiles in faith and truth.

I desire therefore that the men pray everywhere, lifting up holy hands, without wrath and disputing.

THE DRESS AND CONDUCT OF CHRISTIAN WOMEN

In like manner, that women adorn themselves in modest apparel, with shamefacedness and sobriety; not with braided hair, and gold or pearls or costly raiment, but (which becometh women professing godliness) through good works. Let a woman learn in quietness with all subjection. But I suffer not a woman to teach, nor to have dominion over a man, but to be in quietness. For Adam was first formed, then Eve; and Adam was not beguiled, but the woman being beguiled hath fallen into transgression.

THE OFFICE OF BISHOP

This is a true saying, "If a man seeketh the office of a bishop, he desireth a good work." A bishop then must be without reproach, the husband of one wife, temperate, sober-minded, orderly, given to hospitality, apt to teach; no brawler, no striker; but gentle, not contentious, no lover of money; one that ruleth well his own house, having his children in subjection with all gravity (for if a man know not how to rule his own house, how shall he take care of the church of God?); not a novice, lest being lifted up with pride he fall into the condemnation of the devil. Moreover he must have good testimony from them that are outside, lest he fall into reproach and the snare of the devil.

DEACONS AND THEIR WIVES

Likewise must the deacons be grave, not double-tongued, not given to much wine, not greedy of filthy lucre; holding the mystery of the faith in a pure conscience. And let these also first be proved; then let them serve as deacons, if they be blameless.

Even so must their wives be grave, not slanderers, temperate, faithful in all things. Let deacons be husbands of one wife, ruling their children and their own houses well. For they that have served well as deacons gain to themselves a good standing, and great boldness in the faith which is in Christ Jesus.

AGAINST FOOLISH TEACHINGS

Now the Spirit saith expressly, that in later times some shall fall away from the faith, giving heed to seducing spirits, and doctrines of demons, through the hypocrisy of men that speak lies, branded in their own conscience as with a hot iron; forbidding to marry, and commanding to abstain from foods, which God created to be received with thanksgiving by them that believe and know the truth. For every creature of God is good, and nothing is to be rejected, if it be received with thanksgiving: for it is sanctified through the word of God and prayer.

If thou put the brethren in mind of these things, thou shalt be a good minister of Christ Jesus, nourished in the words of the faith, and of the good doctrine, which thou hast followed until now: but refuse profane and old wives' fables. And exercise thyself unto godliness: for bodily exercise is profitable for a little; but godliness is profitable for all things, having promise of the life which now is, and of that which is to come. Faithful is the saying, and worthy of all acceptation. For to this end we labor and strive, because we have our hope set on the living God, who is the Saviour of all men, especially of them that believe.

These things command and teach.

THE PREPARATION OF THE CHRISTIAN LEADER

Let no man despise thy youth; but be thou an example for the believers, in word, in manner of life, in love, in faith, in purity.

Till I come, give attention to reading, to exhortation, to teaching. Neglect not the gift that is in thee which was given thee by prophecy, with the laying on of the hands of the presbytery.

Be diligent in these things; give thyself wholly to them; that thy progress may be manifest to all. Take heed to thyself, and to thy teaching. Continue in these things; for in doing this thou shalt save both thyself and those who hear thee.

DUTIES TO THE WIDOWS

Rebuke not an elder, but exhort him as a father; the younger men as brethren; the elder women as mothers; the younger as sisters, in all purity.

Honor widows that are widows indeed. But if any widow have children or grandchildren, let them learn first to show piety toward their own family, and to requite their parents; for this is acceptable in the sight of God. Now she that is a widow indeed, and desolate, hath her hope set on God, and continueth in supplications and prayers night and day. But she that giveth herself to pleasure is dead while she liveth. These things also command, that they may be without reproach. But if any provideth not for his own, and especially for those of his own household, he hath denied the faith, and is worse than an unbeliever. Let none be enrolled as a widow under threescore years old, having been the wife of one man, well reported of for good works; if she hath brought up children, if she hath used hospitality to strangers, if she hath washed the saints' feet, if she hath relieved the afflicted, if she hath diligently followed every good work.

But younger widows refuse; for when they have begun to chafe against Christ, they desire to marry; having condemnation, because they have rejected their first pledge. And withal they learn to be idle, wandering about from house to house; and not only idle, but tattlers also and busybodies, speaking things which they ought not. I desire therefore that the younger widows marry, bear children, rule the household, give no occasion to the adversary for reviling; for some have already turned aside after Satan.

THE OFFICE OF ELDER

Let the elders that rule well be counted worthy of double honor, especially those who labor in the word and in teaching. For the scripture saith, "Thou shalt not muzzle the ox that treadeth out the grain," and, "The laborer is worthy of his hire."

Against an elder receive not an accusation, except at the mouth of two or three witnesses. Those who sin rebuke in the sight of all, that the rest also may be in fear. I charge thee in the sight of God, and Christ Jesus, and the elect angels, that thou observe these things, without prejudice, doing nothing by partiality.

DUTIES OF CHRISTIAN SERVANTS

Let as many as are servants under the yoke count their own masters worthy of all honor, that the name of God and the doctrine be not blasphemed. And they that have believing masters, let them not despise them, because they are brethren; but let them serve them the rather, because they that partake of the benefit are believing and beloved. These things teach and exhort.

GODLINESS AND MONEY

If any man teacheth a different doctrine, and consenteth not to sound words, even the words of our Lord Jesus Christ, and to the doctrine which is according to godliness, he is puffed up, knowing nothing, but doting about questionings and disputes of words, whereof cometh envy, strife, railings, evil surmisings, wranglings of men corrupted in mind, and bereft of the truth, supposing that godliness is a way of gain. From such withdraw thyself.

But godliness with contentment is great gain: for we brought nothing into this world, and it is certain we can carry nothing out; but having food and covering let us be therewith content.

But they that are minded to be rich fall into a temptation and a snare, and many foolish and hurtful passions, such as drown men in destruction and perdition. For the love of money is the root of all evil: which some reaching after, have been led astray from the faith, and have pierced themselves through with many sorrows.

But thou, O man of God, flee these things; and follow after righteousness, godliness, faith, love, patience, meekness. Fight the good fight of the faith, lay hold on the life eternal, whereunto thou wast called, and didst confess the good confession in the sight of many witnesses. I charge thee in the sight of God, who giveth life to all things, and of Christ Jesus, who before Pontius Pilate witnessed the good confession; that thou keep the commandment, without spot, without reproach, until the appearing of our Lord Jesus Christ: which in its own times he shall show, who is the blessed and only Potentate, the King of kings, and Lord of lords; who only

THE VIGIL
From a painting by John Pettie

In preparation for receiving the accolade and being admitted to the order of knighthood, the law of chivalry required a candidate to place his armor before the altar and spend a whole night in watching and prayer. With such a spirit of consecration the Apostle Paul hath immortality, dwelling in light unapproachable; whom no man hath seen, nor can see: to whom be honor and power everlasting. Amen.

Charge them that are rich in this world, that they be not high-minded, nor have their hope set on the uncertainty of riches, but on God, who giveth us richly all things to enjoy; that they do good, that they be rich in good works, that they be ready to distribute, willing to communicate; laying up in store for themselves a good foundation against the time to come, that they may lay hold on the life which is life indeed.

O Timothy, guard that which is committed unto thee, turning away from the profane babblings and oppositions of the knowledge which is falsely so called; which some professing have erred concerning the faith.

Grace be with you.

The Second Letter to Timothy

Personal Greetings

Paul, an apostle of Christ Jesus, through the will of God, according to the promise of the life which is in Christ Jesus, to Timothy, my beloved child: Grace, mercy, peace, from God the Father and Christ Jesus our Lord.

I thank God, whom I serve from my forefathers in a pure conscience, how unceasing is my remembrance of thee in my supplications, night and day longing to see thee, remembering thy tears, that I may be filled with joy; having been reminded of the unfeigned faith that is in thee; which dwelt first in thy grandmother Lois, and thy mother Eunice; and, I am persuaded, in thee also.

Wherefore I put thee in remembrance, that thou stir up the gift of God, which is in thee through the laying on of my hands.

For God gave us not a spirit of fearfulness; but of power, and love, and discipline.

PRIDE IN THE GOSPEL

Be not ashamed therefore of the testimony of our Lord, nor of me his prisoner: but suffer hardship with the gospel according to the power of God; who saved us, and called us with a holy calling, not according to our works, but according to his own purpose and grace, which was given us in Christ Jesus before the world began; but hath now been manifested by the appearing of our Saviour Christ Jesus, who abolished death, and brought life and immortality to light through the gospel, whereunto I was appointed a preacher, and an apostle, and a teacher. For which cause I also suffer these things: nevertheless I am not ashamed; for I know whom I have believed, and am persuaded that he is able to guard that which I have committed unto him against that day.

Hold fast the pattern of sound words which thou hast heard from me, in faith and love which is in Christ Jesus. That good thing which was committed to thee guard through the Holy Spirit which dwelleth in us.

THE GOOD FIGHT

Thou therefore, my child, be strong in the grace that is in Christ Jesus. And the things that thou hast heard from me among many witnesses, the same commit thou to faithful men, who shall be able to teach others also.

Thou therefore endure hardness, as a good soldier of Christ Jesus. No soldier on service entangleth himself in the affairs of this life; that he may please him who enrolled him as a soldier. And if a man also contend in the games, he is not crowned, except he hath contended lawfully. The husbandman that laboreth must be the first to partake of the fruits. Consider what I say; for the Lord shall give thee understanding in all things.

Remember Jesus Christ, risen from the dead, of the line of David, according to my gospel: wherein I suffer hardship, as an evildoer, even unto bonds; but the word of God is not bound. Therefore I endure all things for the elect's sake, that they also may obtain the salvation which is in Christ Jesus with eternal glory.

THE SOUND FOUNDATIONS

Of these things put them in remembrance, charging them in the sight of the Lord, that they strive not about words, to no profit, to the subverting of them that hear.

Give diligence to present thyself approved unto God, a workman that needeth not to be ashamed, handling aright the word of truth. But shun profane babblings; for they will proceed further in ungodliness. And their word will eat as doth a gangrene.

Howbeit the firm foundation of God standeth, having this seal, "The Lord knoweth them that are his"; and, "Let every one that nameth the name of the Lord depart from unrighteousness."

Now in a great house there are not only vessels of gold and of silver, but also of wood and of earth; and some unto honor, and some unto dishonor. If a man therefore purge himself from these, he shall be a vessel unto honor, sanctified, and meet for the master's use, and prepared unto every good work.

Flee youthful passions; and follow after righteousness, faith, love, peace, with them that call on the Lord out of a pure heart.

But foolish and ignorant questionings refuse, knowing that they gender strifes. And the servant of the Lord must not strive; but be gentle toward all, apt to teach, forbearing, in meekness correcting them that oppose themselves; if perchance God may give them repentance to the knowledge of the truth; and they may recover themselves out of the snare of the devil, having been taken captive by him unto his will.

This know also, that in the last days grievous times shall come. For men shall be lovers of self, lovers of money, boastful, haughty, railers, disobedient to parents, unthankful, unholy, without natural affection, implacable, slanderers, without self-control, fierce, no lovers of good, traitors, headstrong, puffed up, lovers of pleasure rather than lovers of God; holding a form of godliness, but having denied the power thereof: from these also turn away.

For of these are they that creep into houses, and take captive silly women laden with sins, led away by divers desires, ever learning, and never able to come to the knowledge of the truth.

LOYALTY TO THE SCRIPTURES

All that would live godly in Christ Jesus shall suffer persecution. But evil men and impostors shall grow worse and worse, deceiving, and being deceived. But abide thou in the things which thou hast learned and hast been assured of, knowing of whom thou hast learned them; and that from a child thou hast known the holy scriptures, which are able to make thee wise unto salvation through faith which is in Christ Jesus.

Every scripture inspired by God is also profitable for doctrine, for reproof, for correction, for instruction which is in righteousness: that the man of God may be complete, furnished completely unto every good work.

I charge thee in the sight of God, and of Christ Jesus, who shall judge the living and the dead, and by his appearing and his kingdom: Preach the word; be urgent in season, out of season; reprove, rebuke, exhort, with all longsuffering and teaching.

For the time will come when they will not endure the sound doctrine; but having itching ears will heap to themselves teachers after their own desires; and will turn away their ears from the truth, and turn aside to fables.

But be thou sober in all things, endure afflictions, do the work of an evangelist, fulfil thy ministry.

"TRE FONTANE"—THE THREE FOUNTAINS

Tradition has it that the Apostle Paul was beheaded by the side of the ancient road running southward from Rome. Hence the presence here of these three churches to commemorate the death of the Apostle. In one of these churches are three fountains said to have sprung forth miraculously at the time of Paul's execution. A modern altar decorated with a bas-relief of the head of Saint Paul has been erected over each of the three fountains.

UNCONQUERABLE FAITH

I am now ready to be offered, and the time of my departure is at hand. I have fought a good fight, I have finished my course, I have kept the faith. Henceforth there is laid up for me a crown of righteousness, which the Lord, the righteous judge, will give me at that day; and not to me only, but to all them also that love his appearing.

At my first defense no one took my part, but all men forsook me: I pray God that it may not be laid to their account. But the Lord stood by me, and strengthened me; that through me the message might be fully proclaimed, and that all the Gentiles might hear; and I was delivered out of the mouth of the lion.

The Lord will deliver me from every evil work, and will save me unto his heavenly kingdom: to whom be the glory forever and ever. Amen.

The Letter to Titus

PERSONAL GREETINGS

Paul, a servant of God, and an apostle of Jesus Christ, according to the faith of God's elect, and the knowledge of the truth which is according to godliness, in hope of eternal life; to Titus my true child after a common faith: Grace and peace from God the Father and Christ Jesus our Saviour.

THE QUALIFICATIONS OF ELDERS

For this cause left I thee in Crete, that thou shouldst set in order the things that were wanting, and appoint elders in every city, as I gave thee charge; if any man is blameless, the husband of one wife, having children that believe, who are not accused of riot or unruly. For a bishop must be blameless, as God's steward; not self-willed, not soon angry, no brawler, no striker, not greedy of filthy lucre; but given to hospitality, a lover of good, sober-minded, just, holy, temperate; holding to the faithful word which is according to the teaching, that he may be able both to exhort in the sound doctrine and to convict the gainsayers.

For there are many unruly men, vain talkers and deceivers, whose mouths must be stopped; men who overthrow whole houses, teaching things which they ought not, for filthy lucre's sake. One of themselves, a prophet of their own, said: "Cretans are always liars, evil beasts, idle gluttons."

This testimony is true. Wherefore reprove them sharply, that they may be sound in the faith, not giving heed to Jewish fables, and commandments of men who turn away from the truth. To the pure all things are pure; but to them that are defiled and unbelieving nothing is pure; but both their mind and conscience are defiled. They profess that they know God; but by their works they deny him, being abominable, and disobedient, and unto every good work reprobate.

THE PROPER BEHAVIOR FOR CHRISTIANS

But speak thou the things which befit the sound doctrine: that aged men be temperate, grave, sober-minded, sound in faith, in love, in patience; that aged women likewise be reverent in demeanor, not slanderers, not given to much wine, teachers of that which is good; that they may train the young women to love their husbands, to love their children, to be sober-minded, chaste, workers at home, kind, being in subjection to their own husbands, that the word of God be not blasphemed.

The younger men likewise exhort to be sober-minded: in all things showing thyself an example of good works; in thy doctrine showing uncorruptness, gravity, sound speech, that cannot be condemned; that he that is of the contrary part may be ashamed, having no evil thing to say of us.

Exhort servants to be in subjection to their own masters, and to be well-pleasing to them in all things; not gainsaying; not purloining; but showing all good fidelity; that they may adorn the doctrine of God our Saviour in all things.

A SUMMARY OF THE GOSPEL

For the grace of God that bringeth salvation hath appeared to all men, teaching us that, denying ungodliness and worldly desires, we should live soberly, righteously, and godly, in this present world; looking for that blessed hope and the glorious appearing of the great God and our Saviour Jesus Christ; who gave himself for us, that he might redeem us from all iniquity, and purify unto himself a people for his own possession, zealous of good works.

THE EMPEROR NERO

It was under Nero that both Paul and Peter suffered death. This emperor, while by no means the worst in the history of Rome, certainly stands in the popular mind for unbridled lust and cruelty. Though taught in his youth by the philosopher Seneca, on coming to power he forgot the maxims of his tutor and made his own pleasure and aggrandizement his sole object of government. The old story that he set Rome on fire, and then fiddled during the burning while he sang the Homeric song of the sack of Troy, is no longer credited as history; but there is no denying the fact that the blame for that same fire was laid upon the Christians, possibly at his instigation, and that the first Christian persecution was ordered by him. While Paul suffered death outside the city, Peter is said to have been executed in Nero's own circus, at a spot now marked by the obelisk in front of Saint Peter's Church.

OTHER CHRISTIAN DUTIES

Put them in mind to be in subjection to rulers, to authorities, to be obedient, to be ready unto every good work, to speak evil of no man, not to be contentious, to be gentle, showing all meekness toward all men.

For we also once were foolish, disobedient, deceived, serving various passions and pleasures, living in malice and envy, hateful, hating one another. But when the kindness and love of God our Saviour toward man appeared, not by works of righteousness which we have done, but according to his mercy he saved us, through the washing of regeneration and renewing of the Holy Spirit, which he shed on us abundantly, through Christ Jesus our Saviour; that, being justified by his grace, we might be made heirs according to the hope of eternal life.

SALUTATIONS

All that are with me salute thee. Salute them that love us in faith.

Grace be with you all. Amen.

THE SAINTS

Look, what a company of constellations!
    Say, can the sky so many lights contain?
Hath the great earth these endless generations?
    Are there so many purified through pain?

These through all glow and eminence of glory
    Cry for a brighter, who delayeth long;
Star unto star the everlasting story
    Peals in a mystic sanctity of song.

Witness the hour when many saints assembled
    Waited the Spirit, and the Spirit came!
Ay, with hearts tremulous and bones that trembled,
    Ay, with cleft tongues, the Holy Ghost, and flame.

Witness the men whom with a word He gaineth—
    Bold who were base, and voiceful who were dumb:
Battle, I know, so long as life remaineth,
    Battle for all; but these have overcome.

Witness the women, of his children sweetest;
    Scarcely earth seeth them, but earth shall see.
Thou in their woe thine agony completest,
    Christ, and their solitude is nigh to thee.

What is this psalm from pitiable places,
    Glad where the messengers of peace have trod?
Whose are these beautiful and holy faces
    Lit with their loving and aflame with God?

Eager and faint, impassionate and lonely,
    These in their hour shall prophesy again:
This is His will who hath endured, and only
    Sendeth the promise where He sends the pain.

Ay, unto these distributeth the Giver
    Sorrow and sanctity, and loves them well,
Grants them a power and passion to deliver
    Hearts from the prison house and souls from hell.

—*F. W. H. Myers*

CHRISTIAN WORSHIP

Metropolitan Museum of Art

"MY SOUL DOTH MAGNIFY THE LORD"
From a sculpture by Antonio Rosellino

CHRISTIAN HYMNS

THE ANGEL'S MESSAGE

HE shall be great,
And shall be called the Son of the Highest:
The Lord God shall give unto him the throne of his father
    David:
He shall reign over the house of Jacob forever;
And of his kingdom there shall be no end.

THE CHRISTMAS HYMN

An Angelic Chorus

Glory to God in the highest!
And on earth peace, good will toward men

THE MAGNIFICAT

A Song by Mary

My soul doth magnify the Lord,[44]
And my spirit hath rejoiced in God my Saviour.
For he hath regarded the low estate of his handmaiden:
For, behold, from henceforth all generations shall call me
    blessed.
For he that is mighty hath done to me great things;
And holy is his name.
And his mercy is on them that fear him
From generation to generation.
He hath showed strength with his arm;
He hath scattered the proud in the imagination of their
    hearts.
He hath put down the mighty from their seats,

THE YOUNG JOHN THE BAPTIST
From a painting by Pietro Novelli

And exalted them of low degree.
He hath filled the hungry with good things;
And the rich he hath sent empty away.
He hath helped his servant Israel,
In remembrance of his mercy;
As he spoke unto our fathers,
To Abraham, and to his children forever

THE BENEDICTUS

A Song by Zacharias

Blessed be the Lord God of Israel;
For he hath visited and redeemed his people,
And hath raised up a horn of salvation for us
In the house of his servant David
(As he spoke by the mouth of his holy prophets
Who have been since the world began),
That we should be saved from our enemies,
And from the hand of all that hate us;
To perform the mercy promised to our fathers,
And to remember his holy covenant;
The oath which he swore to our father Abraham,
That he would grant unto us, that we, being delivered out
    of the hand of our enemies,
Might serve him without fear,
In holiness and righteousness before him, all the days of our
    life.

And thou, child, shalt be called the prophet of the Highest:
For thou shalt go before the face of the Lord
To prepare his ways;
To give knowledge of salvation unto his people
By the remission of their sins,
Through the tender mercy of our God;
Whereby the dayspring from on high hath visited us,

ELISABETH
From a painting by Guido Reni

To give light to them that sit in darkness and in the shadow
 of death;
To guide our feet into the way of peace.

THE NUNC DIMITTIS

A Song by Simeon

Lord, now lettest thou thy servant depart in peace
According to thy word;
For mine eyes have seen thy salvation,
Which thou hast prepared before the face of all people;
A light to lighten the Gentiles,
And the glory of thy people Israel.

A PROCESSIONAL SONG

The phrases of acclamation that were sung when Jesus entered Jerusalem are found combined in an early hymn. Perhaps this entire processional, given below, was sung as Jesus and the great company that followed him passed over the Mount of Olives.

Hosanna to the son of David!
Blessed is the kingdom of our father David, that cometh in
 the name of the Lord!
Blessed is he that cometh—the King—in the name of the
 Lord!
Peace in Heaven, and glory in the highest!
Hosanna in the highest!
From the highest heavens, send thou, now, salvation!

PRAISE TO GOD OUR SAVIOUR

When the kindness and love of God our Saviour toward man
 appeared,
Not by works of righteousness which we have done,
But according to his mercy he saved us,
Through the washing of regeneration
And renewing of the Holy Spirit,

SAINT CECILIA

From a painting by Raphael

Saint Cecilia was one of the early Roman Christians, who because of her skill in music has become the patron saint of that art. She here stands with her little organ, awaiting the divine inspiration and catching echoes from the celestial choir above. Saint Cecilia's beauty and eloquence were so effective that she converted her husband, her brothers, and even her judges; but at last she was condemned to death. The executioner sent to behead her in her own palace failed to despatch his victim with three blows, and the law forbade more; so she lived three days. The house in which she is said to have died is still shown in Rome under the church that bears her name. Her remains were first buried in the Catacomb of Saint Calixtus, but later were transferred to the church of Saint Cecilia.

Which he shed on us abundantly, through Christ Jesus our
    Saviour;
That, being justified by his grace,
We might be made heirs according to the hope of eternal life.

A HYMN OF THE FAITHFUL

If we be dead with him, we shall also live with him:
If we suffer, we shall also reign with him:
If we deny him, he also will deny us:
If we believe not, yet he abideth faithful:
He cannot deny himself.

A CALL TO THE NEW LIFE

>Awake, thou that sleepest,
>And arise from the dead,
>And Christ shall give thee light.

A CREED ABOUT JESUS IN SONG

>Great is the mystery of godliness:
>He who was manifested in the flesh,
>>Justified in the spirit,
>>>Seen of angels,
>Preached among the nations,
>>Believed on in the world,
>>>Received up in glory.

A CREED OF GOD'S CHILDREN

We know that whosoever is begotten of God sinneth not;
But he that was begotten of God keepeth himself,
And that wicked one toucheth him not.

THE BURIAL OF SAINT CECILIA
From a painting by Luis de Madrazo

But we know that we are of God,
And the whole world lieth in wickedness.
We know that the Son of God hath come,
And hath given us an understanding,
That we may know him that is true,
And we are in him that is true,
Even in his Son Jesus Christ.

THE TE DEUM

This great hymn of triumphant praise is of unknown authorship. It is not found in its present form in the New Testament, but it is wholly a mosaic of Biblical phrases and thoughts, and dates from a time at least as early as that of Saint Augustine (354–430 A.D.).

The Scriptural portions of which this ancient hymn is composed are mostly from the Psalms, the Revelation, and the Epistles to the Hebrews and the Ephesians.

We praise thee, O God,
We acknowledge thee to be the Lord;
All the earth doth worship thee, the Father everlasting.
To thee all angels cry aloud,
The heavens, and all the powers therein,
To thee cherubim and seraphim continually do cry:
"Holy, holy, holy, Lord God of Sabaoth;
Heaven and earth are full of the majesty of thy glory."
The glorious company of the apostles praise thee;
The goodly fellowship of the prophets praise thee;
The noble army of martyrs praise thee;
The holy church throughout the world doth acknowledge
      thee:
The Father, of an infinite majesty;
Thine adorable, true, and only Son;
Also the Holy Spirit, the Comforter.
Thou art the King of glory, O Christ;
Thou art the everlasting Son of the Father.
When thou tookest upon thee to deliver man,

Thou didst humble thyself to be born of a virgin.
When thou hadst overcome the sharpness of death,
Thou didst open the kingdom of heaven to all believers.

"FROM HENCEFORTH ALL GENERATIONS SHALL CALL ME BLESSED"
From a painting by Luini

Thou sittest at the right hand of God, in the glory of the Father.
We believe that thou shalt come to be our Judge.
We therefore pray thee, help thy servants, whom thou hast redeemed with thy precious blood;
Make them to be numbered with thy saints in glory everlasting.
O Lord save thy people,
And bless thy heritage;

Govern them,
And lift them up forever.
Day by day we magnify thee,
And we worship thy name ever, world without end.
Vouchsafe, O Lord, to keep us this day without sin.
O Lord, have mercy upon us, have mercy upon us;
O Lord, let thy mercy be upon us, as our trust is in thee.
O Lord, in thee have I trusted: let me never be confounded

PRAYER

Prayer is the soul's sincere desire,
    Uttered or unexpressed,
The motion of a hidden fire
    That kindles in the breast.

Prayer is the burden of a sigh,
    The falling of a tear,
The upward glancing of an eye,
    When none but God is near.

Prayer is the simplest form of speech
    That infant lips can try,
Prayer the sublimest strains that reach
    The Majesty on high.

Prayer is the contrite sinner's voice
    Returning from his ways,
While angels in their songs rejoice,
    And cry, "Behold! he prays!"

Prayer is the Christian's vital breath,
    The Christian's native air,
His watchword at the gates of death—
    He enters heaven with prayer.

The saints in prayer appear as one
    In words and deed and mind,
Where with the Father and the Son
    Sweet fellowship they find.

Nor prayer is made by man alone—
    The Holy Spirit pleads,
And Jesus, on the eternal throne,
    For sinners intercedes.

O Thou by whom we come to God—
    The Life, the Truth, the Way!
The path of prayer Thyself hast trod;
    Lord, teach us how to pray!

                —*James Montgomery*

CHRISTIAN PRAYERS

This collection of prayers is gathered chiefly from the writings of Paul, the man of prayer, who concludes his wonderful description of the complete armor of a Christian with the words, "Praying always with all prayer and supplication in the Spirit, and watching thereunto with all perseverance and supplication for all saints."

"Paul's prayers," says a great modern scholar, "are the high-water mark of the Epistles in which they occur." He must have been a holy man and a true friend of whom so much can be said. In these prayers we have the tenderest solicitude and the noblest longings anywhere expressed in his marvelous letters.

A PRAYER FOR DELIVERANCE

O LORD, thou that madest the heaven and the earth and the sea, and all that in them is: who by the Holy Spirit, by the mouth of our father David thy servant, saidst:

"Why did the Gentiles rage,
And the peoples imagine vain things?
The kings of the earth set themselves in array,
And the rulers were gathered together
Against the Lord, and against his Anointed":

for of a truth in this city against thy holy Servant Jesus, whom thou anointedst, both Herod and Pontius Pilate, with the Gentiles and the peoples of Israel, were gathered together, to do whatsoever thy hand and thy counsel foreordained to come to pass.

And now, Lord, behold their threatenings; and grant to thy servants that with all boldness they may speak thy word, while thou stretchest forth thy hand to heal; and that signs and wonders may be done through the name of thy holy Servant Jesus.[45]

SOME OF THE PRAYERS OF PAUL

A Prayer for Grace for God's People

For this cause we also, since the day we heard it, do not cease to pray and make request for you, that ye may be filled with the knowledge of his will in all spiritual wisdom and understanding, to walk worthily of the Lord unto all pleasing, bearing fruit in every good work, and increasing in the knowledge of God; strengthened with all power, according to the might of his glory, unto all patience and longsuffering with joy; giving thanks to the Father, who made us worthy to be partakers of the inheritance of the saints in light; who delivered us out of the power of darkness, and translated us into the kingdom of his dear Son; in whom we have our redemption, the forgiveness of our sins; who is the image of the invisible God, the first-born of all creation; for in him were all things created, that are in the heavens, and that are upon the earth, things visible and things invisible, whether thrones or dominions or principalities or powers; all things were created through him, and unto him: and he is before all things, and in him all things consist. And he is the head of the body, the church: who is the beginning, the first-born from the dead; that in all things he might have the preëminence.

A Prayer for Inner Strength and Vision

For this cause I bow my knees to the Father, from whom every family in heaven and earth is named, that he would grant you, according to the riches of his glory, that ye may be strengthened with power through his Spirit in the inward man; that Christ may dwell in your hearts through faith; to the end that ye, being rooted and grounded in love, may be strong to apprehend with all saints what is the breadth, and length, and depth, and height, and to know the love of Christ which passeth knowledge, that ye may be filled unto all the fulness of God.

Now to him who is able to do exceeding abundantly above all that we ask or think, according to the power that worketh in us, to him be the glory in the church and in Christ Jesus unto all generations forever and ever. Amen.

A Prayer for Vision

May the God of our Lord Jesus Christ, the Father of glory, give to you a spirit of wisdom and revelation in the knowledge of him; having the eyes of your heart enlightened, that ye may know what is the hope of his calling, what the riches of the glory of his inheritance in the saints, and what the exceeding greatness of his power toward us who believe, according to that working of the strength of his might which he wrought in Christ, when he raised him from the dead, and made him to sit at his right hand in the heavenly places, far above all rule, and authority, and power, and dominion, and every name that is named, not only in this world, but also in that which is to come: and he put all things in subjection under his feet, and gave him to be head over all things to the church, which is his body, the fulness of him that filleth all in all.

A Prayer for Sincerity and Fruitfulness

And this I pray, that your love may abound yet more and more in knowledge and all discernment; so that ye may approve the things that are excellent; that ye may be sincere and void of offense unto the day of Christ; being filled with the fruits of righteousness, which are through Jesus Christ, unto the glory and praise of God.

A Prayer for More Love

Now may our God and Father himself, and our Lord Jesus, direct our way to you: and the Lord make you to increase and abound in love one toward another, and toward all men, even as we also do toward you; to the end that he may establish your hearts unblamable in holiness before our God and Father, at the coming of our Lord Jesus with all his saints.

A Prayer to Know Christ

May their hearts be comforted, being knit together in love, and to all riches of the full assurance of understanding, that they may know the mystery of God, even Christ, in whom are all the treasures of wisdom and knowledge hidden.

A Prayer for Victorious Living

We pray always for you, that our God may count you worthy of your calling, and fulfil every desire of goodness and every work of faith, with power; that the name of our Lord Jesus may be glorified in you, and ye in him, according to the grace of our God and the Lord Jesus Christ.

A Request for Prayer

With all prayer and supplication pray always in the Spirit, and watch thereunto in all perseverance and supplication for all the saints, and on my behalf, that utterance may be given to me in opening my mouth, to make known with boldness the mystery of the gospel, for which I am an ambassador in chains; that in it I may speak boldly, as I ought to speak.

Prayers of Thanksgiving

We give thanks to God the Father of our Lord Jesus Christ, praying always for you, having heard of your faith in Christ Jesus, and of the love which ye have toward all the saints, because of the hope which is laid up for you in the heavens, whereof ye heard before in the word of the truth of the gospel, which hath come to you; even as it is also in all the world bearing fruit and increasing, as it doth in you also, since the day ye heard and knew the grace of God in truth.

Now thanks be to God, who always leadeth us in triumph[46] in Christ, and maketh manifest through us the savor of his knowledge in every place. For we are a sweet savor of Christ to God, in them that are saved, and in them that perish; to the one a savor from death unto death; and to the other a savor from life unto life.

We are bound to give thanks to God always for you, brethren beloved of the Lord, because God chose you from the beginning unto salvation in sanctification of the Spirit and belief of the truth: whereunto he called you through our gospel, to the obtaining of the glory of our Lord Jesus Christ.

BENEDICTIONS

The grace of the Lord Jesus Christ, and the love of God, and the communion of the Holy Spirit, be with you all. Amen.

To the only wise God, through Jesus Christ, be the glory forever. Amen.

Now the Lord of peace himself give you peace at all times in all ways. The Lord be with you all.

Now to the King eternal, immortal, invisible, the only God, be honor and glory forever and ever. Amen.

The peace of God, which passeth all understanding, shall guard your hearts and your thoughts in Christ Jesus.

Now the God of hope fill you with all joy and peace in believing, that ye may abound in hope, in the power of the Holy Spirit.

PHILIP
Detail from "The Last Supper" by Andrea del Sarto

Now our Lord Jesus Christ himself, and God our Father who loved us and gave us everlasting consolation and good hope through grace, comfort your hearts and establish them in every good work and word.

Now the God of patience and of consolation grant you to be of the same mind one with another according to Christ Jesus: that with one accord ye may with one mouth glorify the God and Father of our Lord Jesus Christ.

And the God of peace himself sanctify you wholly; and may your spirit and soul and body be preserved entire, without blame, at the coming of our Lord Jesus Christ.
Faithful is he that calleth you, who will also do it.

Grace be to you and peace from God the Father, and our Lord Jesus Christ, who gave himself for our sins, that he might deliver us out of this present evil world, according to the will of our God and Father: to whom be the glory forever and ever. Amen.

Blessed be the God and Father of our Lord Jesus Christ, the Father of mercies and God of all comfort; who comforteth us in all our affliction, that we may be able to comfort those who are in any affliction, through the comfort wherewith we ourselves are comforted of God.

Now to him that is able to guard you from stumbling, and to set you before the presence of his glory without blemish in exceeding joy, to the only God our Saviour, through Jesus Christ our Lord, be glory, majesty, dominion, and power, before all time, and now, and forevermore. Amen.

Blessed be the God and Father of our Lord Jesus Christ, who according to his great mercy hath caused us to be born again to a living hope by the resurrection of Jesus Christ from the dead, to an inheritance incorruptible, and undefiled, and that fadeth not away, reserved in heaven for you, who by the power of God are guarded through faith to a salvation ready to be revealed in the last time.

The God of all grace, who called you to his eternal glory in Christ, after ye have suffered a little while, shall himself perfect, establish, strengthen you. To him be the dominion forever and ever. Amen.

Peace be to the brethren, and love with faith, from God the Father and the Lord Jesus Christ. Grace be with all them that love our Lord Jesus Christ in sincerity. Amen.

Now the God of peace, who brought again from the dead our Lord Jesus, that great Shepherd of the sheep, with the blood of the everlasting covenant, make you perfect in every good work to do his will, working in you that which is well-pleasing in his sight, through Jesus Christ; to whom be the glory forever and ever. Amen.

THE LAST SUPPER

From a painting by W. Y. Yeames

SACRAMENTS AND SPIRITUAL GIFTS

CHRISTIAN SACRAMENTS

Baptism

It came to pass, that, while Apollos was at Corinth, Paul having passed through the upper country came to Ephesus; and finding certain disciples, he said to them, "Have ye received the Holy Spirit since ye believed?"

They said to him, "We have not so much as heard whether there is a Holy Spirit."

And he said, "Into what then were ye baptized?"

They said, "Into John's baptism."

Then Paul said, "John baptized with the baptism of repentance, saying to the people that they should believe on him that should come after him, that is, on Jesus."

When they heard this, they were baptized into the name of the Lord Jesus. And when Paul had laid his hands upon them, the Holy Spirit came on them; and they spoke with tongues, and prophesied.

Know ye not that all we who were baptized into Christ Jesus were baptized into his death? Therefore we were buried with him through baptism into death; that like as Christ was raised from the dead through the glory of the Father, so we also might walk in newness of life.

For if we have become united with him in the likeness of his death, we shall be also in the likeness of his resurrection; knowing this, that our old self was crucified with him, that the body of sin might be done away, that so we should no longer be in bondage to sin.

Having been buried with him in baptism, therein we were also raised with him through faith in the working of God, who raised him from the dead.

In one Spirit were we all baptized into one body, whether Jews or Greeks, whether bond or free; and were all made to drink of one Spirit.

As many of you as were baptized into Christ put on Christ.

What shall they do who are baptized for the dead? If the dead are not raised at all, why then are they baptized for them?

The Lord's Supper

I received of the Lord that which also I delivered to you, that the Lord Jesus, the same night in which he was betrayed, took bread; and when he had given thanks, he broke it, and said, "Take, eat; this is my body, which is broken for you: this do in remembrance of me."

After the same manner also he took the cup, when he had supped, saying, "This cup is the new covenant in my blood: this do ye, as often as ye drink it, in remembrance of me. For as often as ye eat this bread, and drink this cup, ye do show the Lord's death till he come."

Wherefore whosoever shall eat this bread, and drink this cup of the Lord, unworthily, shall be guilty of the body and blood of the Lord.

But let a man examine himself, and so let him eat of that bread, and drink of that cup. For he that eateth and drinketh unworthily, eateth and drinketh judgment to himself, not discerning the Lord's body. For this cause many are weak and sickly among you, and many sleep.

"LORD, I AM NOT WORTHY"
From a painting by Martin Feuerstein

The cup of blessing which we bless, is it not a communion
of the blood of Christ?
The bread which we break, is it not a communion of the
body of Christ?

Seeing that we, who are many, are one bread, one body; for we all partake of the one bread.

"SPEAKING WITH TONGUES" AND PROPHESYING

The Comparative Value of These

Follow after love; yet desire earnestly spiritual gifts, but rather that ye may prophesy. For he that speaketh in a tongue speaketh not to men, but to God: for no man understandeth; but in the spirit he speaketh mysteries. But he that prophesieth speaketh to men edification, and exhortation, and comfort. He that speaketh in a tongue edifieth himself; but he that prophesieth edifieth the church.

Now I would have you all speak with tongues, but rather that ye should prophesy: and greater is he that prophesieth than he that speaketh with tongues, except he interpret, that the church may receive edifying.

But now, brethren, if I come to you speaking with tongues, what shall I profit you, unless I speak to you either by way of revelation, or of knowledge, or of prophesying, or of doctrine? Even things without life, giving a voice, whether pipe or harp, if they give not a distinction in the sounds, how shall it be known what is piped or harped? For if the trumpet give an uncertain voice, who shall prepare himself for war? So also ye, unless ye utter by the tongue speech easy to be understood, how shall it be known what is spoken? for ye will be speaking into the air.

There are, it may be, so many kinds of voices in the world, and no kind is without signification. If then I know not the meaning of the voice, I shall be to him that speaketh a barbarian, and he that speaketh will be a barbarian to me. So also ye, since ye are zealous of spiritual gifts, seek that ye may abound unto the edifying of the church. Wherefore let him that speaketh in a tongue pray that he may interpret.

Paul's own Practice

If I pray in a tongue, my spirit prayeth, but my understanding is unfruitful. What is it then?

I will pray with the spirit, and I will pray with the understanding also:
I will sing with the spirit, and I will sing with the understanding also.

Else if thou bless with the spirit, how shall he that filleth the place of the unlearned say the Amen at thy giving of thanks, seeing he knoweth not what thou sayest? For thou verily givest thanks well, but the other is not edified.

I thank God, I speak with tongues more than you all: yet in the church I would rather speak five words with my understanding, that I might instruct others also, than ten thousand words in a tongue.

Paul's Advice as to the Use of "Tongues" in Religious Meetings

Brethren, be not children in mind: yet in malice be ye babes, but in mind be men.

In the law it is written, "By men of strange tongues and by the lips of strangers will I speak to this people; and not even thus will they hear me, saith the Lord." Wherefore tongues are for a sign, not to them that believe, but to the unbelieving: but prophesying is for a sign, not to the unbelieving, but to them that believe.

If therefore the whole church be assembled together, and all speak with tongues, and there come in men unlearned, or unbelieving, will they not say that ye are mad? But if all prophesy, and there come in one unbelieving, or one unlearned, he is reproved by all, he is judged by all; the secrets of his heart are made manifest; and so falling down on his face he will worship God, and declare that God is among you indeed.

What is it then, brethren? when ye come together, every one of you hath a psalm, hath a teaching, hath a tongue, hath a revelation, hath an interpretation. Let all things be done unto edifying.

If any man speak in a tongue, let it be by two, or at the most three, and that in turn; and let one interpret. But if there be no interpreter, let him keep silence in the church; and let him speak to himself, and to God. Let the prophets speak by two or three, and let the others discern. But if a revelation be made to another sitting by, let the first keep silence. For ye all can prophesy one by one, that all may learn, and all may be exhorted; and the spirits of the prophets are subject to the prophets. For God is not a God of confusion, but of peace.

The Prophesying of Women

As in all churches of the saints, let the women keep silence in the churches: for it is not permitted to them to speak; but let them be in subjection, as also saith the law. And if they would learn anything, let them ask their own husbands at home; for it is shameful for a woman to speak in the church. What! was it from you that the word of God went forth? or came it to you alone?

Summary of the Counsel

If any man thinketh himself to be a prophet, or spiritual, let him take knowledge of the things that I write to you, that they are the commandment of the Lord. But if any man is ignorant, let him be ignorant.

Wherefore, my brethren, desire earnestly to prophesy, and forbid not to speak with tongues. But let all things be done decently and in order.[47]

THE APOCALYPSE

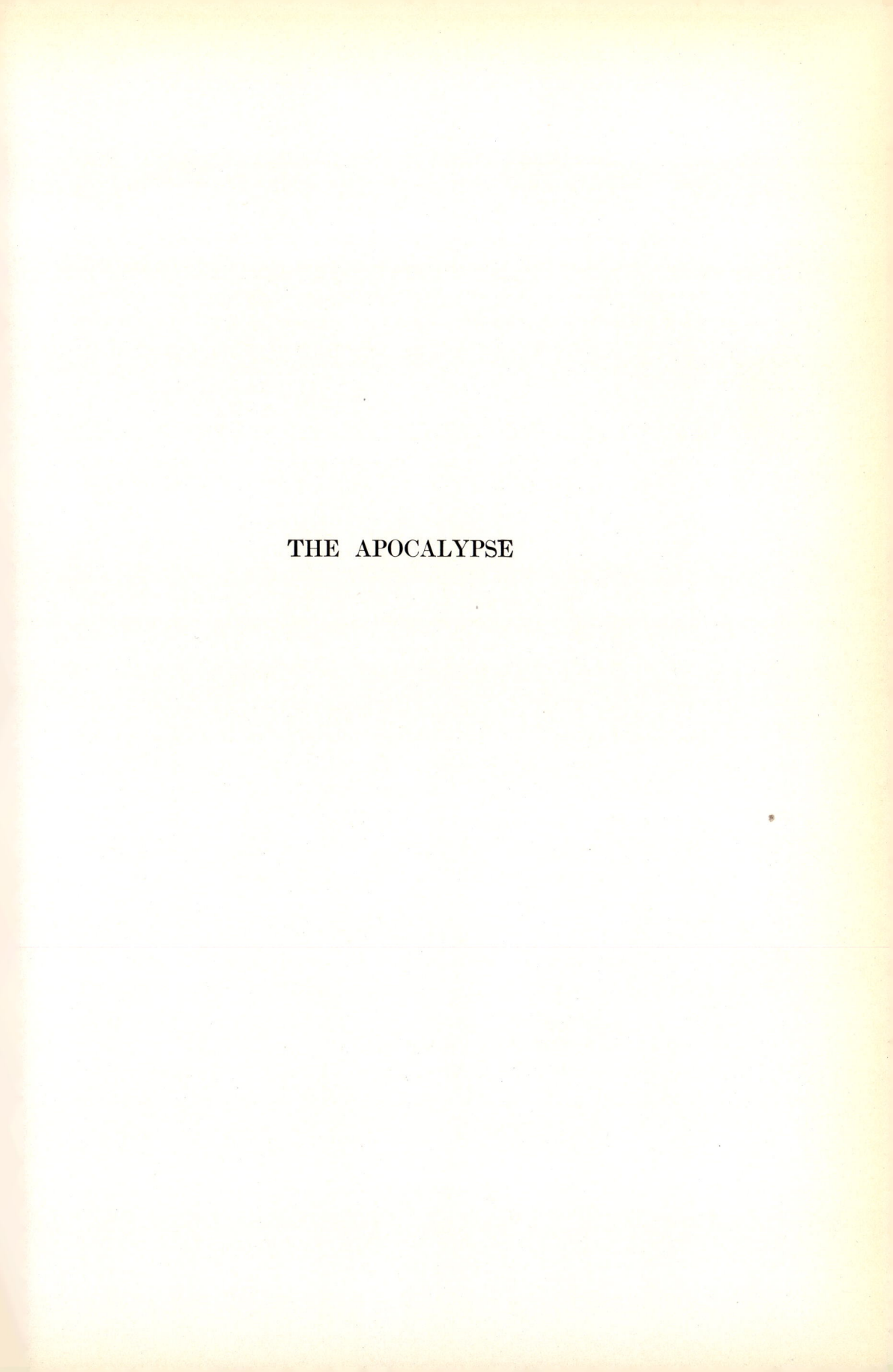

THE REVELATION

WE come now to the climax of the inspired word. Not only does this "revelation" to John contain visions of the things toward which all hearts yearn, but within it, we are told, our glorified Lord unfolds the book of human destiny. It was written during the reign of one of the persecuting Roman emperors, for the benefit of the harassed churches, regarding "the things which must shortly come to pass." This volume contains in its purview the whole of Christian history, past and present, and prophesies things yet to be. To those who faced martyrdom, it foretold the certainty of ultimate victory, as if that victory were close at hand. To us, in easier days, it still foretells such victory.

The Revelation leads our thoughts from experience to expectation, from things as they are to things as they should be. Its title might have been "The Holy War," a title which John Bunyan used, for its theme is the perpetual conflict of the Son of Man with incarnate wickedness. Its purpose is the assurance of the coming of an eternal actuality, the New Jerusalem.

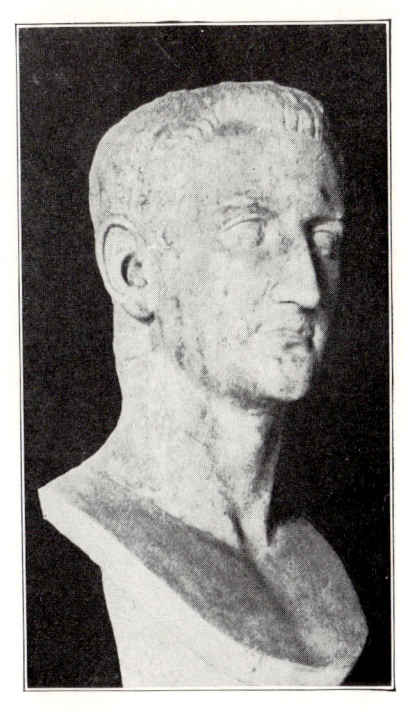

THE EMPEROR DOMITIAN

The early emperors and Roman officials persecuted sporadically and locally, but under Domitian there was a serious attempt on the part of the Roman government to stamp out what was believed to be a dangerous organization. This persecution was especially severe in Asia Minor, and is reflected in the writing of the Book of Revelation.

Sometimes the state of the world seems so hopeless that men can see no solution to its problems through the agencies of gradual betterment, but only through catastrophe. In such days apocalypses are written. They declare that some new force must come into human affairs if they are ever to be straightened out. In the Revelation, that new Life is the glorious Figure with whom the vision opens, who is called the Lamb of God, the Lion of the tribe of Judah, the King of kings. This is "the Revelation of Jesus Christ," who is the Lord of the embattled Church and the bringer of the eternal victory.

It is not within the purpose of this edition of the Scriptures to enter the field of interpretation, least of all of a book concerning which reverent Christians have so thoroughly differed. The great message is here set forth and arranged under its principal divisions, so that whosoever reads may readily catch the thread of thought and "have a strong consolation, having fled for refuge to lay hold upon the hope set before us, which hope we have as an anchor of the soul, both sure and steadfast, and which entereth into that within the veil."

THE REVELATION TO JOHN
PROLOGUE

THE Revelation[48] of Jesus Christ which God gave to him to show to his servants, even the things which must shortly come to pass: and he sent and signified it by his angel to his servant John; who bore witness of the word of God, and of the testimony of Jesus Christ, even of all things that he saw.

Blessed is he that readeth, and they that hear the words of the prophecy, and keep the things which are written therein: for the time is at hand.

DEDICATION

John to the seven churches which are in Asia: Grace to you and peace, from him who is and who was and who is to come, and from the seven Spirits who are before his throne;

And from Jesus Christ, who is the faithful witness,
The first-born of the dead,
And the ruler of the kings of the earth.
Unto him who loveth us,
And loosed us from our sins by his blood;
And he made us to be a kingdom, to be priests to his God
 and Father;
To him be the glory and the dominion forever and ever.

THE VISION OF THE SON OF MAN

I John, your brother and partaker with you in the tribulation and kingdom and patience which are in Jesus, was in the isle that is called Patmos, for the word of God and the

OLD PERGAMUM

These buildings of the Byzantine age are within the area of the city of Pergamum, and may well stand for the church mentioned in the Book of Revelation. The circular one is the church of Saint Antipas, named after the "faithful witness who was slain among you." It is built among the ruins of the great Library of Pergamum, which once contained 200,000 rolls, or volumes. The name "Satan's Seat" has been given to the mountain behind the town, and it may indeed have been the Temple of Rome and Augustus, built on the summit, which the Revelator had in mind when he used the phrase "where Satan's seat is"—for it was in the presence of the statue of Augustus in that temple that the test was made to detect whether a man was or was not a Christian.

testimony of Jesus. I was in the Spirit on the Lord's day, and I heard behind me a great voice, as of a trumpet, saying: "I am Alpha and Omega, the first and the last: and what thou seest, write in a book, and send it to the seven churches which are in Asia; to Ephesus, and to Smyrna, and to Pergamum, and to Thyatira, and to Sardis, and to Philadelphia, and to Laodicea."

And I turned to see the voice that spoke with me. And having turned I saw seven golden candlesticks; and in the midst of the candlesticks one like a son of man, clothed with a garment down to the foot, and girt about at the breasts with a golden girdle. His head and his hair were white as white wool, white as snow; and his eyes were as a flame of fire; and his feet like burnished brass, as if it had been refined in a furnace; and his voice as the voice of many waters. And he had in his right hand seven stars: and out of his mouth proceeded a sharp two-edged sword: and his countenance was as the sun shineth in his strength.

And when I saw him, I fell at his feet as one dead. And he laid his right hand upon me, saying, "Fear not; I am the first and the last, and the Living one; and I was dead, and behold, I am alive forevermore, and I have the keys of death and of Hades.

"Write therefore the things which thou sawest, and the things which are, and the things which shall come to pass hereafter; the mystery of the seven stars which thou sawest in my right hand, and the seven golden candlesticks. The seven stars are the angels of the seven churches: and the seven candlesticks are seven churches."

Having been intrusted with solemn messages of warning and encouragement to the seven churches, and with promises to those who are victorious, the prophet is given a second vision.

THE VISION OF THE CREATOR AND THE REDEEMER IN GLORY

After these things I saw, and, behold, a door opened in heaven, and the first voice which I heard, a voice as of a trumpet speaking with me, one saying, "Come up hither, and I will show thee the things which must come to pass hereafter."

Straightway I was in the Spirit: and behold, there was a throne set in heaven, and one sitting upon the throne; and he that sat was to look upon like a jasper stone and a sardius:

and there was a rainbow round about the throne, like an emerald to look upon. And round about the throne were twenty-four thrones: and upon the thrones I saw twenty-four elders sitting, arrayed in white garments; and on their heads crowns of gold. And out of the throne proceeded lightnings and voices and thunders. And there were seven lamps of fire burning before the throne, which are the seven Spirits of God; and before the throne, as it were a glassy sea like crystal: and in the midst of the throne, and round about the throne, four living creatures full of eyes before and behind. And the first creature was like a lion, and the second creature like a calf, and the third creature had a face as of a man, and the fourth creature was like a flying eagle. And the four living creatures, having each one of them six wings, are full of eyes roundabout and within: and they rest not day and night, saying:

"Holy, holy, holy, Lord God Almighty,
Who was, and is, and is to come."

And when the living creatures shall give glory and honor and thanks to him that sitteth on the throne, to him that liveth forever and ever, the twenty-four elders shall fall down before him that sitteth on the throne, and shall worship him that liveth forever and ever, and shall cast their crowns before the throne, saying:

"Worthy art thou, O Lord, to receive the glory and the honor and the power:
For thou didst create all things,
And because of thy will they were, and were created."

And I saw in the right hand of him that sat on the throne a book written within and on the back, close sealed with seven seals. And I saw a strong angel proclaiming with a great voice, "Who is worthy to open the book, and to loose the seals thereof?" And no one in the heaven, or on the earth, or under the earth, was able to open the book, or to look thereon.

And I wept much, because no one was found worthy to open the book, or to look thereon. And one of the elders saith to me, "Weep not: behold, the Lion that is of the tribe of Judah, the Root of David, hath overcome to open the book and the seven seals thereof."

And I saw in the midst of the throne and of the four living creatures, and in the midst of the elders, a lamb standing, as though it had been slain, having seven horns, and seven eyes, which are the seven Spirits of God, sent forth into all the earth.

And he came, and took the book out of the right hand of him that sat on the throne.

And when he had taken the book, the four living creatures and the twenty-four elders fell down before the Lamb, having each one a harp, and golden bowls full of incense, which are the prayers of the saints.

And they sing a new song, saying:

"Worthy art thou to take the book,
And to open the seals thereof:
For thou wast slain,
And didst purchase unto God with thy blood
Men of every tribe, and tongue,
And people, and nation,
And madest them to be unto our God a kingdom and priests;
And they reign upon the earth."

And I saw, and I heard a voice of many angels round about the throne and the living creatures and the elders; and the number of them was ten thousand times ten thousand, and thousands of thousands; saying with a great voice:

"Worthy is the Lamb that hath been slain
To receive the power, and riches,
And wisdom, and might, and honor,
And glory, and blessing."

And every created thing which is in the heaven, and on the earth, and under the earth, and in the sea, and all things that are in them, heard I saying:

> "Blessing, and honor, and glory, and power
> Be unto him that sitteth upon the throne,
> And unto the Lamb forever and ever."

And the four living creatures said, "Amen." And the twenty-four elders fell down and worshiped.

THE VISION OF THE FOUR HORSEMEN
Conquest, War, Famine, and Pestilence

And I saw when the Lamb opened one of the seven seals, and I heard one of the four living creatures saying as with a voice of thunder, "Come and see!"

And I saw, and behold, a white horse, and he that sat thereon had a bow; and a crown was given to him: and he went forth conquering, and to conquer.

When he opened the second seal, I heard the second living creature saying, "Come and see!"

And another horse came forth, a red horse: and power was given to him that sat thereon to take peace from the earth, and that they should slay one another: and there was given to him a great sword.

When he opened the third seal, I heard the third living creature saying, "Come and see!"

And I saw, and behold, a black horse; and he that sat thereon had a balance in his hand.

And I heard as it were a voice in the midst of the four living creatures saying, "A measure of wheat for a penny, and three measures of barley for a penny; and the oil and the wine hurt thou not."

When he opened the fourth seal, I heard the voice of the fourth living creature saying, "Come and see!"

THE RIDER ON THE WHITE HORSE
From a painting by George F. Watts

"And I saw, and behold, a white horse, and he that sat thereon had a bow; and a crown was given to him: and he went forth conquering, and to conquer."

THE RIDER ON THE PALE HORSE
From a drawing by William Blake
Surely this artist has caught the terror and the energy of that strange and fearful vision when the angel unrolls the scroll to keep pace with the fearful events that are taking place.

And I saw, and behold, a pale horse: and he that sat upon him, his name was Death; and Hades followed with him. And authority was given to them over the fourth part of the earth, to kill with sword, and with famine, and with pestilence, and by the wild beasts of the earth.

One after another the Lamb opens the Seven Seals. At the opening of the sixth seal, the prophet beholds the following vision.

THE VISION OF COMING VENGEANCE FOR THE MARTYRS

When he opened the fifth seal, I saw underneath the altar the souls of them that had been slain for the word of God, and for the testimony which they held[49]: and they cried with a great voice, saying, "How long, O Master, the holy and true, dost thou not judge and avenge our blood on them that dwell on the earth?"

And there was given them, to each one, a white robe; and it was said to them, that they should rest yet for a little time, until their fellow-servants also and their brethren, that should be killed even as they were, should be fulfilled.

And I saw when he opened the sixth seal, and there was a great earthquake; and the sun became black as sackcloth of hair, and the whole moon became as blood; and the stars of the heaven fell to the earth, as a fig tree casteth her unripe figs when she is shaken by a mighty wind. And the heaven was removed as a scroll when it is rolled up; and every mountain and island was moved out of its place.

And the kings of the earth, and the princes, and the chief captains, and the rich, and the strong, and every bondman and freeman, hid themselves in the caves and in the rocks of the mountains; and said to the mountains and rocks, "Fall on us, and hide us from the face of him that sitteth on the throne, and from the wrath of the Lamb: for the great day of their wrath hath come; and who is able to stand?"

SAINT JOHN THE EVANGELIST

From a painting by Carlo Dolci

Saint John is here represented as a young man, which accords with the tradition that he was the youngest of the Twelve. He holds the book which represents his Gospel and the quill with which he is about to write. By his side is his emblem, the eagle. Some say that, as the eagle is able to soar higher than any other and to gaze straight at the sun, so John in his Gospel has reached the loftiest conception of Christ's nature and mission, and gazes full into the heart of the Sun of Righteousness.

Before the last seal is opened, the prophet is given a vision of the servants of God, both those from Israel and from all other nations.

THE VISION OF THE SERVANTS OF GOD IN GLORY

After these things I saw, and behold, a great multitude, which no man could number, out of every nation, and of all tribes, and peoples, and tongues, standing before the throne and before the Lamb, arrayed in white robes, and palms in their hands; and they cry with a great voice, saying:

>"Salvation unto our God
>Who sitteth on the throne,
>And unto the Lamb!"

And all the angels were standing round about the throne, and about the elders and the four living creatures; and they fell before the throne on their faces, and worshiped God, saying:

>"Amen:
>>Blessing, and glory, and wisdom,
>>And thanksgiving, and honor,
>>And power, and might,
>>Be unto our God forever and ever.
>>Amen."

And one of the elders answered, saying to me, "These who are arrayed in white robes, who are they, and whence came they?"

And I say to him, "My lord, thou knowest."
And he said to me:

"These are they who come out of the great tribulation,
And they washed their robes,
And made them white in the blood of the Lamb.
Therefore are they before the throne of God,
And they serve him day and night in his temple;

And he that sitteth on the throne shall spread his tabernacle
    over them.
They shall hunger no more,
Neither thirst any more;
Neither shall the sun strike upon them, nor any heat:
For the Lamb who is in the midst of the throne shall be
    their shepherd,
And shall guide them unto fountains of waters of life:
And God shall wipe away every tear from their eyes."

After the seventh seal had been opened, angels, standing before the throne of God, sounded in turn seven trumpets, each of which brought a portent. Before the last was sounded, the prophet saw himself again before the throne, and thereupon was given a vision of the war in heaven.

There followed great voices in heaven, and they said:

"The kingdom of the world hath become the kingdom of our
    Lord, and of his Christ;
And he shall reign forever and ever." [50]

And the four and twenty elders, who sit before God on their thrones, fell upon their faces and worshiped God, saying:

"We give thee thanks, O Lord God Almighty,
Who art, and wast, and art to come;
Because thou hast taken thy great power, and didst reign.
The nations were wroth,
And thy wrath came,
And the time of the dead to be judged,
And the time to give reward to thy servants the prophets,
And to the saints, and to them who fear thy name, the
    small and the great;
And to destroy those who destroy the earth."

Then there was opened the temple of God that is in heaven; and there was seen in his temple the ark of his covenant; and there followed lightnings, and voices, and thunders, and an earthquake, and great hail.

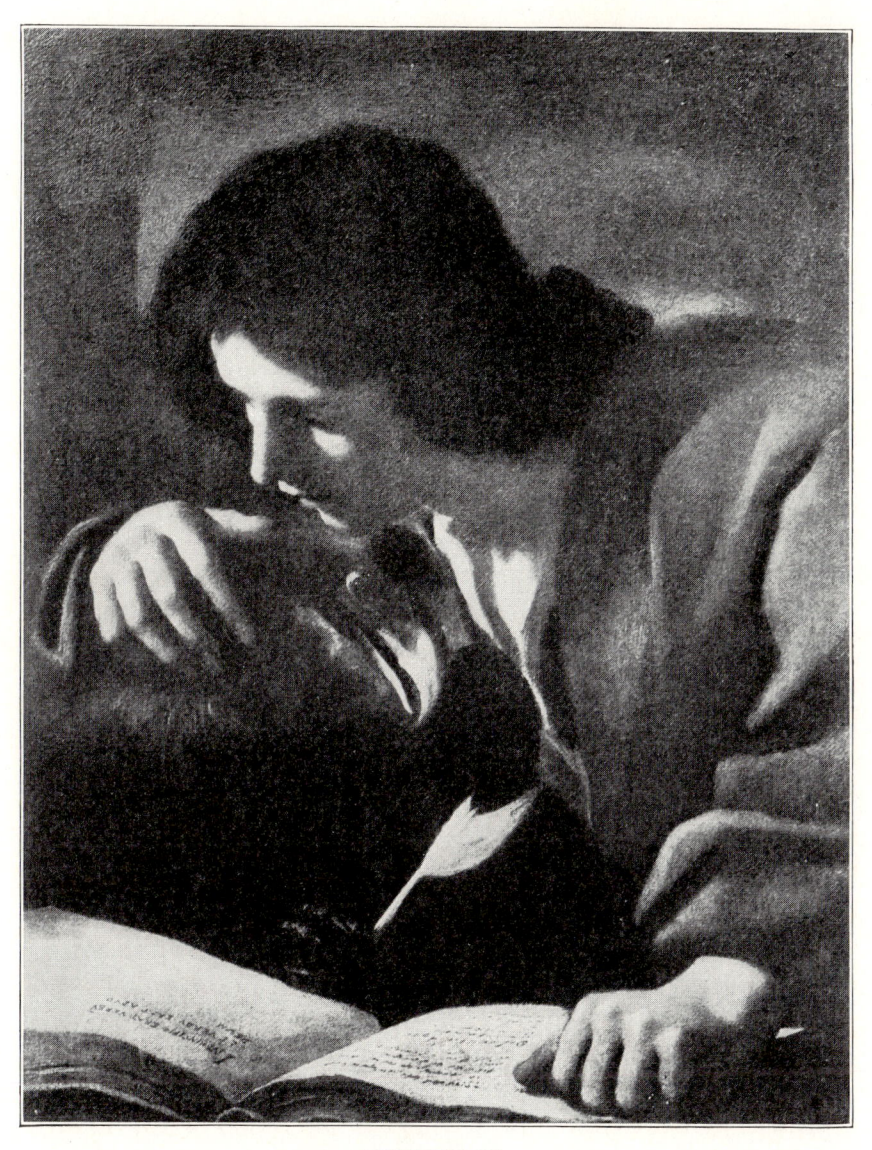

SAINT JOHN
From a painting by Il Guercino

The Evangelist is here gazing with rapture upon the first verse of his Gospel, which he has just inscribed in the book—as if the meaning of it quite transcended his own powers of comprehension, and yet somehow expressed what his heart knew to be true. John's hand rests upon the neck and body of his emblem, the eagle.

THE VISION OF THE WAR IN HEAVEN

And a great sign was seen in heaven: a woman arrayed with the sun, and the moon under her feet, and upon her head a crown of twelve stars; and to her a child was born.

There was seen another sign in heaven: and behold, a great red dragon, having seven heads and ten horns, and upon his heads seven diadems. And his tail drew the third part of the stars of heaven, and did cast them to the earth: and the dragon stood before the woman to devour her child.

Now her child was a son, a man-child, who is to rule all the nations with a rod of iron: and her child was caught up to God, and to his throne. And the woman fled into the wilderness, where she hath a place prepared by God, that there they may nourish her a thousand two hundred and threescore days.

And there was war in heaven: Michael and his angels going forth to war with the dragon; and the dragon warred and his angels; and they prevailed not, neither was their place found any more in heaven. And the great dragon was cast down, the old serpent, he that is called the Devil and Satan, the deceiver of the whole world; he was cast down to the earth, and his angels were cast down with him.

And I heard a great voice in heaven saying:

"Now hath come the salvation, and the power,
And the kingdom of our God,
And the authority of his Christ;
For the accuser of our brethren is cast down,
Who accuseth them before our God day and night.
And they overcame him because of the blood of the Lamb,
And because of the word of their testimony;
And they loved not their life even unto death
Therefore rejoice, O heavens,
And ye that dwell in them!
Woe for the earth and for the sea!

> Because the devil hath gone down unto you, having great wrath,
> Knowing that he hath but a short time."

When the dragon saw that he was cast down to the earth, he persecuted the woman that had the man-child.

And there were given to the woman the two wings of the great eagle, that she might fly into the wilderness to her place, where she is nourished for a time, and times, and half a time, from the face of the serpent.

The serpent cast out of his mouth after the woman water as a river, that he might cause her to be carried away by the stream. But the earth helped the woman, and the earth opened her mouth and swallowed up the river which the dragon cast out of his mouth.

And the dragon became wroth with the woman, and went away to make war with the rest of her family, who keep the commandments of God, and hold the testimony of Jesus.

THE VISION OF THE LAMB

Then I saw, and behold, the Lamb standing on mount Zion, and with him a hundred and forty-four thousand, having his name, and the name of his Father, written on their foreheads. And I heard a voice from heaven, as the voice of many waters, and as the voice of a great thunder: and the voice which I heard was as the voice of harpers harping with their harps: and they sang as it were a new song before the throne, and before the four living creatures and the elders: and no man could learn the song save the hundred and forty-four thousand, even they that had been purchased out of the earth.

> These are they that follow the Lamb whithersoever he goeth.
> These were purchased from among men,
> To be the firstfruits unto God and unto the Lamb.
> And in their mouth was found no lie:
> They are without blemish.

I saw another angel flying in mid heaven, having eternal good tidings to proclaim to them that dwell on the earth, and to every nation and tribe and tongue and people; and he saith

THE ETERNAL SONG OF THE VICTORIOUS
From a painting by Alphonse Osbert

with a great voice, "Fear God, and give him glory; for the hour of his judgment hath come: and worship him that made the heaven and the earth and sea and fountains of waters!"

And another, a second angel, followed, saying, "Babylon is fallen, is fallen, that great city!"

And I heard a voice from heaven, saying: "Write:

"'Blessed are the dead who die in the Lord from henceforth:
Yea, saith the Spirit, that they may rest from their labors;
For their works follow with them.'"

THE VISION OF THE VICTORIOUS

And I saw as it were a sea of glass mingled with fire; and them that come off victorious from the beast, and from his image, and from the number of his name, standing by the sea of glass, having harps of God. And they sing the song of Moses the servant of God, and the song of the Lamb, saying:

"Great and marvelous are thy works,
Lord God Almighty;
Righteous and true are thy ways,

THE COLOSSEUM OF ROME AT SUNSET
From a painting by Oswald Achenbach

Thou King of the ages.
Who shall not fear, O Lord,
And glorify thy name?
For thou only art holy;
For all the nations shall come and worship before thee;
For thy righteous acts have been made manifest."

Then to the prophet it was given to see the pouring forth of the seven bowls, with their portents; and afterwards he heard the doom songs over Babylon the Great, who had drunk the blood of the saints and of the martyrs of Jesus, and who had been overthrown after the outpouring of the seventh bowl.

DOOM SONGS OVER BABYLON

After these things I saw another angel coming down out of heaven, having great authority; and the earth was lightened with his glory. And he cried with a mighty voice, saying:

"Babylon the great is fallen, is fallen![51]
And hath become a habitation of demons,
And a hold of every unclean spirit,
And a hold of every unclean and hateful bird."

And I heard another voice from heaven, saying

"Come forth, my people, out of her,
That ye have no fellowship with her sins,
And that ye receive not of her plagues:
For her sins have reached even unto heaven,
And God hath remembered her iniquities.
How much soever she glorified herself
And became luxurious,
So much give her of torment and mourning:
For she saith in her heart,
'I sit a queen, and am no widow,
And shall in no wise see mourning.'
Therefore in one day shall her plagues come,

Death, and mourning, and famine;
And she shall be utterly burned with fire;
For strong is the Lord God who judged her.

"And the kings of the earth, who have lived luxuriously with her, shall weep and wail over her, when they look upon the smoke of her burning, standing afar off for the fear of her torment, saying:

"'Alas, alas, that great city Babylon,
That mighty city!
For in one hour hath thy judgment come.'

"And the merchants of the earth weep and mourn over her, for no man buyeth their merchandise any more; merchandise of gold, and silver, and precious stones, and pearls, and fine linen, and purple, and silk, and scarlet; and all thyine wood, and every vessel of ivory, and every vessel made of most precious wood, and of brass, and iron, and marble; and cinnamon, and spice, and incense, and ointment, and frankincense, and wine, and oil, and fine flour, and wheat, and cattle, and sheep, and merchandise of horses and chariots and slaves, and souls of men. The merchants of these things, who were made rich by her, shall stand afar off for the fear of her torment, weeping and mourning; saying:

"'Alas, alas, that great city,
That was arrayed in fine linen,
And purple, and scarlet,
And decked with gold,
And precious stones, and pearls!
For in one hour so great riches is made desolate!'

"And every shipmaster, and every one that saileth any whither, and mariners, and as many as gain their living by sea, stood afar off, and cried out as they looked upon the smoke of her burning, saying, 'What city is like this great city?'

THE INTERIOR OF THE COLOSSEUM, ROME

One must do a little reconstructing in the imagination in order to visualize the Colosseum as it existed in Roman times. Part of the surrounding wall and all of the marble seats and trimmings of the interior were used during the Middle Ages to construct either fortifications or churches. That accounts for the ruined appearance of the interior. In the Middle Ages, also, when Rome was torn with the feuds of noblemen, the Colosseum was used as a fortress by the family of Frangipani. They built the brick walls now partly visible in the center of the arena and partly covered up by a modern earth platform where the people are standing. All of this must be cleared away. The original lower tier of seats stopped with the circle of brick structures that bound the platform. It is necessary, therefore, to remove all of this rubbish and discover the true arena some fifteen feet lower than the present floor. The animals, which were admitted at the farther end of this arena, came by an underground passage from their cages some distance away. The emperor's box was in the center of the oval on the right. Huge awnings were stretched from flagstaffs to protect some of the more important seats from the sun. The old amphitheater is said to have held from forty to fifty thousand people. Gladiatorial shows were common here, but the martyrdom of Christians in this arena was not a frequent occurrence.

And they cast dust on their heads, and cried, weeping and mourning, saying:

" 'Alas, alas, that great city,
  Wherein all that had ships in the sea were made rich by reason of her costliness!

>   For in one hour is she made desolate.
>   Rejoice over her, thou heaven,
>   And ye saints, and ye apostles, and ye prophets;
>   For God hath judged your judgment on her.'"

And a strong angel took up a stone as it were a great millstone and cast it into the sea, saying:

> "Thus with a mighty force shall that great city Babylon be cast down, and shall be found no more at all;
> The voice of harpers and minstrels and flute-players and trumpeters shall be heard no more at all in thee;
> No craftsmen, of whatsoever craft, shall be found any more at all in thee;
> The voice of a mill shall be heard no more at all in thee;
> The light of a lamp shall shine no more at all in thee;
> The voice of the bridegroom and of the bride shall be heard no more at all in thee.
> For thy merchants were the princes of the earth;
> For with thy sorcery were all the nations deceived.
> In her was found the blood of prophets and of saints,
> And of all who have been slain upon the earth."

Then to the prophet was given a glorious vision, described in the following section.

THE VISION OF THE PREPARATIONS FOR THE MARRIAGE SUPPER OF THE LAMB

After these things I heard as it were a great voice of a great multitude in heaven, saying:

>   "Hallelujah!
>   Salvation, and glory, and power,
>   Belong to our God:
>   For true and righteous are his judgments:
>   For he hath avenged the blood of his servants."

And again they said, "Hallelujah!" and, "Her smoke goeth up forever and ever."

And the twenty-four elders and the four living creatures fell down and worshiped God that sitteth on the throne, saying, "Amen; Hallelujah!"

And a voice came forth from the throne, saying:

> "Praise our God, all ye his servants,
> Ye that fear him, both small and great."

And I heard as it were the voice of a great multitude, and as the voice of many waters, and as the voice of mighty thunderings, saying:

"Hallelujah!
For the Lord God omnipotent reigneth!
Let us be glad and rejoice,
And give honor to him!
For the marriage of the Lamb hath come,
And his wife hath made herself ready.
And to her is granted that she should array herself in fine
    linen, bright and pure.
For the fine linen is the righteous acts of the saints."

He saith to me,

"Write: 'Blessed are they who are bidden to the marriage supper of the Lamb.'"

And he saith to me,

"These are true sayings of God."

And I saw the heaven opened;
And behold, a white horse:
He that sat thereon was called Faithful and True;
And in righteousness he doth judge and make war.
His eyes are a flame of fire,
And on his head are many diadems;

He hath a name written that no one knoweth but he himself.
He is arrayed in a garment dipped in blood,
And his name is called The Word of God.
And the armies which are in heaven followed him upon white horses,
Clothed in fine linen, white and pure.
Out of his mouth proceedeth a sharp sword, that with it he should smite the nations:
He shall rule them with a rod of iron:
And he treadeth the winepress of the fierceness of the wrath of Almighty God.
And he hath on his garment and on his thigh a name written:
KING OF KINGS AND LORD OF LORDS.

And I saw an angel coming down out of heaven, having the key of the abyss and a great chain in his hand.

And he laid hold on the dragon, the old serpent, who is the Devil and Satan, and bound him for a thousand years, and cast him into the abyss, and shut it, and sealed it over him, that he should deceive the nations no more, until the thousand years should be finished: after this he must be loosed for a little time.

And I saw thrones, and they sat upon them, and judgment was given to them: and I saw the souls of them that had been beheaded for the testimony of Jesus, and for the word of God, and such as worshiped not the beast, neither his image, and received not the mark upon their forehead, and upon their hand; and they lived, and reigned with Christ a thousand years. The rest of the dead lived not until the thousand years should be finished. This is the first resurrection.

Blessed and holy is he that hath part in the first resurrection: over these the second death hath no power: but they shall be priests of God and of Christ, and shall reign with him a thousand years.

THE FALL OF GOG AND MAGOG
From a fresco by John S. Sargent

And when the thousand years are finished, Satan shall be loosed out of his prison, and shall come forth to deceive the nations which are in the four corners of the earth, Gog and Magog, to gather them together to the war: the number of whom is as the sand of the sea. And they went up over the breadth of the earth, and encircled the camp of the saints, and the beloved city: and fire came down from God out of heaven, and devoured them. And the devil that deceived them was cast into the lake of fire and brimstone, where are also the beast and the false prophet; and they shall be tormented day and night forever and ever.

Those who had been the enemies and persecutors of the saints having been overcome by the Lamb, the prophet now sees another vision.

THE VISION OF THE JUDGMENT

And I saw a great white throne,
And him that sat upon it,
From whose face the earth and the heaven fled away;
And there was found no place for them.

THE JUDGE
Detail from "The Last Judgment," by Michelangelo

This beardless young giant is a most extraordinary conception. He possesses none of the traditional characteristics which artists usually assign to Christ. The figure is instinct with energy. His left arm and hand express repudiation, and his right hand seems about to hurl upon the sinners below the judgment that his lips have pronounced. But most unusual is the fact that the face does not express anger, as most interpreters assert it does. Anger is not the

(Continued at bottom of opposite page)

I saw the dead, small and great, standing before God;
And books were opened.
And another book was opened, which is the book of life:
And the dead were judged out of the things which were written in the books,
According to their works.
The sea gave up the dead that were in it,
And death and Hades gave up the dead that were in them,
And they were judged every man according to his works.

Then death and Hades were cast into the lake of fire. And whosoever was not found written in the book of life was cast into the lake of fire.

The triumph of the Lamb being complete, and the heaven and the earth being renewed, the prophet sees a vision of the bride of the Lamb being brought to her bridegroom, now seen under the emblem of a Holy City.

THE VISION OF THE HEAVENLY JERUSALEM

I saw a new heaven and a new earth[52]: for the first heaven and the first earth had passed away; and there was no more sea.

I John saw the holy city, new Jerusalem, coming down from God out of heaven, made ready as a bride adorned for her husband. And I heard a great voice out of the throne, saying:

"Behold, the tabernacle of God is with men,
And he shall dwell with them,

---

function of a judge. Christ is merely pronouncing with distinctness and emphasis a doom the justice of which is imbedded in the moral structure of the universe. He is but the executor of the righteous judgments of heaven. That is why he pays no attention to the prayers of his mother Mary, to the fears of the saints who in a vast throng assemble on his right hand, or to the pleadings of the martyrs like Bartholomew, whose arm and hand are visible in this picture, holding the knife with which his executioners flayed him. He and his companions are those who in the Book of Revelation call from out the altar, saying, "How long, O Master, the holy and true, dost thou not judge and avenge our blood?" What drives the sinners to perdition is not the lightning or the thunder of divine anger reverberating from the throne of heaven, but the consciousness that justice demands precisely this doom.

And they shall be his peoples.
God himself shall be with them,
And be their God.
He shall wipe away all tears from their eyes;
And there shall be no more death,
Neither sorrow, nor crying;
Neither shall there be any more pain:
For the former things have passed away."

He that sat upon the throne said, "Behold, I make all things new."

And he said to me, "Write: for these words are true and faithful."

And he said to me, "They have come to pass! I am the Alpha and the Omega, the beginning and the end. I will give to him that is athirst of the fountain of the water of life freely. He that overcometh shall inherit these things; and I will be his God, and he shall be my son.

"But for the fearful, and unbelieving, and abominable, and murderers, and the vicious, and sorcerers, and idolaters, and all liars, their part shall be in the lake that burneth with fire and brimstone; which is the second death."

Then there came to me one of the seven angels who had the seven bowls full of the last seven plagues; and he talked with me, saying, "Come hither, I will show thee the bride, the Lamb's wife."

And he carried me away in the Spirit to a great and high mountain, and showed me that great city, the holy Jerusalem, descending out of heaven from God, having the glory of God: her light was like a stone most precious, even like a jasper stone, clear as crystal. It had a wall great and high, and had twelve gates, and at the gates twelve angels; and names written thereon, which are the names of the twelve tribes of the children of Israel: on the east were three gates: and on the north three gates; and on the south three gates; and on the

TOMB OF SAINT CECILIA, ROMAN CATACOMBS
From an engraving

The catacombs are huge underground excavations made in the native tufa rock of the Roman plain. The excavations consist of long galleries or streets, on each side of which niches have been cut to receive the bodies of the dead. When necessary for safety or convenience, masonry work was added, as in the picture, where one sees those huge flat bricks in the Roman style that seem to be outlasting time. In important places, the rock and these bricks were covered with a coating of plaster and were frescoed. These frescoes are the earliest specimens of Christian art, some of them dating from the second or even the first century. Specimens of these pictures in their original position are shown in this picture.

While these catacombs were originally merely cemeteries, and were used by pagans and Christians alike, they came to be associated peculiarly with Christians, because during the persecutions the Church often sought protection in them. In the early Middle Ages, all bones found in Roman catacombs were popularly supposed to be the bones of martyrs, and as such they have become cherished relics in many a European church.

west three gates. And the wall of the city had twelve foundations, and on them the names of the twelve apostles of the Lamb.

He that talked with me had for a measure a golden reed to measure the city, and the gates thereof, and the wall thereof. And the city lieth foursquare, and the length thereof is as great as the breadth; and he measured the city with the reed, twelve thousand furlongs. The length and the breadth

THE PASSING OF SOULS INTO HEAVEN
From a fresco by John S. Sargent

and the height of it are equal. And he measured the wall thereof, a hundred and forty-four cubits, according to the measure of a man, that is, of an angel.

And the building of the wall of it was of jasper: and the city was pure gold, like clear glass. The foundations of the wall of the city were adorned with all manner of precious stones. The first foundation was jasper; the second, sapphire; the third, chalcedony; the fourth, emerald; the fifth, sardonyx; the sixth, sardius; the seventh, chrysolite; the eighth, beryl; the ninth, topaz; the tenth, chrysoprase; the eleventh, jacinth; the twelfth, amethyst. And the twelve gates were twelve pearls; each one of the several gates was of one pearl: and the street of the city was pure gold, as it were transparent glass.

And I saw no temple therein:
For the Lord God Almighty
And the Lamb are the temple thereof.
The city hath no need of the sun, neither of the moon, to shine upon it:
For the glory of God did lighten it,
And the lamp thereof is the Lamb.

The nations shall walk amidst the light thereof:
The kings of the earth bring their glory into it.
The gates thereof shall not be shut at all by day
(For there shall be no night there):
They shall bring the glory and the honor of the nations
    into it.
There shall in no wise enter into it anything unclean,
Or he that maketh an abomination and a lie:
But only they that are written in the Lamb's book of life.

Then he showed me a pure river of water of life, clear as crystal, proceeding out of the throne of God and of the Lamb in the midst of the street thereof. And on this side of the river and on that was the tree of life, bearing twelve manner of fruits, yielding its fruit every month: and the leaves of the tree were for the healing of the nations.

And there shall be no curse any more: and the throne of God and of the Lamb shall be therein:

> His servants shall do him service;
> They shall see his face;
> And his name shall be on their foreheads.
> There shall be no night there;
> And they need no light of lamp,
> Neither light of sun;
> For the Lord God shall give them light:
> And they shall reign forever and ever.

And he said to me: "These sayings are faithful and true. And the Lord, the God of the spirits of the prophets, sent his angel to show to his servants the things which must shortly come to pass. Behold, I come quickly: blessed is he that keepeth the sayings of the prophecy of this book."

And I John saw these things, and heard them. And when I heard and saw, I fell down to worship before the feet of the angel who showed me these things.

THE MARTYRS IN THE CATACOMBS
From a painting by Jules Eugène Lenepveu

The catacombs were underground burying places. Niches were hewn in the solid tufa rock; the body was inserted and the marble slab placed in front. In the galleries also were chapels for worship. The palms are symbolic of martyrdom.

Then saith he to me, "See thou do it not: I am a fellow-servant with thee, and with thy brethren the prophets, and with them who keep the sayings of this book: worship God."

And he saith to me, "Seal not up the sayings of the prophecy of this book: for the time is at hand.

"He that is unrighteous, let him do unrighteousness still:
He that is filthy, let him be made filthy still:
He that is righteous, let him do righteousness still:
He that is holy, let him be made holy still."

EPILOGUE

The Message of the Son of Man to Us

Behold, I come quickly; and my reward is with me, to render to each man according as his work is. I am the Alpha and the Omega, the first and the last, the beginning and the end.

Blessed are they that wash their robes, that they may have the right to come to the tree of life, and may enter in by the gates into the city.

Outside are the dogs, and the sorcerers, and the vicious, and the murderers, and the idolaters, and every one that loveth and maketh a lie.

I Jesus have sent mine angel to testify to you these things for the churches. I am the root and the offspring of David, and the bright, the morning star.

The Spirit and the bride say, "Come!"
And let him that heareth say, "Come!"
And let him that is athirst come:
Whosoever will, let him take the water of life freely.

For I testify to every man that heareth the words of the prophecy of this book: If any man shall add to them, God shall add to him the plagues that are written in this book; and if any man shall take away from the words of the book of this prophecy, God shall take away his part from the tree of life, and out of the holy city, which are written in this book.

THE NOBLE ARMY OF THE MARTYRS
From a painting by Frederick Shields

The Closing Word and Benediction

He who testifieth these things saith, "Yea: I come quickly."

Amen: come, Lord Jesus.

The grace of the Lord Jesus be with the saints.[53] Amen.

THE HOLY CITY

O Holy City seen of John,
Where Christ, the Lamb, doth reign,
Within whose foursquare walls shall come
No night, nor need, nor pain,
And where the tears are wiped from eyes
That shall not weep again!

Hark, how from men whose lives are held
More cheap than merchandise,
From women struggling sore for bread,
From little children's cries—
There swells the sobbing human plaint
That bids thy walls arise!

Oh, shame to us who rest content
While lust and greed for gain
In street and shop and tenement

Wring gold from human pain,
And bitter lips in blind despair
Cry, "Christ hath died in vain!"

Give us, O God, the strength to build
The City that hath stood
Too long a dream, whose laws are love,
Whose ways are brotherhood,
And where the sun that shineth is
God's grace for human good.

Already in the mind of God,
That City riseth fair:
Lo, how its splendor challenges
The souls that greatly dare—
Yea, bids us seize the whole of life
And build its glory there!

—*W. Russell Bowie*

EXPLANATORY NOTES
PIONEERS OF THE FAITH

The Scallop Shell was valued in the old days as a useful household implement. It was used as a drinking vessel and as a skimmer for removing cream from milk; it was a ladle, a scoop, and a frying pan. It was so flat that it might be easily carried in the bosom, tucked in the belt, or secreted in a pocket. According to tradition, the early evangelists carried a shell to be used in baptism; hence, in the Middle Ages, shells became popular as receptacles for holy water, and, having a beautiful form, were adopted as a decorative element by the artists of the Renaissance. Crusaders and pilgrims to the Holy Land often carried a shell as a drinking cup.

The scallop shell is appropriate as a symbol for the Pioneers of the Faith, who made long journeys on foot, provided their own means of livelihood, carried the water of life to a weary world, and fostered in it the growth of a new and inspiring hope.

TITUS

Titus and his Roman legions arrived before the walls of Jerusalem a few days before the Passover, A.D. 70. Vast multitudes were assembled to keep the Feast. After Titus broke through the walls of the city, many of the Jews retired to the Temple. He tried to restrain his troops and save the Temple, but the soldiers, maddened by the length of the siege, hurled their torches into the midst of the splendid structure, and it was completely consumed. The whole city was eventually leveled to the ground. During this terrible war which culminated in the destruction of Jerusalem more than a million Jews perished, and ninety thousand prisoners were sold as slaves or used in gladiatorial exhibitions.

PETER AND THE EARLY CHURCH

1. WHY THE DISCIPLES RETURNED TO JERUSALEM. "The return of Jesus' disciples to Jerusalem within a few days after his crucifixion was a bold, seemingly impracticable venture," says Charles F. Kent. "The Jewish authorities who had put their Master to death were still in control. Jewish fanaticism was strongest in Jerusalem. The Roman officials viewed with suspicion any unusual religious movements. Above all, the homes of the majority and the occupations whereby they were able to support themselves were found in Galilee rather than Judea. What were the motives which inspired them? The first was undoubtedly the belief that Jesus would speedily reappear to establish his rule in Jerusalem. They, as his immediate followers, were eager to be present there in order to participate in it. This motive, however, was not alone sufficient to hold them in Jerusalem in the face of disillusionment and persecution. The deeper reason was clearly because Jesus himself in the closing days of his ministry had led them up to Jerusalem and established there, in the very heart of Judaism, the center of their communal life. The only motive that really explains their unusual action is their loyalty to the mission that he had left them. It was because they felt that they were the leaven which must leaven the whole mass of Judaism and that they could do their task better in the capital and temple city as the center than in Galilee or Samaria, where they would fail to touch the streams of Jewish pilgrims which radiated from Jerusalem to the ends of the civilized world. Events quickly demonstrated the truth of their conviction."

2. ASIA. The word is used in the Book of Acts, and refers to the western portion of Asia Minor, nearly corresponding with that section called Anatolia.

3. LATER BUILDINGS IN THE TEMPLE AREA. The Temple itself was destroyed by Titus at the fall of Jerusalem in 70 A.D. In the year 135, the Emperor Hadrian built there a temple to Jupiter. In 363 the Emperor Julian made an attempt to rebuild the Jewish Temple, but was unsuccessful. In 536 the Emperor Justinian erected, at the south end of the area, a magnificent basilica in honor of the Virgin. This building, in the year 691, was made into a Moslem shrine without much alteration other than the substitution of the crescent for the cross upon the dome. This is still standing, and is known as the Mosque El-Aksa. The Moslem shrine, the Dome of the Rock, which now occupies the site of the Temple, was built by the Turks in 688 on the summit of Mount Moriah because it is sacred to them as the reputed landing place of their prophet Mohammed after his miraculous journey through the air from Mecca. The building is called "the Mosque of Omar"; but it has never been a mosque, and Omar had nothing to do with it: its sacredness is due to the rock which it covers.

THE CHURCH OF JUSTINIAN
From a model by Schick

Among the buildings in the temple area is the large structure at the left, the Christian church built by the Emperor Justinian.

4. EARLY CHRISTIAN BENEVOLENCE. Although communism was soon given up in the church, generosity to the unfortunate continued. Justin Martyr, who lived in the second century A.D., in his *Apology*, testifies as follows: "Those who are well to do give as they choose, each as he himself purposes. The collection is then deposited with the president, who succors orphans, widows, those who are in want owing to sickness or any other cause, those who are in prison, and strangers who are on a journey."

There seems to be a tendency toward communism whenever and wherever the thought of equal brotherhood among men is emphasized. Witness the early Wycliffites, the Hussites, and well-known examples in our own day.

5. "A CROWN OF GLORY THAT FADETH NOT AWAY." The phrase "fadeth not away" is, in the Greek, "amaranthine." The amaranth was a fabled flower of a purple-velvet color, which, though gathered, kept its beauty, and when all other flowers faded, recovered its luster by being sprinkled with a little water. It was thus a symbol of immortality. Milton speaks of it as follows:

> "Their crowns enwove with amaranth and gold,
> Immortal amaranth, a flower which once
> In Paradise, fast by the tree of life,
> Began to bloom; but soon, for man's offense,

PANORAMA OF ROME FROM THE DOME OF SAINT PETER'S

The huge Cathedral of Saint Peter is the crowning evidence of the belief of the early church that Peter visited Rome. This edifice stands on the site of Nero's Circus, in which that emperor himself used sometimes to contend in the games as a charioteer. In the immediate foreground, we look down upon part of the church roof with its colossal statues of churchmen; then the noble sweep of the magnificent colonnades, designed by Bernini, which form so fitting an approach to this largest of cathedrals. The ancient Egyptian obelisk standing in the center marks the traditional spot where Peter was crucified head downward. A stretch of the Tiber River is visible toward the middle of the picture.

> To Heaven removed, where first it grew, there grows,
> And flowers aloft shading the tree of life.
> With these, that never fade, the spirits elect
> Bind their resplendent locks enwreathed with beams."

PAUL AND THE WORLD-WIDE CHURCH

6. PAUL'S PERSONAL APPEARANCE. Paul is set before us, by tradition, as having the strongly marked and prominent features of a Jew, yet not without some of the finer lines indicative of the Greek physiognomy. His

stature was diminutive, and his body disfigured by some lameness or distortion which may have provoked the contemptuous expressions of his enemies. His beard was long and thin. His head was bald. The characteristics of his face were a transparent complexion, which visibly betrayed the quick changes of his feelings, a bright gray eye under thickly overhanging, meeting eyebrows, a cheerful and winning expression of countenance, which invited the approach and inspired the confidence of strangers. It would be natural to infer, from his continual journeys and manual labor, that he was possessed of great strength of constitution. But men of delicate health have often gone through the greatest exertions, and his own words on more than one occasion show that he suffered much from bodily infirmity.

7. THE JOURNEYS OF PAUL. These have much interest, especially for young people, because they covered routes that are becoming familiar to them in their school histories. Paul crossed Asia Minor, reversing the route of Alexander when he went forth to conquer the world. He also covered part of the route of Xenophon's *Anabasis*. At Troas, he was within sight of the ruins of the Troy of Homer and Virgil. He crossed the Hellespont, the crossing place of many conquerors before Paul's time and since. He visited Philippi, the scene of the defeat and death of Brutus. He touched at Salamis, the site of one of the world's greatest battles. He landed at Puteoli, whither the dying Alexander had come. He visited Athens, Corinth, Ephesus, and Rome—cities that fill many pages in the world's story.

Paul also saw places that have become renowned in later history. Ptolemais was the Acre of the Crusaders, and Melita was their Malta. Thessalonica, where Paul preached, and to whose disciples he wrote two letters, was the Saloniki of the Great War.

Jerusalem, Damascus, Tyre, Sidon, Crete, and Cyprus, of course had associations reaching back to the history of the ancient peoples and of the Old Testament.

No one can sail the Mediterranean today, especially its eastern end, and among the Grecian islands, without feeling very near to Paul, one of the greatest travelers of olden days.

8. CYPRUS. Cyprus is the Kittim of the Old Testament. Its name is said to have been derived from its rich copper mines. Next to Sicily, it is the largest island in the Mediterranean. In the days of the early Christians, its many inlets, creeks, and havens made it a favorite stopping place for merchants from Egypt and Asia Minor. Its plantations in the interior produced grain in abundance. Large forests furnished timber for shipbuilding, and in its mines and streams were found diamonds, emeralds, silver, lead, and copper. The most famous city of Cyprus was Salamis. The islanders worshiped Aphrodite, who, according to mythology, had

her origin in the sea foam on the shores of the island. Many Jews, some of whom perhaps became Christians on the great day of Pentecost, resided on the island.

9. ICONIUM. Sir William M. Ramsay considers Iconium to be the oldest city in the world, with no possible rival but Damascus. The tradition was that, after men had been made by Jupiter out of images of mud, Iconium was the place in which they first settled. These images were called Eikones, a word similar to the Russian "Icon."

10. MACEDONIA was the region north of Greece, that had been made a famous kingdom by Philip and Alexander the Great. In Paul's time it was a Roman province. It was closely connected with that other Roman province in which Troas was located. Paul's journey from Troas to Neapolis, therefore, did not seem as unusual then as it does now, when we think of it as a passage from one country on the continent of Asia to another in Europe.

The reasonable suggestion has been made that the "man from Macedonia," who appeared in a vision to Paul at Troas, was no other than Luke, who was probably a native of Philippi, and who seems to have joined Paul at that time. It has also been conjectured that, as a physician, he may have formerly been consulted by Paul.

11. PHILIPPI was named after King Philip of Macedon, who prized it for its adjacent gold mines. It was the home of the first Christian church on European soil. Paul, the founder of this church, would be familiar with the famous battle fought at Philippi between Brutus and Cassius with Cæsar's assassins on one side, and Octavius and Mark Antony on the other. Near by, after the battle, Cassius committed suicide. Today the site has no inhabitants; but there are extensive ruins, among which the most significant is a gateway, supposed to be that by which Paul went out to the riverside. Among the other ruins are remains of a theater, broken marble columns, and a portion of the city wall. "Born into the world with the brightest promise, the church of Philippi has lived without a history and perished without a memorial."

12. PAUL'S JOURNEY TO THESSALONICA. Between Philippi and Thessalonica was a mountain ridge rising steeply from the sea, which it was necessary for the Apostles to cross. Here, Brutus and Cassius, Octavius and Antony, pitched their camps, and not far off was fought the Battle of Philippi, as the result of which the republic of Rome perished, and Cæsar Augustus became ruler of the world.

Between Amphipolis and Thessalonica, Paul must have passed the tomb of Euripides and the site of the birthplace of Aristotle.

13. THESSALONICA, the largest town in Macedonia, was on the Egnatian Way, which connected Rome and the Adriatic with the East. It was the chief city on that road, and was one of the three chief centers of

trade in that part of the world: the other two were Corinth and Ephesus. It was a free city and had its own rulers.

In all Greece, if we except Corinth, there is no finer harbor. The anchorage is of the best, the water is as smooth as a lake, and the neighboring valleys give access to roads that lead into the heart of Epirus and Upper Macedonia. The maritime trade was not the only means of livelihood to Thessalonians. A portion of the population was engaged in industrial pursuits. Then, as today, the city was noted for its textile fabrics, brilliant-colored rugs, and coarser stuffs of goat's hair. It was with these weavers and working people that Paul cast his lot. The commercial character of Thessalonica was of great importance in the spread of the Gospel. Ships of every description, hailing from many quarters, set sail from here daily, carrying to far-off lands along with their cargoes such news as could be picked up in the streets of Thessalonica.

For several centuries, it was an important Christian city, and from it missionaries went to teach the Bulgarians and the Slavonians, who have been Christians ever since. The modern city, Saloniki, as it is now called, is large and important. It had a prominent place in the history of the Great War.

14. WORKING AT A TRADE. It was Gamaliel, Paul's teacher, who said: "An excellent thing is study of the Law combined with some worldly trade. All study of the Law apart from manual toil must fail at last and be the cause of sin." Paul's practice of tentmaking was in line with his master's counsel.

During the Middle Ages, some of the best known rabbis supported themselves by laboring at humble occupations, such as carpentering, shoemaking, building, and baking. There are still those,

> "Who carry music in their heart
> Through dusky lane and wrangling mart,
> Who ply their daily task with busier feet
> Because their secret souls a holier strain repeat."

15. BEREA. In the center of Berea is a public square surrounded by enormous cypress trees. It contains a small stone pulpit that is evidently modern, but which may stand upon the place where Paul preached to the people.

16. PAUL'S VOYAGE FROM THESSALONICA TO ATHENS. "Right in front of them, as though stopping their journey, was a shore backed by hills. Among those hills, at the Gates of the Boiling Springs (Thermopylæ), three hundred Greeks defied the armies of Persia in the most famous battle of the world. At length, they came out from this long channel into the open sea once more.

Round another headland, a shining Temple of Athene, built of marble from the quarries of Pentelicus which they passed farther on, showed that

EXPLANATORY NOTES

they were now nearing the wonderful city of this Victory-goddess. At last, in smooth water, they beat up the gulf till the boat slid into the crowded harbor of Piræus."—BASIL MATHEWS

TEMPLE OF THESEUS AND MOUNT LYKABETTUS

Just over the edge of the level square on the right is the hollow in which was the ancient Greek Agora and the court of the Areopagus. From that Agora Paul could easily see this Temple of Theseus. It constituted one other of those objects of adoration the number and variety and costliness of which so impressed the Apostle during his sojourn in Athens. This Temple is contemporaneous with the Parthenon (fifth century B.C.). Though it is named after Theseus, the mythical founder of Athens, no one knows really what its original name and use may have been.

17. THE EPICUREANS, with whom Paul talked in Athens, were followers of Epicurus, a philosopher who "lived in a quiet garden a life of philosophic content, and taught his disciples that the enjoyment of tranquil pleasure was the highest end of human existence." He did not believe, as many suppose, that this meant that each man was to indulge his whims and passions as he chose, but that, before indulging any, he should consider such indulgence in relation to a whole harmonious life and with reference to the consequences to himself and others. He also believed that the gods live a life of serene calm, like that which he himself wished to attain. They therefore were not continually meddling with men, and men were free to make the best of themselves.

While not a complete philosophy, there was much in it which Christians could approve, especially its kindliness and gentleness, its frugality and content with simple pleasures.

Yet the early Christians saw its sensual tendencies more than its charm, and found in it no impulse for the strenuous, sacrificial following of Christ.

18. THE STOICS, whom Paul encountered at Athens, were not the first whom he had met, for Tarsus was a stronghold of Stoicism. Indeed, this philosophy had much in common with Eastern thought. The Stoics exalted as their hero the wise man, who rules his passions by his reason, is unmoved by joy or grief, and endures necessary evils with fortitude. This man alone is free and attains virtue, which, rather than happiness, is the human goal. The Stoics also had a limited belief in a future life.

To the Christians, their system must have seemed to recognize the demands of conscience to a greater extent than any other Greek philosophy did.

19. PAUL'S QUOTATION FROM THE GREEK POETS. Cleanthes, the illustrious pupil of Zeno, composed the immortal hymn to Zeus from which Paul quotes in his famous address to the men of Athens:

> "O God, most glorious, called by many a name,
> Nature's great King, through endless years the same;
> Omnipotence, who by thy just decree
> Controllest all, hail Zeus, for unto thee
> Behooves thy creatures in all lands to call.
> We are thy children, we alone, of all
> On earth's broad ways that wander to and fro,
> Bearing thy image wheresoe'er we go.
> Therefore with songs of praise thy power I will sound forth."

Equally significant is the similar hymn to Zeus that comes from Aratus, the poet of Soli in Cilicia, Paul's native province, whom the apostle possibly also had in mind:

> "Zeus fills all the city streets
> Of the nation's crowded marts; fills the watery deeps
> And heavens. Every laborer needs the help of Zeus.
> His children are we. He, benignant,
> Raises high signals, summoning man to toil,
> And warning him of life's demands."

The phrase, "Evil communications corrupt good manners," used by Paul, is also found in the works of a Greek poet, Menander, and may have been read there by Paul.

20. ANALOGIES BETWEEN PAUL AND SOCRATES. Many interesting parallels may be thought of between the lives and characters of Paul and the noble Athenian philosopher who lived five centuries before him. Both were men of inferior physique, of ascetic lives, and indifferent to persecution and death. Each was a man of singular independence and courage; each depended upon an Inner Guide. Socrates called him his "Mentor"; Paul's was the Spirit of Jesus. Both Paul and Socrates devoted much of their time to the instruction of youth, and inculcated in their disciples

the principle of unselfish love. They both proclaimed their messages in Athens. Socrates was killed there; Paul was rejected there.

21. THE VOYAGE FROM EPHESUS HOME. "Away to starboard," says Basil Mathews, "in the light of the morning, lay Patmos, screened by lesser islands. On the port side the coast faded away into a deep full gulf and then shot out again in a wild riot of rock.

"In the morning, they were away before the gleam of the sun had flushed to life the white columns of the temple behind the little harbor of Cos. Tacking east into the gulf of Halicarnassus, they swung west again round the southern cape, and threaded the channel among the islands till the great island Rhodes loomed ahead of them, her rolling hills and rich valleys covered with the spring green of olive trees and vines.

"Long before Paul sailed into the deep safe harbor of Rhodes, the mighty brazen Colossus, which had once straddled from pier to pier across the harbor, had crashed into the sea under the shock of earthquake.

"Behind all, on the horizon to the northwest, lay the Lycian coast. From the sea the hills lifted themselves, rising past deep, mysterious valleys to the high mountain ridge of the Taurus Range, that caught the sun's first rays as Paul's ship, next day, sailed westward for Patara, the end of the ship's voyage."

At Patara they changed ships, and thence sailed past the distant shore of Cyprus, and along down the Phœnician coast, stopping for a short time at Tyre. Their final port, after a day at Ptolemais, or Acre, was Cæsarea.

22. GALATIA, a province in the eastern central part of Asia Minor, that had been settled by Gauls, men of our own race. Because they were such valuable allies of the Romans, their territory had been extended. We read in Timothy that Crescens had gone to Galatia. Some think that by this was meant the original Gaul, now France.

23. ALEXANDRIA, which is mentioned three times in the New Testament, is of importance in Christian history. There were more Jews living there in New Testament times than there were in Jerusalem: indeed, it was the largest Jewish city in the world. Here, in the version called the Septuagint, the Hebrew Bible had been translated into Greek, in order that these Jews might have the Sacred Writings in the language which they spoke and understood. Here, near the great library and in close contact with Greek philosophy, Jewish scholars reinterpreted the Old Testament, and elaborated great conceptions which influenced the early Christian church. According to tradition, Mark established churches in Alexandria.

24. THE LATER CHARACTER OF THE CORINTHIAN CHRISTIANS. Our latest knowledge of them is favorable. Clement, writing to them near the close of the first century, said: "Day and night you agonized for all the brotherhood, that by means of compassion and care the number of God's

elect might be saved. You were sincere, guileless, and void of malice among yourselves. Every sedition and every schism was an abomination to you. You lamented the transgressions of your neighbors and judged their shortcomings to be your own."

ALEXANDRIA, EGYPT

25. WHERE PAUL MADE HIS DEFENSE IN JERUSALEM. The steps of the present Tower of Antonia, partly hewn in the solid rock, are doubtless the very ones on which Paul stood when he made his defense before the mob in Jerusalem.

26. FELIX was a freedman who had been appointed procurator of Judea by the Emperor Claudius. Tacitus says that he reigned with "the disposition of a slave." His career was full of contests against robbers and revolutionists, and was marked by cruelty and tyranny. His attempt to get a bribe from Paul was characteristic, as was his plan to gain the favor of the Jews by keeping him in prison after it was evident that he was innocent. There were plenty of reasons why Felix should have trembled at the preaching of Paul, not the least of which was that his wife Drusilla, a Jewess, who was present at Paul's hearing, was not his rightful wife.

27. FESTUS, the successor of Felix, seems to have been a more worthy character. He investigated Paul's case with care, but made the imprudent suggestion that he should go back to Jerusalem for trial. He inherited the disturbed conditions that prevailed in Judea during the procuratorship of his predecessor, and died after a few months in office.

28. THE APPEAL TO CÆSAR. Two reasons at least influenced Paul in his appeal to the emperor: first, if Festus should return him to Jerusalem, he would almost certainly either be condemned by a Roman tribunal

or assassinated by the Jews; second, he had for a long time been desirous of visiting the Christians in Rome.

29. CRETE, MODERN CANDIA, an island at which Paul touched on his last voyage, had an important place in history. Once it was the seat of a great civilization, as old perhaps as that of Egypt. Relics have been found indicating long and vigorous prosperity and culture. From this island, probably, originally came the Philistines. Its king was always called Minos, as the Egyptian king was called Pharaoh. The legend of the Minotaur which lived in the Labyrinth, and of the hero Theseus who entered it and slew the monster is a familiar story.

30. THE SHIP, "THE TWIN BROTHERS." "Among the ships in the harbor," says Basil Mathews "was a great grainship from the Egyptian coast, which had put in here for the winter on her way from Alexandria to Italy. On her prow the picture of two men was painted—the twins, Castor and Pollux. These twins were called by the Greeks the Dioscuri, sons of god, because they were believed to be the sons of Zeus. They were gods whom the Romans thought of as their great protectors and helpers in the time of need. Especially the sailors said that, if the Dioscuri came aboard the ship, though invisibly, she would ride through any storm safe to harbor.

"One of the great Roman writers, Epictetus, who himself did not put faith in the twins, told the people to have the faith in God which the sailors had in Castor and Pollux. He says: 'Be mindful of God, call him to be thy helper and defender, as men call upon the Dioscuri in a storm.'"

31. THE WORLD INTO WHICH CHRISTIANITY CAME. "Contemporary representations," says Uhlhorn, "portray the state of morals. What a picture it is! Seneca says: 'All things are full of iniquity and vice. More crimes are committed than can be remedied by force. A monstrous contest of wickedness is carried on. Daily the lust of sin increases; daily the sense of shame diminishes. Casting away all regard for what is good and honorable, pleasure runs riot without restraint. Vice no longer hides itself; it stalks forth before all eyes. So public has iniquity become, so mightily does it flame up in all hearts, that innocence is no longer rare: it has ceased to exist.' Somewhat later Lucian exclaims: 'If any one loves wealth and is dazed by gold, if any one measures happiness by purple and power, if any one brought up among flatterers and slaves has never had a conception of liberty, frankness, and truth, if any one has wholly surrendered himself to pleasures, full tables, carousals, lewdness, sorcery, falsehood, and deceit, let him go to Rome!' Or, if we would have in addition to these somewhat rhetorical representations a sober and calm opinion, we may take that of the historian Livy: 'Rome has become great by her virtues until now, when we can neither bear our vices nor their remedies.' Yet, there was nowhere to be found a power competent to the gigantic

task of a moral renewal of the ancient world. This power must come from another source—from above."

32. THE CHURCH IN THE ROMAN EMPIRE. "With all their faults and failings, they were as salt amid the earth's corruption; the true light had shined in their hearts, and they were the light of the world.

"The art of the world was degraded by such infamous pictures as those on the walls of Pompeii; that of the church consisted in the rude but pure and joyous emblems scrawled on the soft tufa of the catacombs. The amusements of the world were pitilessly sanguinary or shamefully corrupt; those of the Christians were found in gatherings at once social and religious, as bright as they could be made by the gaiety of innocent and untroubled hearts. In the world, infanticide was infamously universal; in the church, the baptized little ones were treated as those whose angels beheld the face of our Father in heaven. In the world, slavery was rendered yet more intolerable by the cruelty and impurity of masters; in the church, the Christian slave, welcomed as a friend and a brother, often holding a position of ministerial dignity, was emancipated in all but name. In the world, marriage was detested as a disagreeable necessity, and its very meaning was destroyed by the frequency and facility of divorce; in the church, it was consecrated and honorable—the institution which had alone survived the loss of Paradise—and was all but sacramental in its heaven-appointed blessedness. The world was settling into the sadness of unalleviated despair; the church was irradiated by an eternal hope, and rejoicing with a joy unspeakable and full of glory. In the world, men were 'hateful and hating one another'; in the church, the beautiful ideal of human brotherhood was carried into practice."—FREDERICK W. FARRAR

33. "AGAIN I WILL SAY, REJOICE!" Thomas Traherne says: "Your enjoyment of the world is never right till every morning you wake in Heaven and see yourself in your Father's Celestial Joys; you never enjoy the world right till the sea itself floweth in your veins, till you are clothed with the Heavens and crowned with the stars, and perceive yourself to be the sole heir of the whole world, and more than so, because men are in it who are every one sole heirs as well as you. Till you can sing and rejoice and delight in God as misers do in gold and kings in scepters, you never enjoy the world. Till your spirit filleth the whole world and the stars are your jewels: till you are as familiar with the ways of God in all ages as with your walk and table: till you love men so as to desire their happiness with a thirst equal to the weal of your own, you never enjoy the world. You never enjoy the world right, till you so love the beauty of enjoying it that you are covetous and earnest to persuade others to enjoy it. The world is a mirror of infinite beauty, yet no man sees it. It is a Temple of Majesty, yet no man regards it. It is the paradise of God, the place of Angels, and the Gate of Heaven."

EXPLANATORY NOTES

THE SEVEN CHURCHES OF ASIA

34. SARDIS. Through the city of Sardis flowed the stream Pactolus, whose sands were laden with gold. Here was found the rich and mysterious metal called electrum. Here had ruled Crœsus, richest of kings, gold coins of whose time were discovered here in 1922. This city held the church whose material wealth and leaning to material things had earned for it the condemnation, "Thou hast a name that thou livest, and art dead."

Sardis was in ancient times the residence of the kings of Lydia, a maritime province in Asia Minor. It was once a commercial mart of great importance, owing partly to the fertile character of the surrounding region and partly to its convenient position for trade. The place is now a complete solitude. The fragmentary remains of the massive Temple of Cybele still bear witness to the wealth and architectural skill of the people who erected it.

CHRISTIAN THOUGHT

35. THE CHIEF CORNER STONE. The great corner stone of the Temple, laid three thousand years ago, has been found. It is beautifully cut and polished, and is three feet eight inches high and fourteen feet long. It is still firmly fixed in the rock on which the Temple stood.

36. A CORRUPTIBLE CROWN. "The prize was symbolical, only a crown of olive, but the real triumph of the victor was the ode in which his praise was sung, the procession of happy comrades, and the evening festival, when, as Pindar has it, 'the lovely shining of the fair-faced moon beamed forth, and all the precinct sounded with songs of festal glee,' or 'beside Castaly in the evening his name burnt bright, when the glad sounds of the Graces rose.' "—G. LOWES DICKINSON

37. THE ARMOR OF A ROMAN SOLDIER. The equipment of a Roman soldier which Paul uses as the basis of his parable of the Christian soldier is described by James Baikie as follows:

"His equipment is as plain and workmanlike as it can well be, for the Roman army is meant not for show, but for business. His head is covered with a perfectly plain round helmet, topped by a metal boss, or button, kept firm on the head by cheek pieces which almost meet under the lower jaw, and bearing a band of metal of double thickness round the forehead, and a projection behind to cover the neck. This, like all the metal-work of his equipment, is browned to a serviceable and inconspicuous tone. His body is guarded by a number of strips of iron which pass round the trunk, forming a kind of jointed breastplate, and these are attached to the shoulderpieces, similar strips of metal which pass over either shoulder and hang down in front and behind for several inches. His thighs are protected by strips of leather which hang from his waist, and his feet are shod with heavy sandals studded with nails, and bound on, well up the leg, with broad leathern thongs.

"In his right hand, the soldier carries a short, stout throwing spear, the famous 'pilum,' which the Roman hurled against the enemy's ranks as he came to close quarters. It measures about six feet nine inches in length, and has a long, heavy iron point, whose socket comes about halfway down the shaft. On his left arm, he bears the great oblong shield of the Roman legionary, four feet from top to bottom and two and a half feet from side to side, curved round at the edges to the shape of a half cylinder, so that it covers the whole of one side of his body. Though the shield is so large, it is not cumbrous, for it is made of cloth and calfskin built up on a wooden framework, and is really wonderfully light.

"Last of all comes the Roman's great weapon, the short sword which won so many battles. A leathern baldric passes over the soldier's left shoulder, and across his chest to his right hip, and there in its sheath hangs a straight, heavy sword, thirty inches long, with a sharp point and two keen edges. Its hilt is perfectly plain, with a simple crossbar, not so much to guard the hand as to keep the fingers from slipping as the swordsman thrusts."

38. THE GIRDLE. James Neil says: "The girdle, being the one tight-fitting part of Oriental dress, stands as a figure of preparation for work, service, traveling, or warfare. Because of this, it is also the emblem of strength."

39. ON LOVE. "Love is a great thing; yea a great good: alone it makes every burden light, and bears evenly all that is uneven. For it carries a burden which is no burden, and makes all bitterness sweet and palatable.

"Love longs to soar and will not be held down by things that are low. Love longs to be free, and estranged from all worldly affection, that its inner eye may not be dimmed, that it may not be caught by any temporal prosperity, or by any adversity cast down.

"Nothing is sweeter than Love, nothing braver, nothing higher, nothing wider, nothing fuller nor better in heaven and in earth; because Love is born of God, and can only rest in God above all things.

"Love often knows no measure; but is fervent beyond all measure. Love feels no burden, counts no pains, exerts itself beyond its strength, talks not of impossibility; for it thinks all things possible and all permitted. It is, therefore, strong enough for all things, and it fulfils many things and warrants them to take effect, where he who loves not faints and lies down.

"Love is watchful, and sleeping slumbers not; though weary it is not tired, though hampered is not hampered, though alarmed is not affrighted; but as a lively flame and burning torch it forces its way upwards and serenely passes through.

"If any man love, he knows what is the cry of this voice."
—Thomas à Kempis

40. Freedom. "I call that mind free which masters the senses, which passes life, not in asking what it shall eat or drink, but in hungering, thirsting, and seeking after righteousness.

"I call that mind free which does not copy the past nor live on old virtues, but forgets what is behind and rejoices to pour itself forth in fresh exertions.

"I call that mind free which sets no bounds to its love, recognizes in all human beings the image of God, and offers itself up a willing victim to the cause of mankind.

"I call that mind free which, through confidence in God, has cast off all fear but that of wrongdoing, which no menace or peril can enthrall, and possesses itself though all else be lost.

"I call that mind free which, conscious of its affinity with God, passes the bounds of time and death, and finds inexhaustible power in immortality."—William E. Channing

41. A Roman Philosopher on Death. The philosopher Seneca, who was a contemporary of Paul, wrote as follows: "This life is only a prelude to eternity, where we are to expect a new life, and another state of things.

"We have no prospect of heaven here, but at a distance. Let us therefore expect our last hour with courage—the last, I say, to our bodies, but not to our minds. The day which we fear as our last is but the birthday of our eternity. What we fear as a rock proves to be a harbor, in many cases to be desired, never to be refused.

"What if death comes? If it stays not with us, why should we fear it? That which we call death is but a pause or suspension; in truth, a progress into life. Only our thoughts look downward upon the body, and not forward upon things to come. A great soul takes no delight in staying with the body; it considers whence it came, and knows whither it is to go. We should live in our bodies as if we were only to lodge in them this night, and to leave them tomorrow. It is the care of a wise and a good man to look to his manners and actions, and rather how well he lives than how long. For to die sooner or later is not the business, but to die well or ill; for death brings us to immortality."

42. The River of Death. "This River has been a terror to many; yea, the thoughts of it also have often frightened me. But now methinks I stand easy; my foot is fixed upon that on which the feet of the priests that

bare the Ark of the Covenant stood while Israel went over this Jordan. The waters indeed are to the palate bitter and to the stomach cold; yet the thoughts of what I am going to and of the conduct that waits for me on the other side do lie as a glowing coal at my heart. I see myself now at the end of my journey, my toilsome days are ended. I am going now to see that head that was crowned with thorns, and that face that was spit upon for me. I have formerly lived by hearsay and faith; but now I go where I shall live by sight, and shall be with Him in whose company I delight myself. I have loved to hear my Lord spoken of, and wherever I have seen the print of his shoe in the earth, there I have coveted to set my foot too. His name has been to me as a civet-box; yea, sweeter than all perfume. His voice to me has been the most sweet, and his countenance I have more desired than they that have most desired the light of the sun. His Word I did use to gather for my food, and for antidotes against my faintings. He has held me, and I have kept me from mine iniquities; yea, my steps hath he strengthened in his way."—JOHN BUNYAN

43. STRANGERS AND PILGRIMS. The saints are called sojourners, because their true citizenship is in heaven, and they are pilgrims going home to God, in whose house they are to dwell forever.

CHRISTIAN WORSHIP

44. CHRISTIAN HYMNS. The early Christians sang the Psalms. The songs in the New Testament, such as the Song of Mary, the Song of the Angels, and those of Elisabeth and Zachariah, soon came into general use.

THE MAGNIFICAT AND OLD TESTAMENT PARALLELISMS

My soul doth magnify the Lord, And my spirit hath rejoiced in God my Saviour.	My soul shall be joyful in the Lord· It shall rejoice in his salvation. Psalm 35:9.
For he hath regarded the low estate of his handmaiden:	Who remembered us in our low estate. Psalm 136:23.
For, behold, from henceforth all generations shall call me blessed.	And Leah said, "Happy am I, for the daughters will call me blessed." Genesis 30:13.
For he that is mighty hath done to me great things;	Thy righteousness also, O God, is very high, who hast done great things. Psalm 71:19.
And holy is his name.	Holy and reverend is his name. Psalm 111:9.

And his mercy is on them that fear him from generation to generation.	The eye of the Lord is upon them that fear him, upon them that hope in his mercy. Psalm 77:18.
He hath showed strength with his arm;	His holy arm hath gotten him the victory.　　Psalm 98:1.
He hath scattered the proud in the imagination of their hearts.	I will cause the arrogancy of the proud to cease, and will lay low the haughtiness of the terrible.　　Isaiah 13:11.
He hath put down the mighty from their seats, And exalted them of low degree.	The Lord cast down the thrones of rulers, and set the meek in their stead. Ecclesiasticus 10:14.
He hath filled the hungry with good things;	They that were hungry ceased. 1 Samuel 2:5.
And the rich he hath sent empty away.	Though he heap up silver as the dust . . . the innocent shall divide the silver. Job 27:16–17.
He hath helped his servant Israel,	But thou, Israel, art my servant. Isaiah 41:8.
In remembrance of his mercy;	Give thanks at the remembrance of his holiness. Psalms 30:4 and 97:12.
As he spoke to our fathers, To Abraham, and to his children forever.	Thou wilt perform the truth to Jacob, and the mercy to Abraham.　　Micah 7:20.

The Benedictus and Old Testament Parallelisms

Blessed be the Lord, the God of Israel;	Blessed be the Lord God of Israel from everlasting and to everlasting.　　Psalm 41:13.
For he hath visited and redeemed his people,	Thou hast with thine arm redeemed thy people. Psalm 77:15.
And hath raised up a horn of salvation for us in the house of his servant David	He is my shield, and the horn of my salvation. 2 Sam. 22:3.

(As he spoke by the mouth of his holy prophets which have been since the world began),	
That we should be saved from our enemies, And from the hand of all that hate us;	He saved them from the hand of him that hated them, and redeemed them from the hand of the enemy. Psalm 106:10.
To perform the mercy promised to our fathers, And to remember his holy covenant;	Thou wilt perform . . . the mercy to Abraham, which thou hast sworn unto our fathers. Micah 7:20.
The oath which he swore to our father, Abraham, That he would grant unto us, that we, being delivered out of the hand of our enemies, Might serve him without fear,	Which covenant he made with Abraham, and his oath unto Isaac; . . . to Israel for an everlasting covenant. Psalm 105:9–10.
In holiness and righteousness before him, all the days of our life. And thou, child, shalt be called the prophet of the Highest:	Worship the Lord in the beauty of holiness. Psalm 29:2.
For thou shalt go before the face of the Lord To prepare his ways;	The voice of him that crieth in the wilderness, "Prepare ye the way of the Lord." Isaiah 40:3.
To give knowledge of salvation unto his people By the remission of their sins,	Thou hast forgiven the iniquity of thy people; thou hast covered all their sin. Psalm 85:2.
Through the tender mercy of our God; Whereby the dayspring from on high hath visited us,	Thy light is come, and the glory of the Lord is risen upon thee. Isaiah 60:1.
To give light to them that sit in darkness and the shadow of death;	He brought them out of darkness and the shadow of death. Psalm 107:14.
To guide our feet into the way of peace.	Ye shall be led forth with peace. Isaiah 55:12.

The Nunc Dimittis and Old Testament Parallelisms

Lord, now lettest thou thy servant depart in peace According to thy word;	Thou shalt go to thy fathers in peace: thou shalt be buried in a good old age. Genesis 15:15.
For mine eyes have seen thy salvation,	With long life will I satisfy him, and show him my salvation. Psalm 91:16.
Which thou hast prepared before the face of all people;	The ends of the earth shall see the salvation of our God. Isaiah 52:10.
A light to lighten the Gentiles, And the glory of thy people Israel.	The Gentiles shall see thy righteousness, and all kings thy glory. Isaiah 62:2.

45. CHRISTIAN PRAYERS. In the first of the Book of Acts, we are told that "they continued in the breaking of bread and in prayers,"—more accurately "*the* prayers"—as if forms of prayer were used from the beginning. This was probably true; we may suppose that the disciples made use of Psalms and of the Lord's Prayer. Soon, other prayers grew up around the breaking of bread and the services of worship. Such prayers are extant, dating from the end of the first century. One of the earliest of these reads, in part: "As this broken bread was scattered as grain upon the mountains, and, gathered together, became one; so let thy church be gathered together from the ends of the earth into thy religion; for thine is the glory and power, through Jesus Christ, forever."

46. THE CHURCH TRIUMPHANT. Before Savonarola was delivered to the secular law for execution, he with his two companions was led into the presence of the Bishop of Vasona. He was formally degraded, and the Bishop said, forgetting the proper formula in his extreme agitation, "I separate thee from the church militant and triumphant." Thereupon, Savonarola calmly set him right, saying, "From the militant, not from the triumphant, for that it is not thine to do." "These words," says the martyr's biographer, Villari, "were uttered in a tone that pierced to the souls of the bystanders, so that all who heard remembered them forever." They live among the great sayings of the world.

47. SERVICES OF WORSHIP. It will be interesting to read contemporary descriptions of the order of public worship among early Christians. Pliny the Younger, the chronicler of the destruction of Pompeii, wrote a letter in the year 109 A.D. to the Emperor Trajan, from which these words are taken: "The Christians assemble on an appointed day at sunrise, and

sing responsively to Christ as God, and then pledge themselves by an oath not to do any evil work, to commit no theft, robbery, nor adultery, not to break their word, nor sacrifice property committed to them."

Justin Martyr, writing about 140, says: "On Sunday a meeting of all is held, and a section from the Memoirs of the Apostles [the Gospels] and the writings of the Prophets [the Old Testament] is read, as long as the time permits. When the reader has finished, the president, in a discourse, gives an exhortation to the imitation of these noble things. After this, we all rise in common prayer. At the close of the prayer, bread and wine with water are brought. The president offers prayer and thanks for them, according to the power given him, and the congregation responds the Amen. Then, the consecrated elements are distributed to each one, and partaken, and are carried by the deacons to the houses of the absent. The wealthy and willing then give contributions according to their free will."

At an early period, Christians began to adorn their services with three ancient accompaniments of veneration—flowers, incense, and ceremonial lights.

THE APOCALYPSE

48. APOCALYPSE is any literature which reveals the future. Irving S. Wood says: "Apocalypse was written from about 200 B.C. to perhaps 200 A.D. by Jews and Christians. It was always written at some time of discouragement, of danger, or actual persecution, when there was special need of courage and faith. It was written in symbolic style. It was not safe to say plainly that the nation which governed them would be overthrown and destroyed. The message must be obscured in symbol and vision, which would say nothing openly, but convey its hidden meaning to the initiated."

49. AN EDICT OF A PERSECUTING EMPEROR. "We were particularly desirous of reclaiming into the way of reason and nature the deluded Christians who had renounced the religion of their fathers, and, presumptuously despising the practice of antiquity, had invented extravagant laws and opinions according to the dictates of their fancy, and had collected a various society from the different parts of our empire. The edicts which we have published to enforce the worship of the gods having exposed many of the Christians to danger and distress, many having suffered death, and more who still persist in their impious folly being left destitute of any public exercise of religion, we are disposed to extend to these unhappy men the effects of our wonted clemency. We permit them, therefore, freely to profess their private opinions and to assemble in their conventicles without fear of molestation, provided they preserve a due respect to the established laws and government. . . . And we hope that our indulgence will engage the Christians to offer up their prayers to the deity whom they adore, for our safety and prosperity, for their own, and for that of the republic."

—THE EMPEROR GALERIUS (371 A.D.)

NERO, VICTOR

From a painting by Edoardo Forti

Nero was one of the Roman emperors who inflicted persecutions upon the Christians. In addition to his cruelty, he was vain. He often competed in person in the public games and chariot races. The picture shows him at the moment of victory receiving the plaudits of his flattering courtiers and people.

50. A NEW KINGDOM. Prophecies about the advent of a great kingdom which was to take its rise in the East had been prevalent in the days of Nero. They were not entirely set at rest by the elevation of Vespasian to the emperorship from the command of the army in Syria. Eusebius says that Domitian's jealousy was excited by rumors that some of the earthly family of him whom Christians adored as the King of the Universe were still living in Palestine. Timid from the sense of his own manifold crimes, Domitian determined to inquire into the matter, and ordered some of these "relations of the Lord" to be brought into his presence. They were grandsons of "Jude, the brother of James," who wrote the Epistle of Jude. When Domitian ascertained that they possessed only a few acres of land, and when he saw that their hands were horny from daily toil, and that they filled no higher rank than that of peasants of Palestine, he dismissed them with disdain to their homes, content with their assurance that the Kingdom of Christ was not of this world.

51. BABYLON AND THE NEW JERUSALEM. "Two Empires," says Bishop Westcott, "two social organizations, designed to embrace the whole world, started together in the first century. . . . In principle, in mode of action, in sanctions, in scope, in history, they offer an absolute

contrast. . . . The history of the Roman Empire is from the first the history of a decline and fall: the history of the Christian Empire is from the first the history of a victorious progress. The outcome of these histories is represented in the fate of two cities, one of which stands for the worldly, the other for the spiritual capital of the earth. The first is the licentious and despotic city named Babylon, but unmistakably identified as Rome, over whose downfall a song like the old-time taunt songs is raised; the second is the holy city, New Jerusalem, which is beheld 'coming down from God out of heaven, made ready as a bride adorned for her husband.'"

52. THE CELESTIAL KINGDOM. One of the cherished writings of the early church, known as the Sibylline Oracles, gives this vision of the coming kingdom:

"Neither entertain in your breast proud anger, which provokes you to quarreling and fighting; but serve the great God, that you may abstain from these things. When this shall be at an end, the great day will come upon good men, the beginning of happy times, for the earth, which is the producer of all things, shall yield to men the best and infinite fruit—corn, wine, oil, and the sweet honey, drink from heaven, the fruits of trees, and the acorns; and fat cattle, and beasts, and lambs from sheep, and kids from goats; and sweet fountains shall flow with the whitest milk, and the cities shall be full of good things, and fields shall be fruitful. And there shall be no sword in the earth nor warlike tumult, nor shall the earth groan any more by an earthquake; there shall be no wars nor drought upon the earth, nor hail to waste the fruit, but there shall be a great peace in all the earth. And one king shall live in friendship with another to the end of the world; and the immortal, who lives in the heavens adorned with stars, shall give a common law to all men in all the earth and instruct miserable men what things must be done. For he is the only God, and there is no other beside him. Then he shall raise a kingdom forever over all men, when he hath given a holy law to the righteous, to all whom he promised to open the earth, and the gates of the blessed, and all joys, and an immortal mind, and eternal cheerfulness."

53. THE EARLY CHRISTIANS (A Contemporary Account). "The Christians know and trust God, the Creator of heaven and earth, in whom are all things and from whom are all things, and who has no other God beside him. From him, they have received the commandments which they have engraved on their minds and keep in the hope and expectation of the world to come. Therefore they do not commit adultery nor fornication; they do not bear false witness; they do not deny what has been deposited with them, nor covet what is not theirs. They honor father and mother and show kindness to their neighbors. If they are judges, they judge uprightly. They do not worship idols made in human form, and whatever

they do not wish that others should do to them, they do not to others. They do not eat of food offered to idols, because they are undefiled. They placate those who oppress them and make them their friends; they do good to their enemies. Their wives are absolutely pure, and their daughters modest. Their men abstain from every unlawful marriage and from all impurity in the hope of future recompense. If any of them have bondmen, bondwomen or children, they persuade them to become Christians for the love that they have toward them; and when they become so they call them, without distinction, brothers. They do not worship strange gods. They walk in all humility and kindness, and falsehood is not found among them.

"They love one another. They do not refuse to help the widows. They rescue the orphan from him who does him violence. He who has gives ungrudgingly to him who has not. If they see a stranger, they take him to their dwellings and rejoice over him as over a real brother; for they do not call themselves brothers after the flesh but after the spirit and in God. When one of their poor passes from the world, any one of them who sees it provides for his burial according to his ability. And if they hear that any one of their number is in prison or oppressed for the name of their Messiah, all of them provide for his needs. And if it is possible to redeem him, they deliver him.

"If any one among them is poor and needy and they do not have food to spare, they fast two or three days that they may supply him with the necessary food. They scrupulously observe the commands of their Messiah. They live honestly and soberly, as the Lord their God commanded them. Every morning and every hour they thank and praise God for his lovingkindnesses toward them; and for their food and drink they give thanks to him. If any righteous man among them passes from this world, they rejoice and give thanks to God, and they escort his body as if he were setting out on a journey from one place to another. If, on the other hand, they see that one of their number has died in his ungodliness or in his sins, they weep bitterly and sigh as over one who is about to go to punishment.

"As men who know God, they ask from him what is proper for him to give and for them to receive. Thus they do throughout their entire life. And inasmuch as they acknowledge the lovingkindnesses of God toward them, lo, because of them, there flows forth all the beauty that is in the world! But the good deeds which they do, they do not proclaim in the ears of the multitude, but they take care that no one shall perceive them. They hide their gift as one who has found a treasure hides it. Thus they labor to become righteous as those who expect to see their Messiah and to receive from him the glorious fulfilment of the promises made to them. Truly, this is a new people and there is something divine in them!"

—Oration of Aristides Before the Emperor Hadrian

BIBLE REFERENCE INDEX

This index shows the Biblical passages used on any particular page of this volume. The figures in heavy type indicate chapters and the figures in light face indicate the verses.

Page		Bible Reference	Page		Bible Reference	Page		Bible Reference
5	Luke	24:44–49	34	Acts	10:17–28	70	Acts	13:4–8
	Acts	1:8	35	"	10:29–32	71	"	13:9–20
6	"	1:12–15	36	"	10:33–36	72	"	13:21–34
	"	1:21–24	37	"	10:37–48	73	"	13:35–46
8	"	1:25–26		"	11:1–2	74	"	13:47–52
	"	2:1–5	39	"	11:3–4	75	"	14:1–10
9	"	2:6–19		"	11:18–24	77	"	14:11–17
10	"	2:20–33		"	11:26–28	78	"	14:18–22
11	"	2:34–47	41	"	11:29–30	79	"	14:23–28
12	"	3:1–8		"	12:1–10		"	15:1–6
13	"	3:9–11	42	"	12:11–17	80	"	15:7–20
	"	4:1–10	43	"	12:18–19	81	"	15:21–32
15	"	4:11–24	44	1 Peter	2:21–25	82	"	15:33–35
16	"	4:25–34		"	5:1–2		Galatians	2:1–10
17	"	4:35–37	45	"	5:3–4	87	Acts	15:36–41
	"	5:1–11	55	Acts	22:3–4		"	16:1–7
18	"	5:12–22		Phil.	3:4–9	88	"	16:8–10
19	"	5:23–35	56	"	3:10–14	89	"	16:11–20
20	"	5:36–42	57	1 Timothy	1:12–16	91	"	16:21–28
	"	6:1–4	58	Acts	7:58	92	"	16:29–40
22	"	6:5–13		"	8:1, 3		"	17:1–3
23	"	6:14–15		"	9:1–6	93	"	17:4–9
	"	7:1	59	"	9:7–11		1 Thess.	2:7–9
	"	7:51–53	60	"	9:12–24		"	1:6–9
24	"	7:54–60	63	"	9:25–30	95	"	2:1–2
	"	8:1–7		Galatians	1:11–14		"	2:13–15
25	"	8:8–22	64	"	1:15–19		Acts	17:10–11
26	"	8:23–25		"	1:21–24	96	"	17:12
27	"	8:26–35		Romans	15:15–21	97	"	17:13–24
29	"	8:36–40		Ephesians	3:8–9	98	"	17:25–31
	"	9:31–35	65	"	3:10–11	99	"	17:32–34
30	"	9:36–39		1 Cor.	9:19–23	101	"	18:1–9
31	"	9:40		Phil.	4:11–13	103	"	18:10–11
32	"	9:41–43	69	Acts	12:25		1 Cor.	2:1–5
33	"	10:1–16		"	13:1–3		"	4:9–13

441

BIBLE REFERENCE INDEX

Page	Bible Reference		Page	Bible Reference		Page	Bible Reference	
103	Acts	18:12–13	123	Acts	20:13–27	161	Col.	3:12–15
104	"	18:14–18	124	"	20:28–38		"	3:17
105	"	18:19–22		"	21:1–5		Ephesians	4:4–6
	Galatians	3:1–2	125	"	21:6–11		"	4:11–13
	"	3:23–27	126	"	21:12–16		"	4:15–16
	"	3:29	127	"	21:17–21	162	Phil.	1:3–5
	"	4:7		"	21:27–29	163	"	1:6
109	Acts	18:23	129	"	21:30–40		"	1:12–14
	1 Cor	16:1–3	130	"	22:12–25	164	"	1:19–25
	Acts	18:24–27	131	"	22:26–30		"	2:16–17
111	"	18:28		"	23:1–6		"	4:4–7
	"	19:1–12	132	"	23:7–18	166	1 Timothy	1:3
113	"	19:18–29	133	"	23:19–32		Titus	3:12
114	"	19:30–41	134	"	23:33–35		2 Timothy	4:13
	"	20:1	135	"	24:1–6		Titus	1:5
115	2 Cor.	2:12–13		"	24:8–15		2 Timothy	4:20
	"	7:5–6	136	"	24:16–27		Philemon	1:22
	"	6:14–16		"	25:1–2	168	2 Timothy	1:15–18
116	"	6:17–18	137	"	25:3–14		"	4:9–12
	"	7:1	138	"	25:15–26	169	"	4:14
	1 Cor.	6:15, 17	139	"	25:27		"	4:16–18
	"	6:19–20		"	26:1–13		"	2:9–10
	"	4:19–21	140	"	26:14–21		Phil.	3:20–21
	2 Cor.	13:1–2	141	"	26:22–32	170	2 Cor.	10:3–5
	"	13:5, 7	145	"	27:1–10	171	2 Timothy	4:6–8
	"	13:10	146	"	27:11–24	177	Rev.	2:1–7
117	"	2:4, 9	147	"	27:25–29	178	"	2:8
	"	7:6–11	148	"	27:30–44	179	"	2:9–11
118	Romans	15:19	150	"	28:1–12		"	2:18–25
	Acts	20:2–3	151	"	28:13–15	181	"	2:26–29
	Romans	1:13–15	153	"	28:16–23		"	2:12–15
	"	15:22–26	154	"	28:24–27	182	"	2:16–17
	"	15:28	155	"	28:28	183	"	3:1–6
119	"	15:29–33		"	28:30–31		"	3:14
	2 Cor.	11:24–28	157	Philemon	1:23–24	184	"	3:15–22
	"	11:32–33		Col.	4:10–14		"	3:7–9
	"	12:2		Philemon	1:10–13	186	"	3:10–13
120	"	12:3–5	159	Phil.	4:18	193	Titus	2:11–14
	"	12:7–9		Col.	1:12–14		1 John	1:5
121	"	12:10		"	2:13		"	3:1
	"	6:4–10		"	2:16–17		"	4:7–10
	Galatians	6:17		"	2:20–22	194	"	4:16, 19
	Acts	20:3–6		"	3:1–2		James	1:17
122	"	20:7–12		"	3:5		2 Cor.	1:21–22

BIBLE REFERENCE INDEX

Page	Bible Reference		Page	Bible Reference		Page	Bible Reference	
194	Phil.	2:13	210	Ephesians	1:12	229	Romans	13:11–14
	Romans	11:33–36	212	"	1:20–23		1 Timothy	6:11–16
	"	2:1–3		Col.	1:27		Phil.	4:1
195	"	2:4–5		Ephesians	3:1–10	231	James	1:2–4
	"	10:12	213	"	3:11–12		"	1:12–15
	"	5:15		"	2:1–15		1 Cor.	10:13
	Hebrews	6:10	214	"	2:16–22		1 Peter	1:6–7
	2 Peter	3:8–9		2 Cor.	5:14–19	233	"	1:8–9
196	Romans	1:16–25		Galatians	2:16		Romans	8:18–24
198	"	2:4–15	216	"	2:20		2 Cor.	6:1
	"	3:9–12		Ephesians	4:17–25		"	6:3–10
199	"	3:20–25		1 Peter	2:3–6	235	1 Peter	4:12–19
	"	5:1–8	217	"	2:7–10		1 Cor.	16:9
200	"	5:9–11		1 Cor.	3:21–23		2 Cor.	4:11–15
201	"	8:1–4, 9		"	4:8	236	1 Cor.	13:1–8
	"	8:12–17		2 Cor.	13:4	238	"	13:9–13
	"	8:26–27		Hebrews	9:28		1 John	3:16–18
202	"	8:28–33	219	Ephesians	4:4–13		"	4:7–12
203	"	8:34–39		"	4:16	239	Galatians	5:13–15
	"	12:1–7	220	1 Cor.	3:4–17		Romans	13:8–10
205	"	12:8		Romans	12:3–4		1 Peter	4:7–10
	"	15:1–3	221	"	12:5–8		Phil.	2:1–4
	"	15:5–6		1 Cor.	12:4–16	240	Romans	12:14–21
	John	3:16	222	"	12:17–31		Ephesians	4:1–3
	1 John	3:23		Romans	7:2–3		"	4:31–32
	1 Cor.	1:23–24	223	"	7:4	242	"	5:1–2
	1 John	1:1–2		1 John	2:12–14		1 Peter	2:21–23
206	"	1:3		Romans	10:13–15		James	5:19–20
	"	2:29	224	Ephesians	5:8–11		Phil.	4:8
	"	2:1–2		1 Cor.	4:1–2		Galatians	6:1
	1 Peter	1:18–21		"	9:16–19		Romans	10:6–7
	1 John	5:11–12		Col.	4:2–4	243	"	10:8–11
	Col.	1:13–16		2 Cor.	3:1–3		1 John	4:2–3
208	"	1:17–22	225	"	3:4–11		"	4:15
	1 Peter	3:18, 22		"	3:17		James	1:21
	2 Peter	1:16–18		1 Cor.	9:24–27		"	4:8–10
	Phil.	2:5–6		Phil.	3:12–13	244	Galatians	6:3–5
209	"	2:7–11	227	"	3:14		1 Peter	5:5
	Galatians	3:23–29		Ephesians	6:10–17	245	"	5:6–7
	"	4:1–7		1 Thess.	5:4–8		1 John	1:8–10
210	"	3:13–14	228	2 Cor.	10:3–6		2 Cor.	10:12–18
	1 John	3:8		Romans	7:14–25		"	11:1–3
	Romans	5:18–19		1 Peter	5:8–9	246	"	11:4–11
	Ephesians	1:4–10	229	"	5:10–11		James	5:7–11

BIBLE REFERENCE INDEX

Page	Bible Reference	Page	Bible Reference	Page	Bible Reference
247	James 1:3–4	266	Romans 8:5–6	281	Romans 8:9–10
	1 Cor. 6:15, 17		1 John 4:4		1 Thess. 4:13–14
	" 6:19–20		Romans 6:16–23	282	" 4:15–18
	" 3:16–17	267	" 6:1–11		Romans 8:11–13
	1 Thess. 4:3–4		Galatians 5:16–23		2 Peter 3:10–14
	" 4:6–8	268	" 5:24–25	283	1 John 2:15–17
	1 Cor. 5:6–8		" 6:14–16		" 3:2–3
248	Romans 8:5–6		2 Cor. 4:1–2	289	James 1:22–27
249	1 Cor. 8:1–13		1 Cor. 4:1–2		" 2:14–18
	" 10:19		Phil. 1:27–30	290	" 2:19–26
251	" 10:20–33	269	" 2:12–15		" 4:17
	" 11:1		1 Thess. 2:12		1 John 4:20–21
252	Romans 14:2–11		Hebrews 10:24–25		" 2:3–6
253	" 14:12–18		1 John 3:4–6	291	" 2:9–11
254	" 14:19–21		2 Peter 1:5–9		" 3:16–18
	2 Cor. 8:21	270	" 1:10–11		" 3:14–15
	Ephesians 5:15–17		1 Peter 1:13–17		" 3:10–11
	Col. 4:5		" 3:15–17		" 1:6–7
	Galatians 4:8–11		" 4:7–11	292	1 Peter 2:11–12
	" 5:1, 7–8	272	Col. 3:1–16		Jude 1:20–23
255	1 Cor. 6:12–13	273	" 3:17		James 2:10–13
	Col. 2:16–19		Phil. 3:1		Galatians 5:25
	2 Cor. 8:7–12		James 5:13–18		" 6:7–9
256	" 9:6–15		Ephesians 5:18–20	293	" 5:16–17
	Galatians 6:6–8		2 Cor. 1:12		1 Cor. 10:21
257	" 6:9–10	275	2 Peter 1:3–4		1 Thess. 5:16–22
	2 Cor. 12:15		1 John 5:14–15		James 4:7–10
259	Col. 2:8–10		2 Cor. 3:13, 18		" 1:19–20
	1 Timothy 1:4–7		Hebrews 6:17–20	294	" 1:26
	Col. 1:21–24		1 John 5:18		" 3:2–12
260	" 1:25	276	1 Cor. 15:19–28		Col. 4:6
	Hebrews 4:1–11		" 15:35–39	295	" 3:9–10
261	" 4:12–13	277	" 15:40–50	296	Ephesians 4:29–32
	" 3:12–13	278	" 15:51–53		James 5:12
	" 2:1–4	279	" 15:54–58		1 Cor. 14:7–9
	" 10:26–29		" 15:32		James 4:11–12
262	" 10:30–31		2 Cor. 4:5–11		1 Peter 3:8–9
	Phil. 3:18–19	280	" 4:16–18	297	" 3:10–11
	2 Peter 2:12–19		" 5:1–10		" 3:15
263	" 2:20–22		Phil. 3:20–21		James 4:4
	Jude 1:3–4	281	1 Peter 1:3–5		2 Cor. 6:14–17
	" 1:11–13		1 Thess. 5:9–11	298	" 6:18
	" 1:16–17		Romans 2:6–7		Ephesians 4:26–27
265	" 1:18–19		Phil. 1:21, 23		Romans 12:9–19

BIBLE REFERENCE INDEX

Page	Bible Reference	Page	Bible Reference	Page	Bible Reference
299	Romans 12:20–21	314	Acts 20:35	341	2 Timothy 2:19–26
	1 Thess. 5:13–15		Romans 13:1–3		" 3:1–2
	1 Cor. 5:6–7	315	" 13:4–7	342	" 3:3–7
	Romans 3:1–2	316	1 Peter 2:13–17		" 3:12–17
	" 9:3–5		1 Cor. 6:1–8		" 4:1–5
300	" 2:17–23	321	Romans 16:1–11	343	" 4:6–8
	James 1:5–8	322	" 16:12–17		" 4:16–17
	" 3:13–16	323	" 16:18–23	344	" 4:18
301	" 3:17–18		" 16:25–27		Titus 1:1–2
	1 Cor. 1:18–28		Col. 4:7–9		" 1:4–14
302	" 1:29	324	" 4:10–18	345	" 1:15–16
	" 2:7–13		1 Thess. 2:17–20		" 2:1–14
305	1 Peter 3:1–7		" 3:6	347	" 3:1–7
	Ephesians 5:21–26	325	" 3:7–10		" 3:15
306	" 5:27–33	2 Thess. 3:1–2	351	Luke 1:32–33
	Col. 3:18–19	326	" 3:3–5		" 2:14
	1 Cor. 11:3–11		Phil. 4:9		" 1:46–52
307	" 11:12–16		1 Cor. 4:15–16	353	" 1:53–55
	" 7:28, 39		Philemon 1:1–9		" 1:68–78
	" 7:10–16	327	" 1:10–14	355	" 1:79
308	" 7:17	328	" 1:15–25		" 2:29–32
	1 Thess. 4:3–4	3 John 1:1–7		Titus 3:4–5
	" 4:6–7	329	" 1:8–14	357	" 3:6–7
	1 Cor. 6:18–20	2 John 1:1–6		2 Timothy 2:11–13
	Ephesians 6:1–4	331	" 1:7–13		Ephesians 5:14
	Col. 3:20–21	1 Timothy 1:1–2		1 Timothy 3:16
309	1 Peter 2:18–25		" 1:12–13		1 John 5:18
	Ephesians 6:5–9	332	" 1:14–19	359	" 5:19–20
311	Col. 3:23–25	333	" 2:1–14	363	Acts 4:24–30
	" 4:1		" 3:1–4	364	Col. 1:9–18
	" 3:11	334	" 3:5–13		Ephesians 3:14–19
	James 1:9–11		" 4:1–7	365	" 3:20–21
	" 4:13–14	335	" 4:8–16		" 1:17–23
312	" 4:15–17		" 5:1–7		Phil. 1:9–11
	" 5:1–6	336	" 5:8–15		1 Thess. 3:11–12
	1 Cor. 7:30–31		" 5:17–21	366	" 3:13
	James 2:1–2		" 6:1–2		Col. 2:2–3
313	" 2:3–9	337	" 6:3–15		2 Thess. 1:11–12
	1 Thess. 4:10–12	339	" 6:16–21		Ephesians 6:18–20
	Ephesians 4:28	2 Timothy 1:1–7		Col. 1:3–6
	2 Thess. 3:6–8	340	" 1:8–14	367	2 Cor. 2:14–16
314	" 3:9–12		" 2:1–9		2 Thess. 2:13–14
	Hebrews 13:16	341	" 2:10		2 Cor. 13:14
	Acts 4:34–35		" 2:14–17		Romans 16:27

BIBLE REFERENCE INDEX

Page	Bible Reference	Page	Bible Reference	Page	Bible Reference
367	2 Thess. 3:16	375	1 Cor. 14:12–24	397	Rev. 18:1–2
	1 Timothy 1:17	376	" 14:25–40		" 18:4–5
	Phil. 4:7	381	Rev. 1:1–6		" 18:7–8
	Romans 15:13		" 1:9	398	" 18:9–13
369	2 Thess. 2:16–17	382	" 1:10–12		" 18:15–18
	Romans 15:5–6	383	" 1:13–20	399	" 18:19
	1 Thess. 5:23–24		" 4:1–3	400	" 18:20–24
	Galatians 1:3–5	384	" 4:4–11		" 19:1–2
	2 Cor. 1:3–4		" 5:1–3	401	" 19:3–9
	Jude 1:24–25	385	" 5:4–12		" 19:11–12
370	1 Peter 1:3–5	386	" 5:13–14	402	" 19:13–16
	" 5:10–11		" 6:1–7		" 20:1–6
	Ephesians 6:23–24	389	" 6:8–17	403	" 20:7–11
	Hebrews 13:20–21	391	" 7:9–15	405	" 20:12–15
371	Acts 19:1–6	392	" 7:16–17		" 21:1–3
	Romans 6:3–6		" 11:15–19	406	" 21:4–13
372	Col. 2:12	394	" 12:1–12	407	" 21:14–16
	1 Cor. 12:13	395	" 12:13–17	408	" 21:17–23
	Galatians 3:27		" 14:1–5	409	" 21:24–27
	1 Cor. 15:29	396	" 14:6–8		" 22:1–8
	" 11:23–30		" 14:13	411	" 22:9–18
374	" 10:16–17		" 15:2–3	412	" 22:19–21
	" 14:1–11	397	" 15:4		